Modern American Drama: Playwriting in the 1980s

DECADES OF MODERN AMERICAN DRAMA: PLAYWRITING FROM THE 1930s TO 2009

Modern American Drama: Playwriting in the 1930s
by Anne Fletcher

Modern American Drama: Playwriting in the 1940s
by Felicia Hardison Londré

Modern American Drama: Playwriting in the 1950s
by Susan C. W. Abbotson

Modern American Drama: Playwriting in the 1960s
by Mike Sell

Modern American Drama: Playwriting in the 1970s
by Mike Vanden Heuvel

Modern American Drama: Playwriting in the 1980s
by Sandra G. Shannon

Modern American Drama: Playwriting in the 1990s
by Cheryl Black and Sharon Friedman

Modern American Drama: Playwriting 2000–2009
by Julia Listengarten and Cindy Rosenthal

Modern American Drama: Playwriting in the 1980s

Voices, Documents, New Interpretations

Sandra G. Shannon

Series Editors: Brenda Murphy and Julia Listengarten

methuen | drama
LONDON · NEW YORK · OXFORD · NEW DELHI · SYDNEY

METHUEN DRAMA
Bloomsbury Publishing Plc
50 Bedford Square, London, WC1B 3DP, UK
1385 Broadway, New York, NY 10018, USA
29 Earlsfort Terrace, Dublin 2, Ireland

BLOOMSBURY, METHUEN DRAMA and the Methuen Drama logo
are trademarks of Bloomsbury Publishing Plc

First published in Great Britain 2018
Paperback edition first published 2021

Copyright © Sandra G. Shannon and contributors, 2018

Sandra G. Shannon has asserted her right under the Copyright,
Designs and Patents Act, 1988, to be identified as author of this work.

Cover design by Louise Dugdale
Cover image: Ronald Reagan at the Berlin Wall. Photo © Bettmann/Getty Images

All rights reserved. No part of this publication may be reproduced or
transmitted in any form or by any means, electronic or mechanical,
including photocopying, recording, or any information storage or retrieval
system, without prior permission in writing from the publishers.

Bloomsbury Publishing Plc does not have any control over, or responsibility for,
any third-party websites referred to or in this book. All internet addresses given
in this book were correct at the time of going to press. The author and publisher
regret any inconvenience caused if addresses have changed or sites have
ceased to exist, but can accept no responsibility for any such changes.

A catalogue record for this book is available from the British Library.

A catalog record for this book is available from the Library of Congress.

ISBN: HB: 978-1-4725-7246-2
PB: 978-1-3502-0453-9
ePDF: 978-1-3501-5363-9
eBook: 978-1-3501-5364-6
Pack: 978-1-4725-7264-6

Series: Decades of Modern American Drama: Playwriting from the 1930s to 2009

Typeset by Fakenham Prepress Solutions, Fakenham, Norfolk NR21 8NN

To find out more about our authors and books visit
www.bloomsbury.com and sign up for our newsletters.

CONTENTS

Biographical Note and Notes on Contributors viii
General Preface Brenda Murphy and Julia Listengarten x

1 Introduction to the 1980s *Sandra G. Shannon* 1
  Politics 1
  The economy 4
  Domestic life 7
  Social issues 9
  Education 15
  Media 16
  Television and film 20
  Technology and science 23
  Travel and leisure 24
  Fashion 25

2 American Theatre in the 1980s *Sandra G. Shannon* 29
  Answering Reagan 29
  Women's theatre 30
  Multicultural theatre 35
  Musical theatre and the 'British Invasion' 36
  Notable playwrights of the decade 39

3 David Mamet: *Edmond* (1982), *Glengarry Glen Ross* (1984), *Speed-the-Plow* (1988), *Oleanna* (1992) *Nelson Pressley* 43
  Introduction 43

Edmond (1982) 47
Glengarry Glen Ross (1984) 52
Speed-the-Plow (1988) 58
Oleanna (1992) 62
Conclusion 69

4 David Henry Hwang: *FOB* (1980), *The Dance and the Railroad* (1981), *Family Devotions* (1981), *M. Butterfly* (1988) *William C. Boles* 71

Introduction 71
FOB (1980) 76
The Dance and the Railroad (1981) 81
Family Devotions (1981) 84
M. Butterfly (1988) 87
Conclusion 93

5 Maria Irene Fornes: *The Danube* (1982), *Mud* (1983), *The Conduct of Life* (1985) *Gwendolyn Alker* 99

Introduction 99
The Danube (1982) 107
 Development, production and reception 108
 The Danube and environmentalism 109
Mud (1983) 111
 Development, production and reception 111
 Mae as a complicated character 112
The Conduct of Life (1985) 115
 Development, production and reception 115
 A feminist re-reading of *Conduct* 116
Conclusion 121

6 August Wilson: *Ma Rainey's Black Bottom* (1984), *Fences* (1987), *Joe Turner's Come and Gone* (1984) *Sandra G. Shannon* 125

Introduction 125

Ma Rainey's Black Bottom (1984) 133
Fences (1987) 137
Joe Turner's Come and Gone (1984) 144

Afterword *Sandra G. Shannon* 153

David Mamet 153
David Henry Hwang 154
Maria Irene Fornes 156
August Wilson 158

Documents 163

Ronald Reagan's Berlin Wall speech 163
The onset of the AIDS epidemic 164
    Epidemiologic notes and reports 165
David Mamet 167
    From Matthew Roudane 167
    'David Mamet's Master Class Memo to the Writers of *The Unit*' 170
David Henry Hwang 172
    Sample 1 173
    Sample 2 178
    Sample 3 184
Irene Fornes 187
August Wilson 190
    From James Earl Jones and Mary Alice 190
    'The Ground on Which I Stand' 191
    From Lloyd Richards 193
    From Suzan-Lori Parks 195
    From Denzel Washington and Viola Davis 196

Notes 199
Bibliography 217
Index 230

BIOGRAPHICAL NOTE AND NOTES ON CONTRIBUTORS

Gwendolyn Alker is Teacher of Theatre Studies in the Department of Drama at Tisch School of the Arts. Her teaching and research interests include gender and performance, Latina/o theatre, and issues of spirituality and embodiment. In 2010 she curated and staged the NYC Fornes Festival. Her article on Fornes, 'Teaching Fornes: Preserving Fornesian Techniques in Critical Context', appeared in *Theatre Topics* in 2009. She has published in various other journals including *Drama Therapy Review*, *Theatre Journal*, *TDR*, *Women & Performance* and *Dance Research Journal*. Gwendolyn is currently the Editor of *Theatre Topics*.

William C. Boles is Professor of English at Rollins College. He is the author of *The Argumentative Theatre of Joe Penhall* (2011) and *Understanding David Henry Hwang* (2013).

Nelson Pressley is a theatre critic for the *Washington Post*. His reviews and features have appeared in *American Theatre*, *Irish Theatre Magazine*, *The Sondheim Review* and *Best Plays*; his book *American Playwriting and the Anti-Political Prejudice* was published in 2014.

Sandra G. Shannon is Professor Emeritus of African American Literature in the Department of English at Howard University. As *the* leading scholar on August Wilson, she is the author of *The Dramatic Vision of August Wilson* and *August Wilson's Fences: A Reference Guide*. In addition, she has edited and co-edited the following key essay collections on Wilson's work: *August Wilson and Black Aesthetics*, MLA *Approaches to Teaching the Plays of August Wilson*, and *August Wilson's Pittsburgh Cycle*. Dr. Shannon has also edited a special issue of the *Zora Neale Hurston Forum* on August Wilson, and she has contributed numerous chapters on his works in collections such as Alan Nadel's *May All Your Fences Have Gates: Essays on the Drama of August Wilson; August Wilson: Completing the Twentieth-Century Cycle;* Philip Kolin's *The Influence of Tennessee Williams*; Harvey Young's *The Cambridge Companion to African American Literature*; Harry Elam and David Krasner's *African American Performance and Theatre History*; and Martin Middeke's *Methuen Drama Guide to Contemporary American Playwrights*. Her essays on August Wilson have appeared in *African American Review, MELUS, College Literature* and *Theatre Survey*.

Dr Shannon previously served as Co-Editor and Editor of *Theatre Topics* journal and Vice President and President of the Black Theatre Network. She is currently Editor of the *College Language Association Journal and* founding board member of *Continuum: The Journal of African Diaspora Drama, Theatre, and Performance*. In spring 2006 following August Wilson's death, she founded the Howard University August Wilson Society and, most recently, served as a key consultant in the making of the acclaimed 2015 PBS-American Masters documentary *August Wilson: The Ground on Which I Stand*. In spring 2018, Dr Shannon will be inducted in the College of Fellows of the American Theatre as a 'distinguished achiever in professional and educational theatre'.

GENERAL PREFACE

Decades of Modern American Drama: Playwriting from the 1930s to 2009 is a series of eight volumes about American theatre and drama, each focusing on a particular decade during the period between 1930 and 2010. It begins with the 1930s, the decade when Eugene O'Neill was awarded the Nobel Prize for Literature and American theatre came of age. This is followed by the decade of the country's most acclaimed theatre, when O'Neill, Tennessee Williams and Arthur Miller were writing their most distinguished work and a theatrical idiom known as 'the American style' was seen in theatres throughout the world. Its place in the world repertoire established, American play writing has taken many turns since 1950.

The aim of this series of volumes is to focus attention on individual playwrights or collaborative teams who together reflect the variety and range of American drama during the 80-year period it covers. In each volume, contributing experts offer detailed critical essays on four playwrights or collaborators and the significant work they produced during the decade. The essays on playwrights are presented in a rich interpretive context, which provides a contemporary perspective on both the theatre and American life and culture during the decade. The careers of the playwrights before and after the decade are summarized as well, and a section of documents, including interviews, manuscripts, reviews, brief essays and other items, sheds further light on the playwrights and their plays.

The process of choosing such a limited number of playwrights to represent the American theatre of this period has been a difficult but revealing one. In selecting them, the series editors and volume authors have been guided by several principles: highlighting the most significant playwrights, in terms both historical and aesthetic, who contributed at least two interesting and important plays during the decade; providing a wide-ranging view of the decade's theatre, including both Broadway and alternative venues; examining many historical trends in playwriting and theatrical production during the decade; and reflecting the theatre's diversity in gender and ethnicity, both across the decade and across the period as a whole. In some decades, the choices are obvious. It is hard to argue with O'Neill, Williams, Miller, and Wilder in the 1940s. Other decades required a good deal of thought and discussion. Readers will inevitably regret that favourite playwrights are left out. We can only respond that we regret it too, but we believe that the playwrights who are included reflect a representative sample of the best and most interesting American playwriting during the period.

While each of the books has the same fundamental elements – an overview of life and culture during the decade, an overview of the decade's theatre and drama, the four essays on the playwrights, a section of documents, an Afterword bringing the playwrights' careers up to date, and a Bibliography of works both on the individual playwrights and on the decade in general – there are differences among the books depending on each individual volume author's decisions about how to represent and treat the decade. The various formats chosen by the volume authors for the overview essays, the wide variety of playwrights, from the canonical to the contemporary avant-garde, and the varied perspectives of the contributors' essays make for very different individual volumes. Each of the volumes stands on its own as a history of theatre in the decade and a critical study of the four individual playwrights or collaborative teams included. Taken together, however, the eight volumes offer a broadly representative critical and historical treatment of eighty years of American theatre and drama that is both accessible to a student first encountering the subject and informative and provocative for a seasoned expert.

Brenda Murphy (Board of Trustees Distinguished Professor Emeritus, University of Connecticut, USA)
Julia Listengarten (Professor of Theatre at the University of Central Florida, USA)
Series Editors

1

Introduction to the 1980s

Sandra G. Shannon

Politics

Ronald Reagan was the face of American-style politics during the 1980s. His rugged good looks, movie-star status and impressive way with words quickly made him a standout within the Republican Party. Reagan combined this charm with a conservative, no-nonsense leadership approach when it came to the safety and security of the United States and, lest foreign countries mistook his predecessor's mistakes as indications of weakness, he let potential adversaries know that the US was not a country to mess with. Evidence that there was 'a new sheriff in town' came within minutes of Reagan's inauguration: Ayatollah Ruhollah Khomeini released the American hostages who had been held captive in Iran for 444 days. Even though Carter had been in ongoing negotiations concerning the hostages' release and terms of the release were in place, Reagan capitalized on the favorable public sentiments that followed the end of the crisis. An end to the hostage crisis also allowed him to focus on the struggling US economy during his first few months in office, rather than conflicts with Iran.

Reagan continued to capitalize on his growing tough-guy reputation as he negotiated on the world stage. According to a published report from the US State Department's Office of the Historian,

The period 1981–1991 witnessed a dramatic transformation in the relationship between the United States and the Soviet Union. During these years the specter of a nuclear war between the superpowers receded as the Cold War ended swiftly, nearly entirely peacefully, and on US terms. When Ronald Reagan became president in January 1981, such outcomes were inconceivable. The Soviets had invaded Afghanistan, causing President Jimmy Carter to withdraw a strategic arms limitation treaty (SALT II) from Senate ratification, boycott the 1980 Olympics Games in Moscow, and ban U.S. grain sales to Moscow. Détente – or, 'relaxation of tensions' – yielded to confrontation.[1]

Clearly, the presidency of Ronald Reagan was transformative as he succeeded in restoring America's image in the world as a formidable superpower, engaged in nuclear arm control talks and attempted to reverse the spread of communism in South America, Africa and South Asia. His nationalist efforts were not without setbacks, however. His introduction of the Strategic Defense Initiative (SDI) program in 1983 was given a cool reception by the Soviet Union, who—fearing that it would pose a threat—withdrew from setting a timetable for further talks. In an ironic reversal, the 1980s saw dramatic increases in the nuclear arms race, which culminated in 1991 at a level of more than ten thousand strategic warheads on both sides.

At the beginning of the 1980s, as the Cold War showed no signs of warming, arms control advocates argued for a 'nuclear freeze' agreement between the United States and the Soviet Union. In 1982, New York's Central Park became the site of what was, arguably, the largest mass demonstration in American history in support of the freeze. Given this mandate, Reagan welcomed the March 1985 appointment of Mikhail Gorbachev as General Secretary of the Communist Party of the Soviet Union. This fellow leader was both amenable to reason and willing to negotiate with Reagan on matters pertaining to nuclear arms control. A series of summits and high-profile meetings occurred between August and September 1986 followed by a meeting between President Reagan and General Secretary Gorbachev in Reykjavik, Iceland, in October 1986. Unfortunately, the Reykjavik summit talks broke down when Soviet leader Mikhail Gorbachev insisted that American research for the Strategic Defense Initiative, also known as "Star Wars," be strictly confined to laboratories for ten years; Reagan refused.

In April 1987, the Soviet Union also proposed a freeze on shorter-range missile deployments and agreed, in principle, to intrusive on-site verification. Although previous major arms talks had collapsed at Reykjavik, Reagan would ultimately win over Soviet leader Mikhail Gorbachev in four summit conferences that yielded the 1987 Intermediate-Range Nuclear Forces (INF) Treaty, an agreement that required the United States and the Soviet Union to eliminate and permanently abandon any aspirations for nuclear and conventional ground-launched ballistic and cruise missiles with ranges of 500 to 5,500 kilometres.[2] These actions accelerated the end of the Cold War (1989–91), which came with the collapse of communism both in Eastern Europe and the Soviet Union, and in numerous Third World countries.

The political landscape in America during the 1980s also included major domestic events apart from international affairs that topped President Reagan's agenda. Issues that arose on the home front were varied and numerous – ranging from shifts in basic family dynamics to the rise of the populist conservative movement known as the New Right and diverse factions of America, such as evangelical Christians, anti-tax crusaders and advocates of deregulation and smaller markets.

Other political mavericks pushed for a more powerful American presence abroad in opposition to agendas espoused by disaffected white liberals and defenders of an unrestricted free market. According to the website U.S. History: Pre-Columbian to the New Millennium,

> Not everyone was happy with the social changes brought forth in America in the 1960s and 1970s. When *Roe vs. Wade* guaranteed the right to an abortion, a fervent pro-life movement dedicated to protecting the 'unborn child' took root. Antifeminists rallied against the Equal Rights Amendment and the eroding traditional family unit. Many ordinary Americans were shocked by the sexual permissiveness found in films and magazines. Those who believed homosexuality was sinful lambasted the newly vocal gay rights movement. As the divorce and crime rates rose, an increasing number of Americans began to blame the liberal welfare establishment for social maladies. A cultural war unfolded at the end of the 1970s ... Enter the New Right ... a combination of Christian religious leaders, conservative business

bigwigs who claimed that environmental and labor regulations were undermining the competitiveness of American firms in the global market, and fringe political groups.[3]

Chief among the New Righters was American media mogul, executive chairman and former Southern Baptist minister Pat Robertson, who generally supported conservative Christian ideals. Robertson was part of a new breed of 'televangelists' who rose to political and cultural prominence in the late 1970s and early 1980s. He used his television station, The Christian Broadcast Network, to deliver a conservative message to millions.[4]

Sociologists link the rise of this New Right to both population shifts and disaffection in the so-called 'Sunbelt', a mostly suburban and rural region that stretches from the Southeastern to Southwestern regions of the country, including states such as Alabama, Arizona, Florida, Georgia, Louisiana, Mississippi, New Mexico, South Carolina, Texas and roughly two-thirds of California. These areas have seen substantial population growth since the 1960s from an influx of people seeking a warm and sunny climate, a surge in retiring baby boomers and growing economic opportunities. Unfortunately, this surge is also accompanied by overcrowding, pollution and crime. Many among this demographic had migrated from the older industrial cities of the 'Rust Belt'. Moreover, many were averse to paying high taxes for social programmes they did not consider effective and became sceptical of the stagnating economy. Many were also frustrated by what they saw as the federal government's constant and unwarranted interference in their lives. The movement resonated with many citizens who had once supported more liberal policies but who no longer believed the Democratic Party represented their interests.

The economy

Like so many other administrations, matters pertaining to war and the state of the economy could determine their legacy. Initially, President Reagan inherited an economy mired in stagnant economic growth, high unemployment and high inflation. Stagnation, as it was called, was brought on by a combination of double-digit economic contraction with double-digit inflation. At the outset of his first term as president in 1981, Reagan set in motion a host of unprecedented economic initiatives that resulted in significant reductions in inflation and annual growth of GDP. He went to work instituting expansionary fiscal policies to stimulate the American economy. He introduced measures to deregulate the oil industry that had the unfortunate byproduct of the 1980s oil glut. The economy was in recession in 1981–3, but recovered and grew sharply after that. From implementing widespread tax cuts and deregulating domestic markets to decreasing social spending while increasing military budgets, Reagan left his mark. In his suggestively titled study, 'Ronald Reagan: Worst President Ever?', Robert Parry writes:

> The American Dream also dimmed during Reagan's tenure. While he played the role of the nation's kindly grandfather, his operatives divided the American people, using 'wedge issues' to deepen grievances especially of white men who were encouraged to see themselves as victims of 'reverse discrimination' and 'political correctness.' Yet even as working-class white men were rallying to the Republican banner (as so-called 'Reagan Democrats'), their economic interests were being savaged. Unions were broken and marginalized; 'Free trade' policies shipped manufacturing jobs abroad; old neighborhoods were decaying; drug use among the young was soaring. Meanwhile, unprecedented greed was unleashed on Wall Street, fraying old-fashioned bonds between company owners and employees. Before Reagan, corporate CEOs earned less than 50 times the salary of an average worker. By the end of the Reagan–Bush-I administrations in 1993, the average CEO salary was more than 100 times that of a typical worker. (At the end of the Bush-II administration, that CEO-salary figure was more than 250 times that of an average worker.)[5]

A major component of the Reagan administration's economic plan was based upon the theory of supply-side economics, which advocated reducing tax rates so, in theory, people could keep more of what they earned. They espoused that lower tax rates would induce people to work harder and longer, and that this, in turn, would lead to more saving and investment, which, also in turn, would result in more production and stimulate overall economic growth. While the Reagan-inspired tax cuts served mainly to benefit wealthier Americans, the economic theory behind the cuts argued that benefits would extend to lower-income people as well because higher investment would lead to new job opportunities and higher wages. Republicans quickly adopted this moratorium on taxes as a major part of their party's platform and, at every turn, held it over the heads of their 'tax and spend' Democratic rivals.

A competing central theme of Reagan's national agenda, however, was his belief that the federal government had become too big and intrusive. In the early 1980s, while he was cutting taxes, Reagan was also slashing social programmes. He also undertook a campaign throughout his tenure to reduce or eliminate government regulations affecting the consumer, the workplace and the environment. At the same time, however, he feared that the United States had neglected its military in the wake of the Vietnam War, so he successfully pushed for big increases in defence spending.

The combination of tax cuts and higher military spending overwhelmed more modest reductions in spending on domestic programmes. As a result, the federal budget deficit swelled even beyond the levels it had reached during the recession of the early 1980s. From $74 million in 1980, the federal budget deficit rose to $221 million in 1986. It fell back to $150 million in 1987, but then started growing again. Some economists worried that heavy spending and borrowing by the federal government would reignite inflation, but the Federal Reserve remained vigilant about controlling price increases, moving quickly to raise interest rates any time it seemed a threat. Under chairman Paul Volcker and his successor, Alan Greenspan, the Federal Reserve retained the central role of economic traffic cop, eclipsing Congress and the president in guiding the nation's economy.[6]

By 1983, the economy had rebounded and the United States entered into one of the longest periods of sustained economic growth since the Second World War. The annual inflation rate remained under 5 per cent from 1983 through to 1987. Still, serious problems remained. Farmers' problems continued; their suffering was compounded by serious droughts in 1986 and 1988. Federal deficits soared throughout the 1980s. From $74 billion in

1980, the federal budget deficit rose to $221 billion in 1986 before falling back to $150 billion in 1987. The US trade deficit hit a record $152 billion that same year. A stock market crash in the autumn of 1987 led many to question the stability of the economy. In fact, the US economy slowed and dipped into recession in 1991 but began a slow recovery in 1992.[7]

As a result of the slowing economy and other factors, the federal budget deficit began heading upward again. Although the stock market recovered, the financial industry was particularly plagued with problems. Numerous savings institutions as well as some banks and insurance companies either faltered or completely collapsed – in many instances, necessitating federal government takeover. Well into the 1990s, credit market and other problems lingered on. By contrast, other sectors of the economy, such as computers, aerospace and export industries generally showed signs of continuing growth.[8]

Domestic life

The 1980s saw the advent of the so-called 'New Man', which was a radical way to describe a male who wholeheartedly accepts equality in domestic life and who believes that women and men are equal and should be free to do the same things, such as share her household workload, show so-called 'feminine' sensitivity and advocate equal pay for equal work. For some people, the new man represented a shift to an emotionally and domestically involved man who was more nurturing and pro-feminist; for others, he was an individualistic and narcissistic man who spent as much on beauty products and who needed just as much time applying them as women did.

The significant numbers among men who took on household chores, tended to children and performed a host of other roles originally ascribed to women increased exponentially in the 1980s as wives, sisters, mothers and daughters traded the home front for the office. With increasing numbers of women entering the workforce and leaving the domestic sphere, the 1980s also saw the rise of the superwomen. According to the website trulovestories.com, they mean business. Striding into court, the boardroom and the corner office, immaculately turned out in power suits, accessorized with a status watch, designer bag and keys to the beamer, the women of the 1980s exuded confidence and success. They surpassed their mothers' wildest dreams. There were no limits to what they could accomplish. Working round-the-clock ensured their flawless performance – mistakes were not an option! But it left little time for themselves – or anyone else. How were they going to fit everything in – a career, a relationship, marriage and children? Could they have it all? *If so, how would they stay awake?*[9]

The 1980s saw significant changes in family dynamics. Shifting attitudes about gender roles resulted in increased numbers of men and women sharing both financial and domestic responsibilities within their families. According to published research, between 1980 and 1990 the average age for marriage among woman was twenty-four while men, on average, went to the altar at around age twenty-six. This same study found that 'between 1986–1990, the total divorce rate was 437 out of 1,000 marriages. Moreover, statistics show that women bore their first child at twenty-seven and in an interestingly circuitous twist, one study reports that "in 1981," about 27% of young adults between ages twenty to twenty-nine were still living with their parents.'[10]

The barriers keeping women out of managerial and professional jobs decreased significantly as millions of women stepped into high-paying positions in areas of banking, law, medicine, science and politics. The United States Supreme Court was exemplary in this regard. By extension, gender equality meant gender-neutral language. For example, 'mankind' became the more politically correct 'humankind'; 'chairman' became 'chairperson' or 'chairwoman'; and 'countryman' became 'country dweller'. The trend in education guaranteed a continuous flow of women executives and professionals for decades. According to this same source, by 1986, women earned more than 50 per cent of college and masters' degrees, and 30 per cent of professional degrees.[11]

In the early 1980s, marketers honed in on the baby boomers, who were entering their prime earning years with significant amounts of disposable income. After an initial downturn in 1981–2, the economy continued an upward trajectory for five consecutive years. Americans' insatiable appetite for conspicuous consumption drove the markets upward as they flaunted newly-acquired 'things'. In an ironic turn, during the late 1980s, popular magazines began addressing what had become a social problem: compulsive shopping. The term 'shopaholics' entered the American lexicon. The ritual of shopping – whether for purchasing actual consumer goods or for being a part of the social scene – took off in the 1980s to become a lasting cultural and social phenomenon.

Further studies on the early 1980s reveal that, in addition to indulging in the excesses of shopping, young adult engagement in premarital sex was not a matter of *if* but *when*. The online study 'The Women of the 1980s' revealed the following sobering statistic: 'by 1980, 80% of men and 65% of women had engaged in premarital sex. Almost 75% of teens had intercourse before they were 20. *Virginity had become a quaint term from a by-gone era!*'[12] Moreover, this study found that the institution of marriage still retained a degree of respect, despite evidence that suggested that increased frequency in cohabitation, premarital intercourse and childbirth impacted the number of couples who would have perhaps made this long-term commitment sooner, if at all. Of course, these alternative living arrangements and relaxed morals regarding sex, childbirth and marriage had a lasting impact upon definitions of the nuclear family.

Social issues

Aside from the less than flattering *Reaganomics* label that characterized Ronald Reagan's signature economic strategy, the 1980s ushered in a host of additional labels that reflected often major shifts in the country's tilting moral compass. Ronald Reagan's presidency (1981–9) was but one part of a complex narrative of the 1980s – a decade that, despite huge gaps between the upper and lower classes, also saw a clamouring among the masses for pop culture icons and a loosening of strict standards of behaviour. Due largely to a new class of young, wealthy, restless, self-centred and often irreverent Americans, terms such as 'hedonism', 'amorality', 'greed', 'materialism', 'substance abuse', 'sexual promiscuity' and 'conspicuous consumption' were also used to describe the decade.

For many people, the symbol of the 1980s was the 'yuppie' – that is, a baby boomer with a college education, a well-paying job and expensive taste. Many people derided yuppies for being self-centred and materialistic, and surveys of young urban professionals across the country showed that they were, indeed, more concerned with making money and buying consumer goods than their parents and grandparents had been. However, in some ways yuppiedom was less shallow and superficial than it appeared. Popular television shows like *thirtysomething* and movies like *The Big Chill* and *Bright Lights, Big City* depicted a generation of young men and women who were plagued with anxiety and self-doubt. They were successful, but they weren't sure they were happy.

While it is difficult to pinpoint a single factor that earned the decade of the 1980s the reputation for birthing the 'me generation' and a bratty population of 'yuppies' or 'young urban professionals', it is much easier to examine the far-reaching impact of this complex and defining era in various aspects of life. Images and trends in the decade's popular culture, for example, seemed indicative of these new standards of behaviour. In music, for example, Madonna's 1984 hit song 'Material Girl' accurately depicted attitudes among conspicuous consumers who had easy access to much more disposable income during this time. In television, *Dallas* (1978–91) and *Dynasty* (1981–9), and in film, *Ferris Beuller's Day Off* (1986) and *Wall Street* (1987) flaunted the spoils of wealth among the pampered elite who abused money as well as the many privileges that came with it. 'Greed is good', the sentiments expressed by Gordon Gekko, Wall Street corporate investor and the film's protagonist, best describes the philosophy of the moneyed class. At one point in the movie, Gekko elaborates:

> The richest one percent of this country owns half our country's wealth, five trillion dollars. One third of that comes from hard work, two thirds comes from inheritance, interest on interest accumulating to widows and idiot sons and what I do, stock and real estate speculation. It's bullshit. You got ninety percent of the American public out there with little or no net worth. I create nothing. I own. We make the rules, pal. The news, war, peace, famine, upheaval, the price per paper clip. We pick that rabbit out of the hat while everybody sits out there wondering how the hell we did it. Now you're not naïve enough to think we're living

in a democracy, are you, buddy? It's the free market. And you're a part of it. You've got that killer instinct. Stick around, pal. I've still got a lot to teach you.[13]

While greed may seem to have been rewarded in the 1980s, gluttony and lust – be it for drugs or sex – proved fatal for large segments of America. The antidote, it seemed, to decades of excess came in the form of widespread and essentially incurable and untreatable disease. As such, the sexual revolution that flourished in the 1960s and 1970s ended abruptly in the 1980s with the epidemic disease that knew no cure or treatment as it ravaged both gay and straight cross sections of various populations of varying income levels, career paths and sexual persuasions. When Rock Hudson – then darling of the big screen – died from an AIDS-related illness in 1985, the nation suddenly sat up and took notice in daily conversations and in various headlines. The hedonism of the 1970s was being re-evaluated in the 1980s.

Drug abuse, like widespread sexual promiscuity during the 1980s, marked a turning point in the zeitgeist of the nation. In 1987, 'Just say no!' or First Lady Nancy Reagan's advice to a school girl's question about accepting drugs sparked a campaign to make schools drug-free zones. In retrospect, however, this catchy phrase seemed but a feeble attempt to raise awareness about a drug culture that was essentially out of control. Considering this, Mrs Reagan's slogan seemed hopelessly ineffectual in curbing this scourge as newer and more dangerous substances like crack cocaine exacerbated the nation's drug problem.

While the 'me generation' garnered much attention during the 1980s, a large and growing population of marginalized groups also demanded equal attention and rights due to them as American citizens. Chief among these disenfranchised minority populations were people of colour, members of the LGBT community, and the poor. In the 1980s, Reagan's presidency ignored most of the issues and interests of African-Americans and appointed conservative judges to a number of federal courts who would, in turn, terminate programmes originally designated to address past discriminatory practices. In ways that appear now to anticipate strategies employed during Donald Trump's 2016 presidential campaign, Ronald Reagan decided 'to mobilize long-simmering racial controversies to build up his own base of political support

... and managed to channel anti-black prejudice into a broader anti-government politics; by cultivating the impression that federal social welfare programs were mostly wasted on "undeserving" black people, Reagan built support for his own anti-government ideology'.[14] Skilled at what became known as 'coded' (aka 'dog whistle') appeals, President Reagan stirred up deep-seated prejudices among northern whites. This tactic was on full display in his decision to construct a mythical black 'welfare queen' to galvanize his campaign against the federal welfare policy. In doing so, he stoked hatred for black Americans from within the Republican Party base that ultimately set the tenor of race relations for much of the 1980s and beyond. The imagined prototype for Reagan's target of white conservative hatred and derision was

> a Cadillac-driving 'Chicago welfare queen,' a black woman in Chicago. She has 80 names, 30 addresses, 12 Social Security cards, and is collecting veteran's benefits on 4 non-existing deceased husbands. And she's collecting Social Security on her cards. She's got Medicaid, is getting food stamps, and she is collecting welfare under each of her names. Her tax-free cash income alone is over $150,000.[15]

Reagan's mythical 'welfare queen' succeeded in affirming what many Northern whites needed to believe about African-Americans: that they were lazy scam artists who took money from hard-working white taxpayers. The collateral damage left in its wake was a polarized nation poisoned by racism and bigotry. Despite the fact that, statistically, the majority of welfare recipients were white, white conservatives clung to the myth that blacks were gaming the system and that whites were footing the bill. Despite these setbacks, in the late 1980s, African-Americans began to wield more political power as increased numbers were elected as mayors and school board members, as well as joining state and local legislative bodies. In 1989, the more moderate George Bush came to the presidency. He respected the counsel of Martin Luther King, Jr. and made possible appointments of increased numbers of minorities to higher governmental positions.

The Hispanic and Latino populations in 1980s America increased significantly due to the ebb and flow of immigration patterns. By 1988 this burgeoning group of American citizens had made a tremendous impact upon American culture in areas such as business, politics, education, music, cinema, literature, dance, food and so on. Latin dances were very popular, and many fashion trends influenced American culture. Nadya Agrawal characterizes the Hispanic influence upon American fashion during 1980s in her *Huffington Post* article 'Six Decades of Mexican and Mexican-American Style Evolution':

> The Chola look of the 1980s was influenced heavily by hip-hop, Pachuco fashion and somewhat by gang culture. It came largely out of the resourcefulness of impoverished Mexican-American women who shared clothes with their brothers and bought workwear labels at local supermarkets. Dark lip-liner, oversized flannel shirts buttoned to the top and hair AquaNetted into the perfect bump all are key components of the Chola aesthetic. Mexican fashion at the time was all about the blush, hairspray and candy lips. The result of American exports, Mexican style looked like a carbon copy of the neon-chic American '80s.[16]

These trends had the greatest impact in border states, yet they also extended to urban areas such as New York and Miami.

According to research findings shared in an article titled 'American Race and Racism 1970 to Present', 'In 1987, Hispanic businesses had numbered approximately 34,0000 with revenues of about $20 billion (Woodger). Their success in the business world had a drastic effect on the economy and attracted many other non-Hispanic businesses to get involved with them.'[17] This source went on to report that financial success notwithstanding, Hispanics and Latinos still experienced a huge divide in terms of their financial status that ranged from the thriving businessman to the impoverished under- or unemployed. Government assistance for many Hispanics and Latinos was meager at best. Despite these circumstances, the close of the 1980s saw an increase in bilingual schools, and Spanish became more acceptable as the national language.

By all accounts, President Reagan had a tenuous relationship with both American Indians and the Japanese-Americans. One group he seemed to perceive as a burden on the country's budget while the other reaped reparation for past grievances. The website micd.org captures the paradoxical nature of his dealings with these two communities, observing that Reagan was

> determined to cut federal spending extended to the Bureau of Indian Affairs as well as to numerous other programs that supported Native Americans. This pushed many of them into poverty and homelessness and deprived them of education and work. A number of land disputes occurred in the early 80s as well, in which the government got involved and often stripped them of their land. In 1980 however, in the Supreme Court Case *United States v. Sioux Nation of Indians*, it was ruled that their land was illegally seized and the government owed them over half a billion dollars in repairs. This was one of the first times the government recognized their wrongdoings and mistreatment towards American Indians. As the decade proceeded, they slowly found more relief.[18]

The early 1980s under the Reagan administration proved to be turbulent times for Japanese-Americans as well; however, the decade ended on a note of reconciliation. In 1988, Congress passed a bill that paved the way for Japanese-Americans who were interned during the Second World War, or their surviving families, to receive reparations. In 1988, President Reagan signed the Civil Liberties Act to compensate more than 100,000 people of Japanese descent who were incarcerated in internment camps during the war. The legislation offered a formal apology and paid out $20,000 in compensation to each surviving victim. The law won congressional approval only after a decade-long campaign by the Japanese-American community. To mark the 25th anniversary of its passage, the Civil Liberties Act was put on display at the National Archives alongside the original Executive Order 9066, which authorized the internment.

Increased numbers among the country's gay population in the 1980s led to increased political clout for the LGBT community. In particular, the 1980s marked a major shift towards the emergence of a global gay culture. Ironically, much of this was driven by adversity surrounding fears about the newly discovered HIV/AIDS virus. While hysteria impacted on the gay community, at the same time, it caused this community to rally both nationally and internationally. Adding to the sense of alienation and isolation among the LGBT community, the US Court of Appeals ruled that there was no 'fundamental right' to be gay, and the Catholic Church continued to shun this lifestyle. In 1986, Pope John Paul II labelled homosexuality as 'evil' and ordered the Church to withdraw all support from gay Catholic organizations.

Of course, the 1980s did not spell complete doom and gloom for the gay community. The United States joined several other countries in introducing anti-discrimination laws. For example, the US Army, which had declared homosexuality to be 'incompatible with military service' in 1982, was forced to admit in 1989 that gay recruits were 'just as good or better' than heterosexuals, which turned out to be long-held but politically suppressed truth.[19]

Education

The 1980s witnessed a shift in priorities for educational policies at the local, state and federal levels. Many attributed America's poor performance within the realm of education to Ronald Reagan's belief that the role of the federal government in education should be reduced.

Numerous studies on the quality of American education were launched, and much of the results showed poor student performance in every subject area when held against past national test scores as well as against scores from other countries. A clarion call went out against the American school system's failure to educate poor and minority children.

One of the most significant shifts during the 1980s occurred in the readjustments made in the country's testing practices. Emphasis was placed upon K-12 standardized testing as the direct result of a national educational reform movement that took shape in the early 1980s. This same issue culminated in 2002 in the passage of No Child Left Behind. Under President Reagan, the federal government took a different approach in establishing national education priorities compared to past administrations. The National Commission on Excellence in Education, under then Education Secretary Terrel Bell, produced *A Nation at Risk: The Imperative for Educational Reform*, the influential 1983 report that said the US educational system was not meeting the national need for a globally competitive workforce. The report, which warned that American schools were failing, alarmed elected officials, corporate executives and education leaders to the point that education reform shifted from a liberal left-of-centre focus on school integration and civil rights to one concerned with setting national standards and building accountability systems. With state governors and presidents George H. W. Bush, George W. Bush and Bill Clinton joining the movement, education reform that embraced standards and accountability measures received bipartisan support during the 1980s and 1990s.[20]

Throughout the decade, advocates reminded educators and the general public that the 'nation at risk' could not afford to ignore its children at risk – those youngsters, largely from poor and minority families, who were more likely to fail in school, drop out, become pregnant or abuse drugs. In the closing years of the decade, support mounted for policies allowing students and their parents to choose the public schools the children would attend. This approach was a far cry from the earlier idea of expanding choice to private schools with vouchers or tuition tax credits.

Perhaps one of the most promising developments of the 1980s was the private sector's recognition of the need for better schools. In many districts, the local business community created partnerships with the public schools, set up scholarship programmes and provided summer jobs for students. At the national level, corporate leaders lent their support to school reform. In the closing months of the decade, President Bush convened a first-ever education summit of the nation's governors. The participants agreed to set national goals for improvement in such areas as academic performance, children's readiness for school, the dropout rate and adult literacy.[21] As the decade ended, however, the tests themselves underwent even more radical changes, such as reducing or eliminating altogether multiple-choice questions.

Media

In the 1980s, many Americans enjoyed significant improvements in their standard of living. One such perk involved having more media options. Increased access to television, for example, clearly played a major role in reshaping the culture of this decade. Thanks to deregulation, more channels were available and content was less restricted. Increased images of sex, violence and previously tabooed subjects permeated the airwaves. Such a seemingly free-for-all environment gave rise to billionaire mogul Rupert Murdoch, whose News Corporation acquired Twentieth Century Fox in 1985 and HarperCollins in 1989. Cable television, although available in the 1970s, became standard for most American households. This change ushered in a whole host of new programming that was not bound to the same regulations as the former monopoly held by NBC, CBS and ABC.

In addition to more adult programming, cable television gave sports-minded Americans 24-hour access to programmes such as ESPN, and children of Baby Boomer parents could indulge in channels such as Nickelodeon and binge-watch news at any time by tuning in to CNN. The decade also saw a boom in the magazine industry, as magazine publishers streamlined their content for specific audiences. At the same time, however, a considerable number of newspapers folded as production costs soared and consolidation became more and more an unregulated and unscrupulous business. The 1980s saw the rise of women in the media, including Oprah Winfrey, Connie Chung and Barbara Walters.

Music Television, or MTV, brought a revolution to the recording industry during the 1980s and redefined popular music. Launched on 1 August 1981 for the main purpose of playing music videos, this sensational media development caught on quickly in America. Its impact was far reaching and especially popular among teenage and young adult audiences. From risqué fashion trends to musical icons who challenged the establishment values and the emergence of a new lexicon, MTV essentially staged a pervasive countercultural insurgence that continues to have an impact on Americans into the twenty-first century. Michael Jackson and Madonna, for example, owed much to this medium as it created the perfect conditions for launching their solo music careers. Michael Jackson's *Thriller*, which was released on 30 November 1982, enabled Jackson to break down racial barriers in pop music via his appearances on MTV, and his 1984 meeting with President Reagan at the White House validated his work and provided major exposure.

Thriller was one of the first albums to use music as a successful promotional tool.

The lyrics to Madonna's 'Papa Don't Preach' caused quite a stir, as the subject of this popular MTV song was teenage pregnancy and abortion. Its release prompted heated discussions about its lyrical content. Spokespersons for women's organizations and family planning programmes lambasted Madonna for what they interpreted as promoting teenage pregnancy. Conversely, pro-life groups saw the song as having a positive, life-affirming message. Controversy over Madonna's song extended to the Vatican: she dedicated it to Pope John Paul II. His answer was to urge Italians to boycott her concerts during the 1987 'Who's That Girl' world tour. In a similar vein, Cindy Lauper's MTV hit 'Girls Just Want to Have Fun', released in 1983, gained recognition as a feminist anthem and was packaged and promoted in the form of a Grammy-winning video.

The expansion and dominance of FM radio – which has better audio quality but a more limited broadcast range than AM – represented the major technical change in radio during the 1970s and 1980s. FM radio (aided by the development of smaller portable radios and 'Walkman' headsets) dominated music programming, while AM shifted to talk and news formats. Talk radio became more popular during the 1980s because of improved satellite communications and the repeal of the Fairness Doctrine. On 4 August 1987, the Federal Communications Commission voted unanimously to abolish its fairness doctrine because it unconstitutionally restricted the free-speech rights of broadcast journalists. They charged that the 38-year-old Fairness Doctrine was stifling the democratic debate it was supposed to promote.

Radio formats proliferated in the 1980s with the increased prominence of progressive or album-oriented rock (AOR) stations that arose in the early 1970s as part of a concerted effort by radio executives along with major record labels to standardize FM playlists. It was geared to the album rather than to 45-rpm single sales; many of the playlist selections were never released as singles. This move toward the album represented a break with the long tradition of the three-minute single by playing full versions of songs such as 'Stairway to Heaven', while 'Freebird' college radio was emerging as an alternative music force.

The biggest 'new media' stories in the early 1980s were the

start of CNN in 1980 and *USA Today* in 1982. Launched by Al Neuharth, head of the Gannett newspaper chain, *USA Today* was the first true national daily newspaper and continues to be the most widely read newspaper in America. Founded by media mogul Ted Turner, CNN was first channel to provide 24-hour television news coverage, and the first all-news television channel in the United States.[22]

At the movie theatre, the 1980s was the age of the blockbuster. Movies like *E.T.: The Extra-Terrestrial*, *Return of the Jedi* and *Raiders of the Lost Ark* appealed to moviegoers of all ages and made hundreds of millions of dollars at the box office. The 1980s was also the heyday of the teen movie. Films like *The Breakfast Club*, *Some Kind of Wonderful* and *Pretty in Pink* are still popular today. At home, people watched family sitcoms like *The Cosby Show*, *Family Ties*, *Roseanne* and *Married ... with Children*. They also rented movies to watch on their new VCRs. By the end of the 1980s, 60 per cent of American television owners had cable service and the most revolutionary cable network of all was MTV, which made its debut on 1 August 1981. The music videos the network played made stars out of bands like Duran Duran and Culture Club and made megastars out of artists like Michael Jackson (1958–2009), whose elaborate *Thriller* video helped sell 600,000 albums in the five days after its first broadcast. MTV also influenced fashion: people across the country (and around the world) did their best to copy the hairstyles and fashions they saw in music videos. In this way, artists like Madonna became (and remain) fashion icons.

As the decade wore on, MTV became a forum for those who went against the grain or were left out of the yuppie ideal. Rap artists such as Public Enemy channeled the frustration of urban African-Americans into their powerful album *It Takes a Nation of Millions to Hold Us Back*. Heavy metal acts such as Metallica and Guns n' Roses also captured the sense of malaise among young people, particularly young men. Even as Reagan maintained his popularity, popular culture continued to be an arena for dissatisfaction and debate throughout the 1980s.[23]

Television and film

The 1980s ushered in a challenge to the dominant big three networks by new competitors, Fox and cable. Launched on 9 October 1986 as a competitor to ABC, NBC and CBS, Fox went on to become the most successful attempt at a fourth television network.[24]

The website Archives in American Television provides a comprehensive overview of the reach and growing popularity of television in the 1980s. It observes that, at the dawn of the decade, media mogul Ted Turner ignored sceptics and launched Cable News Network (CNN). Two years later, CNN Headline News premiered. By 1987, CNN was the only network providing live coverage of what turned out to be the tragic NASA *Challenger* space shuttle launch. It was moments like these that proved that CNN was making its mark as a leading news source. Also, at a huge risk to his fledgling operation, Turner sued the Reagan administration and the big networks for access to the White House pool. CNN won and earned the respect of the industry.

The 1980s also marked changes for veteran newsmen. David Brinkley began hosting duties for ABC with *This Week with David Brinkley*. The 'most trusted man in America', Walter Cronkite, retired as CBS news anchor and passed the baton to Dan Rather. News coverage of the protests in Beijing's Tiananmen Square reached around the world and shone a grim light on modern communism. CBS News correspondent Richard Roth was imprisoned because of his reporting, and the television image of a lone man defying an approaching tank remains a symbol of modern anti-government protest. The decade finished with the worldwide coverage of the fall of the Berlin Wall. Newsman Tom Brokaw reported the momentous occasion live, as the symbol of the Iron Curtain was dismantled, piece by piece. A powerful way to end the 1980s.

At the beginning of the decade, new breakthrough sit-coms were scarce. Even an old standard like *M*A*S*H* aired its final episode in 1983, garnering 107 million viewers – the largest US audience for a single TV programme. Some of the hits from the previous decade began to lose steam, including *Taxi* and *Soap*. However, many drama shows from the late 1970s continued their success into the 1980s.

The new decade signalled a shift in series themes as well. After years of watching shows that tackled tough issues such as the Vietnam War, inflation and women's rights, the public's interests shifted to escapist themes. One way to deliver that was to peek inside of the lives of the super-rich. Shows such as *Dynasty*, *Dallas*, *Hotel* and even *Lifestyles of the Rich and Famous* fed that appetite. Millions of loyal viewers watched as Luke and Laura exchanged vows in a storybook wedding on the daytime soap, *General Hospital*.

The police drama again became popular with shows such as *Hill Street Blues*, *Magnum P.I.* and *Simon and Simon*. Some of the drama programmes in this genre included *The Fall Guy*, *Father Dowling Mysteries*, *Murder She Wrote* and *Wise Guy*.

In terms of comedy, *The Cosby Show* was the keystone of NBC's Thursday night 'Must See TV' mantra. Audiences became interested in comedies again. The other networks filled their slates with family sit-coms – nuclear and non-traditional ones. The success of *Cosby* turned Carsey-Werner Productions into an independent powerhouse. They solidified their ability to deliver hit shows with the blue-collar family comedy *Roseanne*, which redefined the idea of a functional family.

Some favourite stars made their return to television throughout the decade including Lee Majors, Bob Newhart, Bill Cosby, Beatrice Arthur and Tom Bosley. Programmes which introduced the talents of individuals who would make their mark in television history included Tom Selleck in *Magnum P.I.*, Tom Hanks in *Bosom Buddies* and Michael J. Fox in *Family Ties*. Oprah Winfrey also emerged, as *The Oprah Winfrey Show* became nationally syndicated from Chicago. Another daytime programme, *The David Letterman Show*, premiered on NBC, but soon moved to nighttime.

Programmes emerged during the 1980s that arguably laid the groundwork for a whole new genre that has apparently reached its pinnacle in popular shows such as *American Idol*, *America's Got Talent* and *Dancing with the Stars*. Programmes such as *Solid Gold*, *Star Search*, *It's Showtime at the Apollo* and the first annual *Soul Train Music Awards* showcased the talents of newer singers and dancers. The variations of the comedy genre continued to evolve towards the end of the decade, including *Moonlighting*, which introduced the hour-long romantic comedy to the world. This was soon followed by *thirtysomething*. Comedy programmes of the era include *The Cosby Show*, *Family Ties*, *The Golden Girls*, *Married ... With Children* and *Moonlighting*. In children's television, the decade may be remembered for introducing us to *The Smurfs* and *Pee Wee's Playhouse*.

Toward the end of the 1980s, *The Wonder Years* became a nostalgic favourite, and the weekly real-life problems of Roseanne began directly competing with Bill Cosby's family dilemmas. And as the decade began to dim, the fledgling Fox network caught a hit with the controversial domestic show *Married ... With Children*, triggering a wave of irreverent, often racy programming.[25]

By 1989, over half of homes with TVs in America had cable service. Its offerings were limited to CNN, MTV, ESPN and Nickelodeon, but these networks paved the way for an explosion of other such channels. News organizations shifted their goals from serving the public good to generating profits. Comedy was very popular, and the public's desire to keep up with the rich was seemingly insatiable. VCR sales sky-rocketed, and gave viewers freedom to watch what they wanted, whenever they wanted. Movie-goers fled to the theatres to watch comedies, chick-flicks, traditional fare and blockbusters with special effects.[26]

In film, perhaps the most iconic representation of attitudes in the 1980s is *Ferris Bueller's Day Off*, a 1986 American comedy film written, produced and directed by John Hughes. The film follows high school senior Ferris Bueller (Matthew Broderick), who skips school and spends the day in downtown Chicago along with his girlfriend Sloane Peterson (Mia Sara) and best friend Cameron Frye (Alan Ruck). He creatively avoids his school's dean of students Edward Rooney (Jeffrey Jones), his resentful sister Jeannie (Jennifer Grey) and his parents. During the film, Bueller regularly breaks the fourth wall by speaking directly to the camera to explain to the audience his thoughts and techniques.

Released by Paramount Pictures on 11 June 1986, *Ferris Bueller's Day Off* became one of the top-grossing films of the year and was enthusiastically received by critics and audiences alike. Yet, aside from its commercial success, *Ferris Bueller's Day Off* tapped into prevailing notions in the 1980s about wealth, privilege and self-indulgence. In essence, then, Bueller seems to be cut from the same cloth as his successor Gordon Gekko, the ruthless, greedy, shamelessly aggressive baron in the 1987 film *Wall Street*. The 1980s was indeed a pivotal decade that saw unprecedented greed and hedonism on one hand and, on the other, startling innovations and exponential cultural shifts. The imprint of this decade lasts well into the twenty-first century.

Technology and science

Arguably, the product that had the greatest impact on American lifestyles in the 1980s was the personal computer. Introduced by Apple in 1977, the personal computer, in effect, gave consumers a glimpse of the world beyond the confines of their homes. Also available was the ability to connect these computers over local or even national networks. Through a device called a modem, individual users could link their computer to a wealth of information using conventional phone lines. What lay beyond the individual computer was a vast domain of information known as cyberspace.

In the 1980s, when the underlying structure for the internet was developed, the foundation was laid for one of the biggest communication technology advances of the twentieth century and beyond. California's Silicon Valley, which produced equipment for these computers, became the symbolic heart of the American technological economy. The personal computer also became a fixture in middle-class American homes and offices and set the stage for the growth of the information highway a decade later.

What came with this worldwide access, however, was a mixed bag of seemingly boundless benefits tempered by a host of frightening prospects – some of which have already begun to surface in the growing practice of hacking into computer databases by foreign government operatives, identity thieves or mischievous computer whizzes bent on creating mayhem. On the one hand, classrooms were populated with teacher- and student-friendly computers for educational purposes; consumers could order goods via the internet; and businesses could manage payrolls, mailing lists and inventories from one small machine. On the other hand, child predators, internet scams and identity theft seemed relentless and difficult to police.

Travel and leisure

The 1980s is touted as the 'travel decade'. Though the decade began in recession, by the mid-1980s – for better or worse – excess prevailed. This was the age of conspicuous consumption, of *Dallas* and *Dynasty,* and Americans were swooning over – if not all living – the luxurious life. Those with the financial means to afford hotel, food and fees for various methods of travel fare regarded travel as a right, not just a privilege. Travellers in this decade spent billions of dollars on trips to places 100 miles or more from home. It is estimated that more money was spent on travel than was spent on clothing, cars or national defence. Travel during this decade reflected a desire for bigger and better methods of transport, affecting everything from the family car to the largest corporate jets. During this time, Chrysler unveiled its minivan, marketing it for suburban families on the go. Honda and Toyota, Japanese corporations, brought out new cars promising better mileage than any American-made car on the market. In an effort to keep pace with these foreign vehicles, Ford released its Taurus, a newly designed sedan.

The convenience of air travel made Americans more mobile than ever. This mobility became most apparent during the holiday season. The chaotic atmosphere intensified as regular business and corporate travellers were joined by vacationers, college students and military personnel.[27] Ironically, the decade in aviation began with a hilarious and popular movie that spoofed air travel. *Airplane!*, the uproarious satire about the pitfalls associated with modern day flying, skewered the various industry tropes that had become familiar in movies and on television. The slapstick comedy that featured a familiar line-up of celebrities, ranging from O. J. Simpson to Priscilla Presley and Peter Graves, playfully mocked airport security, flight crew and passenger behaviour and in-flight rituals. The film was an elaborate exaggeration of the travails of air travel in the 1980s.

Because the average workday increased between 1980 and 1985, leisure time actually declined in the 1980s. According to online published research at The 80s Club: Politics and Popular Culture of the 1980s,

> between 1980 and 1984, leisure time declined from 19.2 hours to 18.1 hours. This was due in part to the increase in

white-collar salaried jobs and a decrease in blue-collar 'time clock' jobs. Previously, it had been predicted that technology would increase leisure time; that didn't seem to be the case.[28]

This study also reveals that Americans spent the majority of their leisure time at home in passive activities like reading or watching television, or even talking on the home telephone. Going to the cinema was less of a pastime then as many Americans obviously preferred to watch their own television sets. Other popular pastimes included reading newspapers, attending the theatre and reading books.

Walking, hiking or simply going for a drive were popular outdoor activities during this decade. A majority of Americans gravitated toward gardening as a favourite outdoor activity. Exercise was taken seriously as Americans participated in activities such as hiking, aerobics and jogging. This 80s Club website also reports that,

> In 1986, nearly 70% of Americans were exercising, with almost half exercising 1.5 hours a week or less, and 27% working out five hours or more. In 1985, 20% participated in aerobics. (Nonetheless, nearly 60% of us were overweight in 1985.) Gardening was the number one outdoor activity; it occurred in 82% of households. In 1986, nearly 105 million Americans took a vacation, with about one in ten traveling to foreign countries for that purpose. Golfing and skiing were by far the most popular recreational activities during a vacation.[29]

Fashion

According to Jan Deleon, author of 'The 80s Greatest: "80s Fashion Trends"', the 1980s were such a simpler time. Reagan was in the White House, the internet was relegated to underground military bunkers, and computers were the size of your living room. Fashion was also at its most bold. In an age of excess, style reflected the zeitgeist perfectly.[30] That zeitgeist of the era was in step with styles made popular by television and movie celebrity icons, by high-profile recording artists and by the lure of pop culture. Parachutes and baggy pants, bright-coloured accessories, teased hair, loud make-up and neon were popularized by pop music stars. The Ray-Ban sunglass fad was popularized by Tom Cruise in the 1980s, and the T-shirt worn under a designer sports jacket was popularized by *Miami Vice* actors; Members Only jackets were also popular in the 1980s.

Fashion designers soon discovered another unisex fashion trend in the shoulder pad, through which consumers sought the illusion of power, confidence and command in their persona. With this in mind, various designers worked to achieve an all-important menacing look by creating the appearance of broad shoulders and a drop-down waist. While mostly women adopted the trend, some rockers like Prince went further by enhancing this design. The early 1980s saw many fashion-conscious sports fans wearing lots of browns, tans, plaid and oranges in their regard for golfers such as Tom Watson and Jack Nicklaus.

Actress, activist and exercise guru Jane Fonda popularized spandex during the decade with a series of popular videotapes of various workout routines featuring her wearing this form-fitting attire. Interestingly, for the 1980s viewers, the lure of the svelte Fonda's videos went beyond her stretch routines to her outfit. Thus, spandex left the gym and found its way onto the streets and public spaces of America – much to the chagrin of the fashion conscious. The influence of dance wear outfits, especially among women, was further popularized by the release of *Flash Dance* (1983) and the desire among many women to emulate actress Jennifer Beals. Makers of Jordache jeans deposed Levi's Wrangler, Lee and other heretofore popular brands and upped its sales by engaging in sensual advertising campaigns for their product. Consumers responded by making Jordache jeans a covetable fashion item; sales skyrocketed.

By and large, 1980s apparel tended to be very bright and vivid in appearance. Female consumers went for the look of wealth and success through shiny costume jewelry, such as large faux-gold earrings, pearl necklaces and clothing covered with sequins and diamonds. Popular clothing in the early 1980s for men included tracksuits, V-neck sweaters, polyester and velour polo-neck shirts, sports jerseys, straight-leg jeans, polyester button-ups, cowboy boots, beanies and hoodies. Men wore sports coats and trousers to places that previously required a suit. Throughout the 1980s, the punk style was popular among people aged eighteen to twenty-two, characterized by multi-colored Mohawks, ripped skinny jeans, worn band T-shirts and denim or leather jackets. Although difficult to summarize in broad strokes, it is safe to conclude that fashion trends in the 1980s ran the gamut from tastefully conservative to downright racy, gaudy or in overall poor taste. One might argue that the extreme fashion trends of this decade were exponential in their reflection of excess, greed and self-centredness on the one hand, and poverty and neglect on the other.

In spring 2016, Cable News Network (CNN) premiered a seven-part documentary series, *The Eighties*, which, according to its trailer, 'explored individuals and events that shaped a decade of exceptionalism and excess'. Through rarely seen archival footage and interviews with journalists, historians, musicians and television artists who had their finger on the pulse of this decade, *The Eighties* looked back upon the age of Reagan, the AIDS crisis, the end of the Cold War, Wall Street corruption, the tech boom and the expansion of television and the evolving music scene. For many, the series dredged up nostalgic memories of a decade marked by reckless abandon and hedonistic pleasure fuelled by the arrogance of American exceptionalism promoted and championed by the Reagan presidency. For others, the series became a bothersome reminder that twenty-first-century America under President Donald Trump will resurrect this same divisiveness, racism, inequality and greed that, unfortunately, had so characterized the Reagan era.

2

American Theatre in the 1980s

Sandra G. Shannon

Answering Reagan

'Any book on the 1980s inevitably turns into a Reagan book'. Author Bradford Martin set out to disprove his friend's prediction in *The Other Eighties: A Secret History in the Age of Reagan* (2011), a book that argues that 'there was more to the story' and that 'the foregrounding of Reagan in historical interpretations of the 1980s, though partially justified, displaces many important actors, events, and movements whose stories deserve telling'.[1] Theatre in 1980s America can be construed as an antidote to the toxic ideology of the Reagan Right, on the one hand, and, on the other, a cautionary tale about the greed, waste, sexual promiscuity and overall moral decay that so characterized this time in America. Histories will show that theatre in the 1980s stood in the crossfire while, on the domestic front, programmes designed to support the underprivileged Other were significantly reduced or completely gutted. Theatre in the 1980s also raised awareness while simultaneously offering solace as the AIDS epidemic ran amok and as crack cocaine took its toll in poor urban black communities. Theatre in the 1980s called out deregulation of the banking industry that, in one instance, yielded record profit for a new class of white millionaires and, in another, prompted dramatic increases in welfare recipients. Theatre in the 1980s – as it does in the 2000s – drew attention to the uneven scales of justice as women, gays, both legal and naturalized Americans, and other minorities, clamoured for equal and fair treatment. In this decade marked by extremes, playwrights – as they did in the past – transformed theatre spaces into sites of contestation and enlightenment where audiences could grapple with a host of these hot button issues specific to the decade.

Women's theatre

Bradford Martin's rejection of Reagan as the litmus for life in 1980s America paves the way for a much-needed discussion of the dominant role that theatre played as part of that era's countercultural revolution. In addition to the many functions listed above, theatre in the 1980s was in the forefront of galvanizing a movement that turned conservatism on its head and that created space for much needed dialogue on issues of race, class, gender and ethnicity. Women's theatre, for example, came in on that wave of liberalism and owes as much to increased attention to feminist concerns as it does to a noticeable increase among their ranks. In the forefront of this movement was a group of gifted and influential women writers, such as Beth Henley (*Crimes of the Heart*, 1979), Marsha Norman (*'night, Mother*, 1981) and Wendy Wasserstein (*The Heidi Chronicles*, 1989). Both Henley and Wasserstein won the Pulitzer Prize for their work. Writing in their book, *Women in American Theatre* (2006), Helen Chinoy and Linda Jenkins capture what they believe was behind this gradual increase in numbers and recognition accorded this heretofore relatively unnoticed group:

> Since the enterprise of theatre has been mainly run by men, women in both the business and the art of theatre have usually been seen only in terms of male definitions of success. A shift of focus shed light on their obscured accomplishments ... Out of the renewed feminism came not only feminist theatres but also major new awards for women, such as the Susan Smith Blackburn

Prize. Major older awards, such as the Pulitzer Prize, which hadn't been given to a woman since 1958, were awarded in 1988 to Beth Henley for *Crimes of the Heart*, in 1983 to Marsha Norman for *'night, Mother*, and in 1989 to Wendy Wasserstein for the *Heidi Chronicles* ... Although Broadway remained largely inhospitable, more work by women was seen in the emergent Off Broadway and Off-Off Theatres and in the regional theatres. A few anthologies of scripts and several important theoretical, critical, and historical studies were published. It looked like the 1980s would finally be the decade of women in the theatre.[2]

The number of exceptional plays, innovative subjects and techniques increased significantly in the late 1970s on into the 1980s, as women dramatists addressed tensions between societal expectations and women's realities. Marsha Norman's *Getting Out* (1978), for example, presented the same woman in two characters, her mature self and her rebellious teenage past. Wendy Wasserstein's *Uncommon Women and Others* (1978) achieved widespread national exposure. Regarded as one of the first plays about contemporary women's issues, it commanded the attention and demanded to be taken seriously. In fact, it became one of the most commonly reproduced plays in colleges in the years after its premiere. Not only did it encourage a movement, but this coming-of-age story embraces the theme of finding oneself in the midst of adulthood – a theme that is relevant to all genders throughout time. Emily Mann's *Still Life* (1981) brought home the effects of the Vietnam War, and Mann was the first woman to direct her own play on Broadway. Norman's *'night Mother* (1983) continued the story of generational differences. Beth Henley, winner of the Pulitzer Prize and the New York Drama Critics' Circle Award, had major plays with *Crimes of the Heart* (1981), a character study of three sisters, each of whom is coping with some kind of personal crisis, and *The Miss Firecracker Contest* (1980), a two-act Southern Gothic drama that boldly dissects traditional 1950s and 1960s small town values, particularly how they affect the women.

The number and diversity of women dramatists in the 1980s were welcome reversals of trends that characterized previous decades. This decade also saw a phenomenal development of feminist drama and an exponential increase in the number of theatres that featured women's realities. Early feminist theatre, as Martin Banham notes, evolved from what was deemed to be radical feminism, drawing attention to issues that eventually came to be celebrated in women's culture. New York's It's Alright to Be a Woman Theatre was a pioneer in this regard.[3] From 1970 to 1976, this theatre group set up headquarters in New York City and travelled to women's centres and college campuses across the US. The performances that they offered – based upon their own lived experiences – inspired audiences everywhere, and many credit them with having prompted the movement that is now known as 'Second Wave Feminism'.

While prevailing attitudes of separatism prompted the rise of groups such as the Living Theatre, the Open Theatre and the Performance Group, in the 1980s liberal feminism continued to develop an audience. This individualistic form of feminist theory focuses on women's ability to maintain their equality through their own actions and choices and gave women's issues an entrée into public discourse and legislation. Although persistent attempts to pass the Equal Rights Amendment failed, continued lobbying around women's issues led to a focus on the 'gender gap' in American politics. The fate of black women and other minorities received little attention on the liberal feminist agenda, yet the movement's focus on political and economic equity for white middle-class women became a force with which the dominant culture had to contend.

As a result of the liberal feminist agenda, mainstream theatre in the 1980s began to include the work of female playwrights in major awards ceremonies. For example, one can argue that the raised profile of women playwrights led to three Pulitzer Prizes for women in that decade: Beth Henley for *Crimes of the Heart* (1981), Marsha Norman for *'night, Mother* (1983) and Wendy Wasserstein for *The Heidi Chronicles* (1989). Lily Tomlin and Jane Wagner's *Search for Signs of Intelligent Life in the Universe* (1985) proved a major Broadway success. Women's caucuses in professional theatre organizations and the vitality of Julia Miles's Women's Project at the American Place Theatre helped women playwrights, directors, producers, designers and actors seem suddenly to appear where they had never been before in the ranks of Broadway and regional US theatres.

Much of feminist theatre of the 1980s highlighted consciousness-raising technique, such as overt use of sex-role reversal, realistic portrayal of women's oppression, and historical characters in and out of historic context as role models of feminism. Mainstream plays by women, however, conformed to more traditional forms and styles, such as psychological realism and social comedy. Feminist theatre troupes in the 1970s and 1980s continued to search for a 'feminine' or 'feminist' aesthetic that would give voice to new content by developing new theatre forms and modes of production. Because of increasing economic burdens and the fractionalization of radical feminism as a concerted political movement, however, the tradition of flourishing, alternative feminist theatres failed to sustain itself.

Of the numerous radical feminist theatre groups that began in the 1970s, only Spiderwoman Theatre, a collective of Native American women operating in New York, and At the Foot of the Mountain Theatre in Minneapolis continued to produce and tour by the early 1990s. The multicultural or ethnic focus of these groups indicates the growing awareness in US feminism in the 1990s of differences between and among women. Split Britches, a popular feminist and lesbian troupe that began in the 1980s in the East Village lesbian community in New York City, appropriates popular cultural forms once avoided at all cost by feminist theatre to investigate sexuality as well as gender. While alternative feminist theatre practice declined in the 1980s, the decade witnessed the beginning of committed feminist criticism and theory that has become a vital site for activist and intellectual work in the theatre profession and in academia.

While women playwrights could certainly boast historic gains in the 1980s, each advance in the discipline seemed to be met with equal – if not even greater – setbacks. For instance, women's theatre faced relentless backlash during the Reagan years. 'One tactic', according to Chinoy, 'was to blame feminism for the evident malaise among women.'[4] This, of course, provided ample reason to slash or completely obliterate funding to support a women's theatre movement. Also, attempts to utilize the stage to raise public consciousness and argue the rights of lesbians further splintered the movement and further solidified opposition against federal funding.

African-American women playwrights of the decade had to wage a similar war to gain exposure for their work. A major battle for them involved wresting a share of the limelight from two formidable male forces that Peterson and Bennett referred to as 'two brothas: August Wilson and George C. Wolfe ... While Wolfe and Wilson maintain their presence on Broadway', they argued, 'African-American women playwrights remain outsiders.'[5] What's more, in addition to the dominance of theatre by Wolfe and Wilson, author Carlos Cortes observes in his edited study *Multicultural America: A Multimedia Encyclopedia* that:

> Between 1971 and 1982, African-American novelist, performer, and filmmaker Melvin Van Peebles had four shows on Broadway, two of which he also produced. The most noteworthy of them were *Ain't Supposed to Die a Natural Death*, a social commentary on inner city life, and *Don't Play Us Cheap*, a lighthearted fantasia on contemporary black identity. Finally, fictionalized accounts of black historical figures, including Jackie Robinson (*The First*) and Diana Ross and the Supremes (*Dream Girls*), launched the careers of a number of successful African-American performers, including David Alan Grier, Loretta Devine, and Sheryl Lee Ralph, Jennifer Holliday, Janet Hubert-Whitten, and Phylicia Rashad.[6]

Still, a growing list of women playwrights – Aisha Rahman (*The Mojo and the Sayso*, 1989), Suzan-Lori Parks (*Imperceptible Mutabilities in the Third Kingdom*, 1989) and Cheryl West (*Before It Hits Home*, 1990) – were beginning to gain access to that inner circle. Rahman's plays are widely anthologized in several collections including *Nine Plays, Moon Marked and Touched by Sun* and *Plays by African Americans*. Her plays were produced across the United States at theatres including the Public Theatre, Ensemble Theatre, BAM and in universities. She explained to theatre scholar and anthologist Sidne Mahone her motivation for writing *The Mojo and the Sayso*, her best known work:

> I was trying to dramatize the unconscious or emotional levels of character. And that's why I find that I always have to make some kind of leap that might be described in some Eurocentric term like 'absurdist.' But I don't think of it that way ... My work is in the tradition of what I call the 'jazz aesthetic,' which acknowledges the characters' various levels of reality. They have a triple-consciousness: of the unborn, the living and the dead.[7]

Multicultural theatre

The 1980s drew the curtain back on theatre that thrived outside of mainstream white culture. The driving force among plays of this ilk was the will to overcome all forms of discrimination, including racism, sexism and homophobia. This resistance movement yielded three types of theatre: theatre of identity, theatre of protest and cross-cultural theatre. Theatre of identity promotes a particular people's cultural identity and invites members of that culture and others to experience their joys, problems, history, traditions and point of view. Theatre of protest objects to the dominant culture's control and demands that a minority culture's voice and political agenda be heard. Cross-cultural theatre mixes different cultures in an attempt to find understanding or commonality among them.

Ideally, the mission of multicultural theatre is to reflect America's acknowledgement of the many different cultures that coalesce in this country's melting pot. It stood to reason, therefore, that the stage should be an ideal place to portray that reality. Such was the case during the 1980s and 1990s, when many mainstream theatres opened their doors to works that depicted issues of cultural and social relevance to various minorities. Hispanic/Latino theatre, Asian theatre and Native American theatre, for example, found venues for plays steeped in the myths, rituals, cultural sensibilities and real life experiences of these various ethnic groups. Moreover, plays that addressed such social issues as AIDS also found receptive mainstream audiences.

Pulitzer Prize-winning Hispanic playwright Nilo Cruz became interested in theatre in the early 1980s as an actor, and in 1988 he directed *Mud*, by playwright Maria Irene Fornés, who in 1990 became the only other Latin-American ever nominated for a Pulitzer Prize for drama. José Rivera also raised the profile of Hispanic/Latino theatre in the 1980s with the *House of Ramon Iglesia* (1983) and *The Promise* (1988). The most commercially successful Asian-American play was David Henry Hwang's play *M. Butterfly*, which became the first Asian-American play to be produced on Broadway and won the Tony Award for Best Play in 1988. The success of *M. Butterfly* created a national interest in Asian-American plays, and regional theatre companies around the country began to produce plays by Hwang and other second wave

Asian-American writers such as Philip Kan Gotanda and Velina Hasu Houston.

Jeffrey Huntsman's remarks in his Introduction to *New Native American Drama: Three Plays by Hanay Geiogamah* (1980), which includes *Body Indian*, *Foghorn* and *49*, underscore the importance of multicultural perspectives on the American stage:

> As the first plays published by a Native American, Hanay Geiogamah's dramas represent a newly emerging theatrical impulse from a group of Americans who have already found moving artistic expression in song, poetry, prose, painting, and sculpture. These plays grew out of their author's desire to present Native Americans to Native Americans in ways that are vivid and compelling and free from the more pernicious of the Euro-American stereotypes.[8]

According to *Cambridge Guide to Theatre* editor Martin Banham,

> Ethnic theater allowed Asian-, African-, Mexican-, and Native-American actors as well as those of other minorities to move beyond the stereotypical roles usually assigned them in mainstream entertainment. It gave a new generation of playwrights an opportunity to use the language of the ethnic ghetto and to express sensibilities rooted in the unique historic experience of their own communities.[9]

Multicultural theatre of the 1980s continued to challenge dominant (primarily white, middle-class) cultural standards. Successful awareness campaigns opened mainstream theatres to plays about groups previously marginalized or ignored, to establish theatres to give these groups their own voices.

Musical theatre and the 'British Invasion'

Scott Miller sums up the state of musical theatre during the 1980s as 'the most mediocre' crop to have made it to Broadway in quite a few years.[10] His lukewarm criticism of what many believed to be an exclusively American-made art form was a commentary upon its diminished popularity among 1980s audiences. Quite frankly, American musical theatre at this time had all but lost its domestic audience to what many dubbed as a 'British Invasion'. London's West End had come up with a winning formula that captured and kept the attention of Broadway audiences for some time with a string of commercially successful, long-running mega-musicals. In her book, *British and American Musical Theatre in the 1980s and 90s*, Miranda Lundskaer-Nielsen observed

> a common feeling of bemusement and resentment at the British musicals on Broadway – the inner sanctum of the American musical theatre. These feelings of hostility may explain the common reference to this period as the 'British Invasion' with its connotations of the Revolutionary War and an unwelcome presence ... In the case of the musical, the phrase serves to reveal the intense American sense of ownership surrounding the art form that is so deeply embedded in American culture.[11]

The influx of musicals such as *Evita*, *Cats*, *Les Miserables*, *Me and My Girl*, *Phantom of the Opera*, *Starlight Express*, *Miss Saigon*, *Aspects of Love* and *Sunset Boulevard* drew anger from parts of the Broadway theatre establishment and forced serious discussions about certain *American* characteristics of the genre that they felt were under assault.

As the British musical effectively sidelined the American brand in the 1980s, American playwrights and producers fought to regain the patronage of their American audiences. Fortunately, as the decade ended, two Broadway musicals broke through to popular success: *Grand Hotel and City of Angels*. *Grand Hotel* – premiering in 1989 – was a resurrected project that had closed in 1958. Based on the classic novel, play and MGM film, it told of the intertwined fates of guests at a posh Berlin hotel in the early 1930s. The revised show got mixed reviews, but a combination of limited competition, good word of mouth and strong marketing kept the show running for several years. Big-name cast replacements – including screen dance legend Cyd Charisse – helped make *Grand Hotel* the first American musical since *La Cage Aux Folles* to top 1,000 performances on Broadway.

City of Angels, which also premiered in 1989, enjoyed 878 performances and went on to win the 1989 Tony for Best

Musical. The musical weaves together two plots: the 'real' world of a writer trying to turn his book into a screenplay, and the 'reel' world of the fictional film. The musical is a homage to the film noir genre of motion pictures that rose to prominence in the 1940s. As these American musical successes waned, the mega-musicals *Les Miserables* and *Phantom of the Opera* were still playing to capacity audiences, with multiple companies enjoying brisk ticket sales worldwide. Yet Americans would soon succeed in wresting back control of the genre from the British mega-musical.

Despite worrisome competition from British musical theatre and waning audiences, the characteristically American strands of the genre continued unabated throughout the 1980s. The decade did not conclude, however, without a number of spectacular performances. The original Broadway production of *42nd Street*, for example, opened on 25 August 1980 and played for 3,486 performances, which amounted to eight years on Broadway at the Winter Garden, Majestic and St James Theatres. One of show business's most classic and beloved examples of musical theatre, *42nd Street* has the record for being the longest running show in Broadway history. This quintessential backstage musical comedy classic is the song and dance fable of Broadway with an American Dream story and includes popular tunes such as 'We're in the Money', 'Lullaby of Broadway', 'Shuffle Off to Buffalo', 'Dames', 'I Only Have Eyes for You' and, of course, '42nd Street', telling the story of Peggy Sawyer, a talented young performer with stars in her eyes who gets her big break on Broadway.

In 1982, African-American talent was on full display in *Dreamgirls* and *Sophisticated Ladies*. *Dreamgirls*, which premiered in 1981, is based on the show business aspirations and successes of R&B acts such as the Supremes. Three black singers – Deena, Lorrell and Effie – begin as a group called the Dreamettes. They start as three talented, close friends and gradually sharpen their act and rename themselves *The Dreams*. Little do they know of the hard, competitive world of show business. This young female singing trio from Chicago get their big break at an amateur competition and begin singing backup vocals for James 'Thunder' Early. However, things begin to spin out of control when their agent, Curtis Taylor, Jr, makes Deena and not Effie the star of what will become known as 'The Dreams'.

Regarded as a tribute to the big-band music of legendary composer Duke Ellington, the lavish musical revue *Sophisticated Ladies* premiered at Broadway's Lunt-Fontanne Theatre in March 1981. In two acts this stylish and brassy retrospective recreates the Duke Ellington big-band sound and features all of his most famous numbers – from the infamous Speak Easy era of the Cotton Club up to his death – including 'It Don't Mean a Thing If It Ain't Got That Swing', 'Take the "A" Train', 'Satin Doll' and the haunting 'In a Sentimental Mood'. Ultimately, the Broadway musical genre forged ahead and found its way to the stage, including *Joseph and the Amazing Technicolor Dreamcoat* (1983), *The Wiz* (1984), *Singing in the Rain* (1985), *Lady Day at Emerson's Bar and Grill* (1986), *Cabaret* (1987), *Sarafina* (1988) and *Sweeney Todd* (1989).

The slide in popularity among American musicals during the 1980s cannot be attributed solely to competition from London's West End. If truth be told, the American musical form had run its course, with formulaic renditions heavily invested in safe but predictable conventions. Scott Miller identifies a string of flawed American musicals as 'forgettable mistakes'.[12] His list includes *Bring Back Birdie* (1981), *Merlin* (1983), *Doonesbury* (1983), *The Tap Dance Kid* (1983), *The Rink* (1984), *Leader of the Pack* (1984), *Starlight Express* (1984), *Harrigan 'n Hart* (1985), *Grind* (1985), *Big Deal* (1986), *Raggedy Ann* (1986), *Smile* (1986), *Chess* (1986), *Teddy and Alice* (1987), *Legs Diamond* (1988) and *Aspects of Love* (1989). He went on to charge that 'Some of these were written by top-notch talent (like Kander and Ebb's *The Rink*), and some had strong material derailed by bad productions (like Tim Rice's *Chess*)', but many of them, as Miller notes, 'were just bland'.[13] Still, some critics charge that the demise of the American musical has been greatly exaggerated and attribute the temporary lapse in this genre's popularity to its slow evolution into the twenty-first century.

Notable playwrights of the decade

The American theatre community coalesced during the decade of the 1980s to prod the country's conscience and expose its many contradictions, especially in terms of what it meant to be

American. In particular, four socially, politically and artistically engaged playwrights – David Mamet, David Henry Hwang, Maria Irene Fornes and August Wilson – took on this challenge.

Mamet wrote plays to deconstruct myths of prosperity and equal access supposedly assured by the American Dream and portray a country – indeed an entire world – plagued by irreparable moral decay. Similarly, David Henry Hwang situates his plays around the experiences of the Other as he relays the immigrant experience in America and challenges traditional beliefs about gender, race and identity. The 1980s avant-garde plays of Cuban-American Maria Irene Fornes bring to light issues related to groups outside mainstream America – including women and the poor. Her plays use humour and movie-like visuals to address social and personal issues. Her most notable works from this decade include *The Danube* (1982), *Mud* (1983) and *The Conduct of Life* (1985). Known in both Hispanic-American and experimental theatre in New York, Fornes adopted a writing style that mirrored avant-garde techniques developed in the early years of the Off-Off-Broadway movement. The spectator's identification and empathy with characters is seen as the core of her theatrical philosophy. August Wilson gave new meaning to Cornell West's mantra 'race matters' as he began writing a series of plays that focused upon black life in America in the twentieth century with an unabashed black cultural nationalist agenda.

The work of these playwrights, then, tells the 'other story' of this decade through the prism of twelve plays written by a sampling of the era's most influential dramatists. Plays such as Mamet's *Glengarry Glen Ross* (1984), *Speed-the-Plow* (1988) and *Oleanna* (1992) mirror a remorseless society grown ruthless in its pursuit of money, power and status. Mamet himself is known to have raised a few eyebrows among critics who saw him as a misogynistic, America-bashing, foul-mouthed cynic, yet his reputation remains as one who captured the zeitgeist of the decade with his characteristic, sharp dialogue (aka 'Mamet speak') and irreverent casts of characters. The so-called 'invasion of the yuppies and all of their requisite tastes, styles, and linguistic inflections' was in full swing in 1984, providing Mamet with fodder for the bulk of his dramatic output during this decade.

The 1980s, also known as the 'Me Decade', saw attention shift toward more personal concerns and away from larger social issues.

Minority writing became a major fixture on the American literary landscape, and increasing numbers of African-Americans, Asian-Americans and Mexican-Americans had major breakthroughs in this regard. The timing was right for David Henry Hwang, a California-born son of Chinese immigrants, who made his mark in drama with plays such as *Family Devotions* (1981), *The Sound of a Voice* (1983) and *M. Butterfly* (1986). Described by the *New York Times* as 'a true original', he is best known as the author of a string of 1980s plays that explore the complicated relationship of Chinese-Americans to family, culture and religious belief.

Theatre audiences in the 1980s were also introduced to the work of Pittsburgh, Pennsylvania native August Wilson, who escaped poverty in the Hill District of Pittsburgh to become a highly acclaimed, two-time Pulitzer Prize-winning playwright who – shortly before his death – completed the *American Century Cycle*. Now considered his magnum opus, these ten plays chronicle select moments in the history of African-American life in the twentieth century. The plays that comprise this unprecedented project encompass an over 90-year time frame from 1904 to 1997 and demonstrate African-Americans' engagement with pivotal moments in history, such as the Reconstruction era, the Great Migration, the Great Depression, the Second World War, and the pre-civil rights and pre-Obama eras. In one sense, the plays that make up this historic ten-play cycle can stand alone; in another sense, collectively they form an elaborate instructive narrative of a resilient people. Toward this end, the bookend plays, *Gem of the Ocean* (set in 1904) and *Radio Golf* (set in 1997), frame the rituals, the beliefs, the history and the culture of many whose stories had not yet been given voice.

And yet the decade did not belong exclusively to the above playwrights, nor the Broadway musicals. For example, the plays of Christopher Durang – known for outrageous and often absurd comedy – include the Obie Award-winning *The Actor's Nightmare* (1981), *Sister Mary Ignatius Explains It All for You* (1981–3), *Beyond Therapy* (1982), *Baby with the Bathwater* (1983), *The Marriage of Bette and Boo* (1985) and *Laughing Wild* (1987). Wendy Wasserstein's 1983 one-act play *Tender Offer*, which was produced at the Ensemble Theater, explores poignantly the relationship between a girl and her father. *Isn't It Romantic*, presented by Playwrights Horizons in New York in 1983, explores upper middle-class, expensively educated, single women. Her Pulitzer Prize-winning play, *The Heidi Chronicles* (1988), was workshopped at the Seattle Repertory Theater and then presented by Playwrights Horizons. In 1989 it moved to Broadway's Plymouth Theater, where it won the New York Drama Critics' Circle Award, the Drama Desk Award and the Susan Blackburn Prize, in addition to the Tony. Lee Blessing's *A Walk in the Woods* (1988) was reportedly based upon a real-life incident that occurred in 1982 when two negotiators left the official Geneva nuclear arms talks for an unofficial 'walk in the woods', which turned into a diplomatic breakthrough. Lanford Wilson, author of *A Tale Told* (1981), *Angels Fall* (1982), *Burn This* (1986) and *Abstinence* (1989), received the Pulitzer Prize for Drama in 1980. His earthy, realist, greatly admired, widely performed work centred on the sheer ordinariness of marginality. American theatre in the 1980s was both eclectic and influential in reflecting the changing American landscape and in shaping the field for further developments in the 1990s.

3

David Mamet: *Edmond* (1982), *Glengarry Glen Ross* (1984), *Speed-the-Plow* (1988), *Oleanna* (1992)

Nelson Pressley

Introduction

David Mamet emerged in Chicago's proudly rough-edged theatre scene with a reputation for social critique. That status was founded on the breakout success of his 1975 *American Buffalo*, a three-character drama about a junk shop owner, the owner's young hireling and a neighbourhood thief turning on each other during a small-time heist. Symbolically, much was made of the play's title, derived from the iconic object of the theft: an old buffalo head nickel, which seemed to invoke a nation historically known to prey on the weak (from animals to Native Americans) in pursuit of profit. *American Buffalo* catapulted to Broadway in a 1977 production starring Robert Duvall, resurfaced Off-Broadway with Al Pacino in 1981 and returned to Broadway with Pacino in 1983. The popular (if profane) drama was received as a pungent critique of flimsy American business ethics: 'A violent vision of the dog-eat-dog jungle of urban American capitalism', Frank Rich wrote in the *New York Times*.[1] That response was typical, and it clinched an identity for Mamet as an incisive sage. That would last through the famously pro-business decade that was presided over by Ronald Reagan and marked by a high-flying Wall Street newly fuelled by junk bonds and leveraged buyouts. If Oliver Stone's 1987 film *Wall Street* endures as a window into that era, so do Mamet's great money plays, *American Buffalo* and his 1983 Pulitzer winner, *Glengarry Glen Ross*.

Mamet's 1980s works clinched his position near the top rank of American dramatists, yet the subversive political power of the plays may have been overstated – and by the end of the long decade, with the 1992 *Oleanna*, Mamet stumbled badly. That terse, two-character drama about a female college student and her male professor merits full consideration in this study as the conclusion of a decade that saw Mamet's spectacular ascendance and surprising critical backlash; the play was billed as a battle of the sexes, and it polarized – even inflamed – audiences that sometimes heckled the woman as she warped her professor's words and actions into a career-killing charge of rape. *Oleanna* was Mamet's most political play yet, but with this ill-conceived attack on political correctness his reputation experienced a thorough about-face. Was it possible that this vital American voice was misogynistic?

Mamet's achievement may be better understood as deriving from a unique suite of skills involving character, plot and a language so distinct that it is still commonly referred to in theatre reviews as 'Mamet-speak'. The elements that made Mamet's dramas so magnetic through the 1980s had little to do with his political insight, though that reputation did not come in for a full reappraisal until his apostasy with the famed *Village Voice* essay 'Why I Am No Longer a Brain-Dead Liberal' in 2008, and even more thoroughly with Mamet's subsequent liberal-bashing non-fiction essay collection *The Secret Knowledge* (2011). Politically, the arc of Mamet's 1980s plays hardly traces an ascendency to 'voice of a generation' status, *a la* Arthur Miller or Tony Kushner. Instead, it traces Mamet's cultural fall from grace, despite a popularity so stupendous that his 1988 Hollywood satire *Speed-the-Plow* was marked by the decade's splashiest bit of celebrity casting on Broadway, as sturdy stage actors Joe Mantegna and Ron Silver were joined by pop star Madonna. Even the intensely controversial *Oleanna* was widely staged and nationally debated. But *Oleanna* marked the end of the epoch when Mamet's dramas were guaranteed a place in the nation's dramatic repertoire.

After the gnomic and unpopular *Edmond* in 1982, Mamet's star rose spectacularly with the crackling foul-mouthed knavery of the Pulitzer Prize-winning *Glengarry Glen Ross* (1983) and *Speed-the-Plow* (1985). Both dramas were received by critics as brilliant lampoons of an American culture sketched as sharks preying upon the weak. 'His plays stand as a consistent critique of a country whose public myths he regards as destructive, and whose deep lack of communality he finds disturbing,' Christopher Bigsby wrote in 1985.[2] The combative quality of Mamet's work may have been bred in the bone: Mamet's unhappy upbringing with his sister Lynn is described in his essay 'The Rake' (in the 1992 collection *The Cabin*) and elsewhere. 'The Rake' describes the brutal punishments the children received after the testy young Mamet bloodied his sister in the yard,[3] and in 1997 Lynn Mamet described her brother as 'the angriest man who was ever born'.[4] Their father, Bernie Mamet, was a labour lawyer and demanding kitchen table rhetorician. In 1985, Mamet told the *New York Times*, 'In my family, in the days prior to television, we liked to wile away the evenings by making ourselves miserable, solely based on our ability to speak the language viciously. That's probably where my ability was honed.'[5] Bernie Mamet was in part the model for the title figure in the 1991 film *Hoffa*, written by Mamet.[6] In 1959, Mamet's parents divorced. The climate of emotional instability was surely aggravated when Mamet's mother remarried in three days.

Mamet wrote for the men's magazine *Oui* briefly in the 1970s, and married actress Lindsay Crouse in 1977; they divorced in 1990. As the industrious Mamet won the 1984 Drama Pulitzer for *Glengarry*, he also established himself as the successful Hollywood screenwriter of *The Postman Always Rings Twice* (1981) and *The Verdict* (1982), and then as the writer-director of *House of Games* (1987) and, with co-author Shel Silverstein, *Things Change* (1988). Mamet married Scottish actress-singer Rebecca Pidgeon in 1991; she would originate the role of Carol in *Oleanna* and go on to appear in many of Mamet's films.

The insightful subtitle of John Lahr's 1997 *New Yorker* profile, 'Fortress Mamet', read 'Where did the playwright get his gift for the swagger of American speech?' The brilliant and searing profanity wielded by the play's largely male and often underworld (or at least insulated) characters had long been a popular way to tag Mamet. A much-cited line from *Buffalo* illustrates the violent yet comic allure and the precise rhythmic calibration of Mamet's pungent speech: 'Only, and I'm not, I don't think, casting anything on anyone: from the mouth of a Southern bulldyke asshole ingrate of a vicious nowhere cunt can this trash come.'[7] The spectacular profanity hardly eclipsed the sharp craft of Mamet's terse plays, which typically run 90 minutes or less even thirty years later: see *Race* (2009), *November* (2008), *The Anarchist* (2012) and *China Doll* (2015). Characters are rendered in swift strokes. Plots tighten fast, especially as Mamet's 1980s writing evolves under Hollywood's influence. In performance, the bite and the economy of the plays were striking, and Mamet earned a reputation as a minimalist. 'The trick is leaving out everything except the essential,' Mamet said. 'As Bettelheim says in "The Uses of Enchantment", the more you leave out, the more we see ourselves in the picture, the more we project our own thoughts onto it.'[8]

Perhaps above all, the image of Mamet that emerged as he triumphed in both theatre and film throughout the 1980s was that of a hustler. Mamet's fascination with the con is well chronicled, from hanging out in pool halls and poker rooms to directing shows by card sharp and close friend Ricky Jay. His scripts and screenplays are rife with heists: *Glengarry*, *The Shawl* (1985), *House of Games* (1987), *The Spanish Prisoner* (1998) and *Heist* (2001) are merely a portion of his works that turn on deception and misdirection. Mamet has displayed a career-long interest in the shady practices and exclusionary idioms of insiders. He is a fan of the con, and a sharp himself. Mamet's particular stock in trade, firmly established in the 1980s, is an exuberantly rarefied and action-packed language. The character that knows the angles and commands speech nearly always rakes in the chips. This edgy, richly competitive and powerfully actable language remains the enduring accomplishment of his plays.

Edmond (1982)

Edmond is a drama about a confused man who stumbles his way into committing murder; it has been compared to Buchner's *Woyzeck* and to Richard Wright's *Native Son*. The title character is clueless about the rules of the game he is convinced he wants to play. In 1982, Mamet saw *Edmond* as diagnostic of society's ills, and a portrait of a seedy New York City. 'It's a society that's lost its flywheel, and it's spinning itself apart. That's my vision of New York. It's a kind of vision of hell,' he told the *New York Times*.[9]

The plot is a swift, thorough descent as Edmond tersely leaves his wife and home and ventures into the streets looking for hired sex. Violence ensues, and he finally winds up in jail – where, in a strangely tranquil finale, Edmond is at peace. This is a cryptogram, to invoke the title of his 1994 drama *The Cryptogram*, that demands decoding, a cloaked parable puckishly inviting interpretation. What can Edmond's grim yet satisfied final situation possibly imply? What does the precise string of events suggest? Is it to do with free will? Is it a joke on conservatives as Edmond (whose full name is Edmond Burke, after the eighteenth-century conservative philosopher) reveals himself to be a deadly misogynist and racist?

'I love and have always loved jargon,' Mamet declared at the outset of the essay collection *Make-Believe Town*. Expounding on the allure of encrypted language, he wrote, 'The codes mean to me that something of surpassing interest was in progress – that something was being done up to the Green River, which River, surely as the Cocktail follows the Abby Singer, exists nowhere but on the ricasso, between the hilt and the choil.'[10]

Arguably, Mamet has always been writing about poker rooms: each of the plays examined in this chapter can be viewed in that light. His essay 'Gems from a Gambler's Bookshelf' limns his knowledge of cards and other forms of gambling, and the descriptions echo his plays. The dramas are competitions; they are not about characters in the way that most American theatre-makers discuss 'character'. Mamet says this repeatedly, insisting upon it in the context of teaching acting: 'The actor does not need to "become" the character. The phrase, in fact, has no meaning. There *is* no character. There are only lines upon a page,' he writes in *True and False: Heresy and Common Sense for the Actor*.[11] This is a Mamet drumbeat: 'As a playwright and lover of good writing, I know that the good play does not *need* the support of the actor, in effect, narrating its psychological undertones, and that the bad play will not benefit from it,'[12] and 'It will not help you in the boxing ring to know the history of boxing, and it will not help you onstage to know the history of Denmark. It's just lines on a page, people.'[13] Mamet deliberately steers the focus away from character and toward action; his combative dramas are about winning and losing, survival and defeat. What changes are the settings and the terms of engagement, and what fascinates the playwright is the specificity of the closed society, or the poker room, in which his figures match wits.

Edmond dashes through its twenty-three scenes, illustrating that Mamet was still under the influence of the blackout sketch technique (short punchy comic bits) that characterized much of his 1970s work: *Lakeboat* (written in 1970, produced in 1980), *Sexual Perversity in Chicago* (1974), *A Life in the Theatre* (1977). The play features thirty characters. Two have names: Edmond and Glenna, the waitress-actress Edmond kills in a sudden fit. The drama opens with a Fortune Teller introducing Edmond to his fate: 'You are unsure what your place is. To what extent you are cause and to what an effect ...' (221).

The unnamed wife Edmond abruptly leaves in the thinly motivated second scene has a scant twenty-eight lines; she erupts in fury as the inexpressive Edmond says little beyond the vague 'I can't live this kind of life.' The first substantial thing that Edmond says occurs at the beginning of Scene Three, when he agrees with a man at a bar who declares, 'I'll tell you who's got it *easy* ... The niggers' (226). The taproom philosophizer introduces race theory about inflexible hemispheric anthropological differences (expanding in a racist mode on the Fortune Teller's foreboding hints of predetermination), and about social pressure from which modern man needs release. He cites '*Pussy*', '*Power*', '*Money*', '*adventure*', 'self-*destruction*', '*religion*', '*release*' and 'rati*fi*cation' as pathways (227) – and as is highly characteristic of Mamet, all capitalizations and italics are his. (The punctuation in Mamet scripts is exacting in emphasis and cadence.) This seemingly unhinged litany is a road map of what's to come, though one wonders if the calamity implicates Edmond simply because, as one character will threateningly tell another in *Glengarry Glen Ross*, Edmond *listens*.

As if obeying a Greek oracle, Edmond takes the man's tip and heads to the bar recommended to him for getting laid. Edmond claims to be a novice in this situation and certainly acts like one, naively trying to negotiate what he thinks is a fair price for the services. He is quickly bounced from the place and is next at a peep show, where things go just as badly. Edmond clings to his money rather than settle for an ersatz experience with a woman behind Plexiglas, sounding idiotic as he bargains. A whorehouse scene becomes a protracted commercial negotiation, too. When Edmond gets roped into a three-card monte game on the street and accuses the hustlers of cheating, he is, of course, beaten. A hotel clerk declines to help the obviously distressed Edmond, who asks whether the phone needs a dime. Ignored, Edmond erupts, 'Do you want to live in this kind of world? Do you want to live in a *world* like that?' (249). The hard-to-reconcile paradox is that Edmond has painstakingly sought this demi-monde, which he doggedly refuses to take on its own terms. That is something for which the happily streetwise Mamet (whose non-fiction writings so often romanticize the ways and means of hustlers) punishes his naïve title figure.

The milieu and its codes are clear. The mystery is Edmond. His quest seems direct: hired sex. But he does not know how to conduct the transaction, which makes him a fool. He is a social misfit, but it seems pivotal – if often overlooked in analyses of the play – that the society in which he struggles is not his native environment, or even a civilized environment (which he fled), but a frontier of his choosing. The issue of free will Mamet introduces is tantalizing, but it may be a highbrow MacGuffin, to use Alfred Hitchcock's term for a plot device or protagonist's goal that may ultimately prove to be tangential. Mamet has primed viewers for a socio-philosophical inquiry, but the play is a tragedy about a man who cannot conduct the transactions he craves, and who cannot speak the terse but *learnable* language of business in the commercial world he has picked.

The pawnshop provides another tutorial about basic transactions. Edmond hawks his ring and acquires a survival knife, no doubt because of the allure of the tool's name. His lines in the following scene are psychopathically whiplash and vile, as he idly remarks to a woman on a subway platform that her hat reminds him of his mother's. When she moves away, he grabs her and curses her – again, with flamboyant vitriol and crude creativity ('Did I say, "I want to lick your pussy?"'). Emotionally, he is snapping: 'I worked all of my life!' he roars nonsensically. Negotiations with a pimp break down in the following scene: the pimp attempts to mug Edmond, but Edmond fights back – though all that is really audible by the scene's end, after palaver about fair prices and what percentage the girl gets, is Edmond's hailstorm of racist epithets as he beats the man (the stage directions do not indicate that Edmond uses the knife). This hateful and emotional excess can only be the point: as forecast at the play's beginning, Edmond has found something that 'opens his nose'.

Scene Fifteen directly echoes the third scene with the anonymous philosopher; here with Glenna, Edmond philosophizes that the white race is 'dead', too passive and law-abiding (263). He says to her the same simple, primal thing he has been saying throughout the play: he wants to have sex. He brags, tells Glenna he stabbed the pimp, and says, 'when I spoke *back* to him, I DIDN'T WANT TO FUCKING UNDERSTAND ... let him understand me ... I wanted to KILL him. (*Pause.*) In that *moment* thirty years of prejudice came out of me' (265). 'It's always struck me what a great achievement it would be if I could one day write a scene to make people understand why somebody killed,' Mamet said at the time.[14]

A code of truth-telling is forged as Glenna declares that she hates 'faggots', but it backfires as she tells Edmond that she is an actress. He refuses to accept her self-definition: in fact, she makes her living as a waitress. The scene turns on Edmond's ignorance and inarticulacy as he suggests that perhaps there are plays called *Juliet* and she says there aren't; his following angry stammer puts the chill of violence in the air. He describes madness as 'self-indulgence' even as he indulges his self-righteous rages. 'Are you insane?' he asks her after he's killed her.

Edmond, a man without a history and inhabiting the kind of poetic, closed, warped society that characterizes much of Mamet's work, begins to sound unreliable. He lies to the police, telling them his name is Gregory Brock (276). Can we believe him when he tells the officer he is going back his wife? That he left because he was 'bored'? When he says, 'I've learned my lesson' (280)? His function as an incoherent protagonist is clinched when his wife visits him in jail and he is nonsensical. The difficulty with the play is not merely its harshness; it is its embrace of meaninglessness and shock tactics.

What drives the final scenes is not Edmond's crackpot philosophy that white people should be in jail with blacks because whites are lonely, but the chilling, authentic-sounding statements from the cellmate instigating the ritual prison rape. This is a pointedly perverse portrait of the domestic comfort Edmond renounced at the beginning of the play; the drama's challenge (and tease) is to extrapolate meaning from this. The fundamental inarticulacy is underscored when Edmond stammers in reply to a chaplain's query of why he killed Glenna; Mamet's penultimate scene is a letter expressing insecurely that he was attractive to his prom date, and that she went with him willingly. 'I think it's a very, very hopeful play,' Mamet said at the time,[15] perhaps playing the inscrutable subject that many scholars and journalists have described in interviews with the playwright.

Edmond is one of Mamet's grunting, severely limited male figures. Mamet has penned a cargo's worth of such men; the all-male *Lakeboat* features a braggadocio-fuelled monologue by a character named Fred, the point of which is to illustrate that 'a lot of women find that [being hit] attractive'. 'I hit her in the mouth. I don't mean slapped, Dale, this is important,' says Fred (162). The line-up of men who become violent with women includes Bernie Litko in *Perversity* and the inarticulate Nick in the two-character *The Woods* (1977), who assaults the woman with whom he is on a presumably romantic retreat. 'You talk too much,' Nick grouses of Ruth, though her dialogue does not register as notably nattering or nagging, and he fails to pick up any conversational threads. The question was raised early in Mamet's career: is he a misogynist? Or does he simply write such stunted men unnervingly well? The pattern, and the question, would accelerate through *Oleanna*.

Like his 1977 anti-capitalist fable *The Water Engine*, *Edmond* labours as a sweeping paranoid American statement – as a version of what the British call 'state of the nation' plays. 'The myth of the so-called American Dream doesn't work anymore and as a result the people it has sustained, the white males, are going nuts,' Mamet said regarding *Edmond*.[16] Brenda Murphy writes that Edmond finds what he wants, that the final relationship has the basic hallmarks of quality – honesty, and 'most important, no element of monetary exchange'.[17] But that non-mercantile quality, to say nothing of the 'honesty' (Edmond is irrefutably raped in his first sexual encounter with his cellmate), is highly qualified, if not entirely compromised, by the brutal circumstances and incarceration. If this is Edmond's wish, it is meant to be hard for audiences to follow along. Largely, they haven't: the play is seldom revived, though Kenneth Branagh starred in a 2003 production at London's National Theatre, and William H. Macy starred in the little-seen 2005 film version. Mamet experienced much greater success as he returned to the kind of highly specific setting and menacing yet sprightly gang operation of *American Buffalo*.

Glengarry Glen Ross (1984)

Glengarry Glen Ross was instantly hailed as a compelling expose of underhanded real estate salesmen peddling questionable parcels to hapless marks. Mamet knew his territory; for a period in Chicago, he worked in just such a sales office, observing the work habits of men hustling for their daily bread.

The play was seen as a ruthlessly unsentimental companion to Miller's American masterpiece *Death of a Salesman*, likewise calling into question the pie-eyed view of capitalism as the nation's chief engine of happiness; Brenda Murphy called it 'Mamet's most devastatingly direct treatment of US business'.[18] In his autobiography *Timebends*, Miller wrote that he intended *Salesman* as a portrait of 'the bullshit of capitalism'.[19] But in *Glengarry Glen Ross*, so enthralled is the writer to his weasels (*Weasels and Wisemen* is the apt title of Leslie Kane's long study) and so irresistibly thrilling is the life-and-death action of the sales force's language that Mamet actually has us rooting for the bad guys.

'A particular way of using language ... is central to the characters' identities and relationships to each other,' David Worster writes in 'How to Do Things With Salesmen: David Mamet's Speech-Act Play'.[20] Worster notes that 'say', 'said', 'tell', 'told', 'talk', 'talking' and 'speaking' are used more than 200 times in this short drama, which is apt for a play dedicated to British dramatist Harold Pinter, a master of infusing talk (and silence) with portent. To talk is to sell; to sell is to win. Where the riddling *Edmond* is mystical obfuscation, *Glengarry* is pure persuasion.

The two-act play breaks its first act into three scenes, each a confidential dialogue in a Chinese restaurant booth. The character list describes men (no women) in their forties and fifties, and the first scene begins *in media res* as an older, down-on-his-luck salesman named Shelly Levene pleads with his younger boss John Williamson. In Levene's short first speech, Mamet puts 14 words in italics: Mamet is ever-emphatic, yet he almost never resorts to exclamation marks. (For contrast, see the forest of exclamation marks in Miller's 2002 *Resurrection Blues*, which set a hysterical tone without providing nearly as nuanced a guide to speech as Mamet accomplishes.) Mamet's cadences are geared to appeal to the listener's ear while guiding performers, who are required to discriminate between shadings of words that may be capitalized, italicized or garbed in ironic quotation marks, as in this line from Levene: 'Sixty-*five*, when we were there, with Glen *Ross* Farms? You call 'em downtown. What was that? *Luck*? That was "luck"? *Bull*shit, John' (3).

Levene's pathetic position conspicuously echoes *Salesman*. Levene cites his productive years and demands loyalty, then begs for mercy: 'My stats for those years? Bull*shit* … over that period of time …? Bull*shit*. It wasn't luck. It was *skill*. You want to throw that away, John …? You want to throw that away?' (3). Williamson explains the policy that hands the quality leads to the men at the top of the board. Levene recognizes that the system is rigged against him: 'Then how do they come up above that mark? With *dreck* …? That's *nonsense* … I want sits. I want leads that don't come right out of a *phone book*' (5–6).

The bargaining is bare-knuckled as Levene talks tough and resorts to bribes and kickbacks. Williamson is cool and unmoved, so lacking in empathy that no sooner do the words 'John: my daughter …' come out of Levene's mouth than Williamson cuts him flat with 'I can't do it, Shelly' (9). Does Levene actually have a daughter? This, and one more similar supplication very late in the play, is all the evidence we have. Mamet has frequently stated disdain for the poignant backstory, which he criticizes as cheap emotion and a dramatic crutch. (Mamet did expand on the existence of Levene's daughter for the film, which is 'seriously overwritten and overplayed' in the judgement of director Sam Mendes.[21] Like Williamson, Mamet is not interested in Levene's unseen, unnamed daughter – she's not part of the action. Yet the brief mention increases our own empathy for Levene, and diminishes our view of the reptilian Williamson.

The second scene between colleagues Moss and Aaranow modulates the rhythm toward vaudeville. Banter overlaps and sentences fragment, but thoughts run in tandem. We hear the men bond, particularly as they (like Levene) disparage the unseen bosses Mitch and Murray in cadences worthy of Pinter and Beckett:

Aaranow They came in and they, you know ...
Moss Well, they fucked it up.
Aaranow They did.
Moss They killed the goose.
Aaranow They did.
Moss And now ...
Aaranow We're stuck with *this* ...
Moss We're stuck with this fucking shit ...
Aaranow ... *this* shit ...
Moss It's too ...
Aaranow It is.
Moss Eh? (13)

The dyspeptic co-workers finish each other's thoughts; they reinforce each other in a bitter solidarity that quickly turns underhanded, shrewdly guided by Moss. If Levene displays the ultimate hard sell, desperately pressing his adversary without guile or tact (and therefore destined to fail – it's too clear he doesn't have the cards), Moss is subtler. He manoeuvres Aaranow so effectively that very quickly Aaranow says, 'That's right' (with small variations) five times in a row, followed by a flurry of plain yes/no responses (14–15). Moss carefully works up to the idea that Mitch and Murray have wrecked the enterprise (Levene has said much the same thing). 'And you know who's responsible?' Moss asks once he has Aaranow properly wound up with indignation. The bosses will have it coming if – say – the office gets robbed of the leads the executives are squandering, and if the talent – namely, Moss and Aaranow – walk across the metaphorical street to the competition, Jerry Graff. The trick for Moss is to make the case so persuasively that he can strut past any doubts – and there are doubts. How much are the leads worth? How well is Graff doing? We only have Moss's word for such matters, and his picture changes. 'Somebody told me' and 'You hear a *lot* of things' he says (16) as he ballparks pretty pictures for Aaranow.

The whiny, ineffectual, go-along Aaranow is perhaps the least persuasive character in the play. For an experienced salesman in such a ferociously competitive climate, he shows no appetite, little savvy and a dull nose for detecting Moss's manipulations. He doesn't even function particularly well as the moral outlier, a resistant straight-arrow compass by which we gauge how amoral this gang is. The primary weakness of the first act is the way Moss supposedly has Aaranow in an inescapable vice by virtue of having shared his plot to knock off the office and raid the leads. Mamet himself pulls off an artful con job, seducing audiences with a semantic distinction that is one of the play's most famed passages. Moss and Aaranow debate over whether they're genuinely 'talking' about the heist as an actionable plan – 'We're not actually *talking* about it,' the fretful Aaronow clarifies – or merely 'speaking' about it ('As an *idea*,' Moss parses). But Aaronow apparently is helpless to resist when Moss threatens to implicate him if the cops come asking after the fact. Moss has his man, closing the scene with the flamboyantly insidery 'Because you listened' (27).

Act One climaxes with the finest sales pitch of the three, one so smooth we don't even recognize it for what it is until it's practically over. In contrast to the nervous energy of the previous dialogues, the velvety Richard Roma delivers what is all but a monologue to his mark, whose scant six lines of dialogue include one complete sentence ('I don't know'). The seductive philosophy Roma espouses is a rascal's code casting shadows on 'middle class morality' and whether 'bad people go to hell', tossing off impressive comments about sexual escapades. Roma endeavours to personify fearlessness while enlisting his companion into his ethos of risk, action and life aggressively lived. The talk is so familiar and chummy that it is a striking surprise when Roma asks his companion's name. Roma finally comes to the point about land, a pitch that he introduces with his own soft sell utterance of 'Florida. *Bullshit.*' Roma gets his teeth into the man, James Lingk, with 'Listen to what I'm going to tell you now.'

The second act is one unbroken scene in the sales office, which has been ransacked overnight. A detective is on hand to investigate, and any doubt about the firm's unsavoury ethics are erased when Williamson privately informs Roma that if stolen contracts need to be re-signed, they will be taken care of by Murray with a made-up song-and-dance: 'He'll be the *president*, just come *in*, from out of *town*' (39). Levene, who seems to know nothing about the robbery, enters with a heroic war story of a sale he just made; Roma salutes his comrade's success, and Levene, back on top, declares haughtily to Williamson that 'A man's his job' (49). The act turns, though, as Lingk, under orders from his unseen wife, arrives to renege on his sale with Roma. Mamet has Roma go into his wiliest tap dance: Roma quickly enlists the revitalized Levene to impersonate a big-shot buyer so they can buffalo Lingk. The performance under pressure by Levene and Roma is virtuoso, and Roma is on the brink of getting away with it when Williamson intervenes and reassures Lingk that his check has already been taken to the bank – exactly what Lingk did not want to hear. The vituperation for the bumbling manager Williamson from the workingmen is a blast of invective. The furious Roma delivers the belittling lesson: 'You never open your mouth 'til you know what the shot is' (66).

Leslie Kane illuminates the Jewish component in Mamet's work throughout her compelling *Weasels and Wisemen*:

> So skillfully has Mamet universalized his themes, however, that critics have failed to note that from its opening beat *Glengarry Glen Ross* is a profoundly Jewish play ... Framed as a brilliantly conceived maze of questions – 'Do I want pity?' (22), 'You need money?' (46), 'What does that mean?' (43) – that are themselves typically Jewish, *Glengarry Glen Ross*'s intrinsically Jewish concerns are evident in its linguistic rhythms, comic irony, and consideration of conduct in a society rarely hospitable to human aspirations and dignity.[22]

Kane deciphers the characters' names, finding strong biblical connections between Aaranow, Moss and Levene and Aaron, Moses and the Levites. In 1983, as *Glengarry* emerged, the Goodman Theatre produced Mamet's *The Disappearance of the Jews*, and Mamet's exploration of Jewish identity would intensify in the 1990s. In 2005, Mamet argued Willy Loman's largely overlooked Jewishness in London's *Guardian* newspaper: 'It is a Jewish play,' he concludes simply.[23] This potent facet of Mamet's writing is worth noting here; Kane's study fully develops similar compelling arguments regarding *Speed-the-Plow* and *Oleanna*.

If *Glengarry* follows the form of a 'gang comedy', though, as Mamet has said, the mischievous heroes are the polished salesman Roma and the redeemed old warrior Levene, with Williamson as the villain. Scholarship often focuses on the ethical outsider Aaranow, but in performance it can be difficult for that reticent character to gain traction. The dominant macho swagger and linguistic panache are powerful; the sheer forward-pressing action is seductive. Bigsby writes of the salesman, 'So long as he keeps talking, his hopes are alive and, to a degree, so are those of his listeners. For this reason it would be a mistake to see *Glengarry Glen Ross* as simply an attack on American business ethics, though it is certainly that ... That it has the power to entrance is the origin of a certain fascination and even exultance.'[24] Bigsby adds the important point that Mamet does not 'write about his salesmen with contempt'.[25]

That leaves the moral compass spinning. The climax has the audience rooting for Roma's attempted heist, and plot-wise, the play essentially is the ruination of Levene, who reveals himself as the office thief due to the simplest of verbal slips. *Glengarry Glen Ross* is one of the most exciting plays about con men ever written, but it is not clear that it holds water as an indictment of American capitalism. 'I don't think I was ever a critic of capitalism ... Anything I might know about capitalism is not going to be found in a play,' Mamet said in 1994.[26] Despite its reputation as an anatomy of unchecked market forces, the play is, in fact, an expert display of sales techniques and misdirection. 'David loves these guys,' Mendes said as he directed *Glengarry* at London's Donmar Warehouse in 1994. 'No question about it. All of them ... It's a hymn to their absurd genius.'[27]

Unapologetic self-interest is an ethos Mamet has frequently embraced in his abundant non-fiction, culminating in his conservative political book *The Secret Knowledge* (2011). The characters in *Glengarry* appear not to reverse or to recognize anything deeper than a winning gambit and a losing hand. They simply act, and tally results. 'Attention must be paid,' Linda Loman says in *Salesman* at her husband's grave, the kind of sweep and sentiment that Mamet forbids. Like *Edmond*, *Glengarry* offers no solace, and no nod to a rounder environment. Roma exits brusquely toward the restaurant as this particular ungoverned underworld spins on.

Speed-the-Plow (1988)

Mamet returned to the art of the deal with a jaunty three-character parody of a very soft target: Hollywood. The comic *Speed-the-Plow* falls into the deep furrows of playwrights savaging the Philistine playground where movies (and money) get made and where anti-intellectualism and inanity rule. The language of the two film producers is the same as that of the salesmen in *Glengarry*, with the same ABC ('Always Be Closing') culture. There is a film deal to be made. The dramatic question within the play's semi-romantic triangle is who the partners will be and which project is the better 'lede': a vehicle for the unseen action picture star Doug Brown, or an angst-riddled philosophical novel with the ludicrously clumsy title *The Bridge: or, Radiation and the Half-Life of Society. A Study of Decay*, penned by what the producers call 'an Eastern Sissy Writer'.

In the play, *The Bridge* is inscrutable: there is no way to fix its value (something Steven Price explores).[28] Plainly, though, within the confines of 'Hollywood', the 'highbrow' and 'meaningful' are antithetical to what the self-acknowledged 'whores' (or 'executives') have to produce: commercial hits. 'That's what we're in business to do,' Gould tells Karen. '*Make the thing everyone made last year*' (74). The only thing that matters besides hits, the men agree, are fun, and – the thing to be tested, the only ethic by which they actually swear and the thing that Mamet shows that they do not believe in at all – loyalty.

With *Speed-the-Plow* Mamet balanced on a fine point between the high art of literary drama and the low (yet lucrative and heady) enterprise of moviemaking. *Glengarry* positioned him as the country's leading dramatist, with a forceful linguistic and dramatic style singularly his own. But he was also a rapidly rising Hollywood hand by the 1988 Broadway debut of *Speed-the-Plow*, and the play was his brightest, most accessible to date, notwithstanding its rampant cursing and knife-in-the-back plot. *House of Games* had just established Mamet as a film director, and in 1987 he penned the screenplay for the Brian DePalma blockbuster *The Untouchables*, starring Kevin Costner and Robert DeNiro. *Speed-the-Plow* itself was a conspicuous celebrity event with Madonna in the cast as Karen, the secretary who argues for *The Bridge*. Like the compulsive female psychiatrist alone among con men and learning their ways and means in *House of Games*, Karen tries to make herself a player.

Like *Oleanna*, *Speed-the-Plow* is published with an epigraph; the lines from Thackeray's *Pendennis* praise the work ethic. Bobby Gould's foreboding opening line echoes *Edmond*: 'When the gods would make us mad, they answer our prayers' (1). This is what happens to Gould: as a studio executive whose new job, he says, 'is one thing: the capacity to make decisions' (30), he prays for a hit. It seemingly arrives in the form of an action picture brought to him by his associate Charlie Fox. The colleagues banter in a way that Mamet polished steadily since *Lakeboat*, with Gould outlining workplace code by reiterating to Fox the 'channels' for getting scripts read (5). The news from Fox is that megastar Doug Brown will 'cross the street' to make an action picture with their studio; Fox only needs Gould to green-light the project (7). Just as Levene raved about his triumphant sale in *Glengarry*, Fox and Gould revel at the windfall fortune at their fingertips. Their language is juiced with the adrenaline of the *Glengarry* salesmen (Gould repeatedly demands coffee for his partner-to-be), so exhilarated as to be nearly drunken, powered by brothers-in-arms camaraderie, telling with relish the tale of the kill. At the same time, there is broad satire in the description of the proposed Doug Brown picture, and even in how the producers value it:

> **Fox** Now that's the *great* part, I'm telling you, when I saw this script ...
> **Gould** ... I don't know how it got past us ...
> **Fox** When they get out of *prison*, the Head Convict's Sister ...
> **Gould** ... a buddy film, a prison film, Douggie Brown, blah, blah, some girl ...
> **Fox** Action, a social ...
> **Gould** Action, blood, a social theme ...
> **Fox** (*simultaneously with 'theme'*): That's what I'm *saying*, an offbeat ...
> **Gould** Good. Good. Good. Alright. Now: Now: when we go in ...
> **Fox** That's what I'm saying, Bob.
> **Gould** Don't even say it.
> **Fox** Bob.
> **Gould** I understand. (15)

This is not Beckett and Pinter so much as it is Laurel and Hardy, growing more comic as these executives gush with mutual appreciation and dreams of lucre.

Surely only irony and subversion can be indicated by the quotation marks Mamet writes in this line for Gould: 'And it was "loyalty" kept you with us ...' (17). The plot twists with a phone call and a delay that will put 'loyalty' to the test: instead of meeting almost immediately with Gould's superior, the deal can't be clinched until the next morning (20). (Mamet profoundly intensifies the office telephone as an interrupter and bearer of bad news in *Oleanna*.) Still, the producers' spirits remain playful, and they bond philosophically. 'Fuck people,' Gould says, adding one line later, 'But don't fuck "people"' (26), which quickly spins into Fox's declaration that within this 'People Business', 'We're gonna kick the ass of a lot of them fucken' people' (27).

They carry on in this key as Gould's temporary secretary Karen arrives with the coffee. In the atmosphere of triumph she gets drawn into the conversation, gingerly interrogating their terms as they celebrate the creation of 'garbage':

Karen But why should it all be garbage?
Fox Why? Why should nickels be bigger than dimes? That's the way it is.
Gould It's a business, with its own unchanging rules. (37)

Karen tests this when Gould – who has taken an ironically termed 'gentlemen's bet' (50) with Fox that he can sleep with her – asks if she would like to give the radiation novel the 'courtesy' read that he owes his studio head, who of course has no intention of turning such a book into a movie. Replying to her innocent question about the Doug Brown project ('Is it a good film?'), Gould details the Hollywood process to Karen. (This is obviously a seductive manoeuvre, meant to impress, so he can win his bet and, in accordance with the already ratified principle of meaningful existence, have some fun.) Karen is interested in the business, in 'The making decisions' (58). She continues to ask about the book's actual potential and, by overt implication that Gould acknowledges, about his own 'purity' as he decides. 'Hey, I prayed to be pure,' he says (57).

The second act is a tête-à-tête with Karen at Gould's house.

The surprise is that Karen is smitten by the apocalyptic/mystical novel and gives Gould a hard sell that appeals to his sense of greater purpose. She claims to have been 'empowered' by the book's import (64). She presses the case that people don't want the degrading pictures Hollywood peddles; Gould replies, 'Of course they do.' She reminds him that he offered her hope of genuine participation: in a sense, they entered into a deal. She adds that she came to the house knowing he wanted to sleep with her; this unbalances him. 'You say that you prayed to be pure,' Karen says, pressing her advantage as smoothly as Richard Roma (though we don't yet see her angle). 'What if your prayers were answered? You asked me to come. Here I am' (79).

The third act takes place the following morning before the decisive meeting with Gould's superior, and Gould – positioned by Mamet on the horns of a moral choice – is now opting to pitch *The Bridge* and dump Fox's project. Fox crudely but accurately refers to Karen (who acknowledged to Gould, 'I don't have any skills' [69]) as 'the temporary girl' (83), and he furiously, flamboyantly does most of the talking ('Listen to me now,' he repeats) as he fights Gould's decision:

> Now, listen to me: when you walk in his door, Bob, what you're paid to do ... now, listen to me now: is make films that make money – you are paid to *make films people like*. And so gain for yourself a *fortune* every day. This is what Ross *pays* us for. This is the thing he and the stockholders want from us. This is what the, listen to me now, 'cause I'm going to 'say' it, Movie Going Public wants from us, excuse me, I'm talking to you like some Eastern Fruit, but *this*, what I've just told you, is your job. You cannot make the radiation book. (87)

In his precise, even lawyerly rants about loyalty and logic, Fox displays strong echoes of Roma's bravura in *Glengarry* and the Mamet-ish ethos that 'a man's his job'. He invokes the Hollywood code Gould is brazenly violating, and when Fox summons Karen for a cross-examination it's hard not to root for him, scoundrel and champion of 'garbage' that he is. Fox, who did Gould a favour by bringing the Doug Brown opportunity to him, is treated unfairly. We have been given no reason to pull for the high-toned 'intellectual' picture, which Mamet describes in preposterous terms.

Fox is a classic Mamet operator, which, in this strictly delimited milieu, makes him heroic, misogynist crudities notwithstanding: 'You squat to pee,' he says to Gould as he physically beats (fisticuffs again) his colleague-turned-nemesis (92).

Mamet proves brilliant at engineering Fox's cross-examination climax and the unmasking of Karen. In the first act Fox tells Gould, 'I don't think she is so *ambitious* she would schtup you just to get ahead,' with Gould saying a few lines later, 'You mean nobody loves me for myself.' Fox says, 'Not in *this* office ...' (46–7). By Act Three, Fox recognizes that Karen *is* in fact acting like a member of said office, and is – like the men – trying to get ahead. She is using Gould, who was seduced and deluded by her cant of higher purpose, a brand of romanticism that cannot succeed. *She* is not 'pure'. Gould returns to whorish form, since that is their stated business, and evaluates accordingly. Karen 'played' him, but badly. Commercially, her project is second-rate. She loses.

Structurally, the piece is a return to *American Buffalo*, with Gould as shop owner Donny Dubrow, Fox as a mature, decidedly assertive (but still subservient) Bobby, and Karen horning in on the operation *a la* Teach. Ethically, it's *Glengarry*: a venal system defends itself and destroys the weakest player. Because this weak player is a woman who uses sex to buy her way into the game, critics began to note the paucity of distinct, rounded female characters – often of *any* female characters – in Mamet's work. That feature, coupled with an accumulating record of violence against women in Mamet's fictions, became a sizable cultural flashpoint as Mamet went from Karen to Carol in *Oleanna*.

Oleanna (1992)

With *Oleanna* Mamet continued to demonstrate a gift for intriguingly poetic, obscure, indelibly self-branding titles. While 'Speed-the-plough' is a traditional prayer for a rich harvest, Oleana was the name of a failed utopian community in nineteenth-century Pennsylvania. 'An overtly dystopian play,' Murphy writes of *Oleanna*,[29] with an up-to-the-minute university as the setting for brave new relativistic values that come to ruin. The subject is 'this political correctness thing', said Pidgeon, who played the floundering female student Carol opposite William H. Macy's self-absorbed professor named John.[30]

Carol comes to John's office for guidance, but in three short meetings communication fails so completely that she destroys John's career, specifically by ruthlessly recontextualizing his inept words into a transparently false charge of rape. The play ends as he beats her, an action that audiences often greeted with cheers.[31] The public reception of the American Repertory Theatre premiere (at Harvard University) was inflamed: 'I think doing this play in Cambridge is like doing "The Diary of Anne Frank" at Dachau,' Mamet said to a reporter observing two weeks of rehearsals during the premiere.[32] 'Vagina dentata goes to college,' linguist Deborah Tannen wrote when the production moved to New York.[33]

The May 1992 premiere came less than a year after Supreme Court nominee Clarence Thomas was accused of sexual harassment by Anita Hill during confirmation hearings that became a national 'he said/she said' scandal. Mamet told Bruce Weber he wrote a draft of *Oleanna* eight months prior to the Hill–Thomas hearings, an event that led him to finish the script. He also spoke of a 'longtime friend' who had been targeted with a harassment charge on a college campus[34] (Mamet said the same thing to Charlie Rose in 1994).[35] Two years later, Weber would note that *Oleanna* 'solidified his image as a man who writes out of a particularly chauvinistic brand of male rage'.[36]

Structurally, *Oleanna* follows *Speed-the-Plow*: a terse three-act drama set in a closed society with its own codes and language, and with a plot upset by the introduction of a woman unversed in that society's ways. The epigraph quotes Butler's *The Way of All Flesh*: 'The absence of a genial mental atmosphere is not commonly recognized by children who have never known it,' and the play's mental atmosphere is extraordinarily fraught. Mamet consciously submitted *Oleanna* during an inflamed national debate – 'with impeccable timing has marched right into the crossfire', Rich wrote,[37] and Mamet has John, on the phone, say three times in the opening seconds, 'What about the land?' (1) – a phrase that initially sounds as if it may have national implications. The query, we will learn, is about a house John and his wife are buying, but the phrasing resonates with Mamet's utopian theme as he subverts the notion of ideal communities.

Linguistically, *Oleanna* marshals Mamet's strengths with perhaps more blunt force than anything he had written to that point. The telephone is a natural way of introducing the jabbing speech fragments that dominate much of the first act. Mamet uses ellipses 27 times in John's first phone monologue (with Carol mutely sitting by), and the staccato cadence helps set the urgent stakes for John: 'We aren't *going* to lose the house,' he says, as the subject (real estate again) comes into view (2). Carol's first question, asked twice, regards a phrase John has used, 'term of art', which introduces the idea of specialized languages – codes, jargon, the old poker room patois. John's answer is imprecise. 'I'm not sure that I know what it means,' he says, backing down meekly after brandishing the phrase (3). That is a far cry from Fox's cocky 'nickels and dimes' line. John is vulnerable: he cannot talk the talk.

Still, the first act is his as he tries to deal with Carol's plaintive requests for help while answering repeated phone interruptions from a broker named Jerry. 'I can't talk now,' John says with variations, and the impotent repetitions do double duty, since 'talk' is the subject with Carol (10). The struggling student doesn't understand what this professor is teaching: 'I don't ... lots of the *language* ...' and 'The *language*, the "things" that you say ...' she tries to explain. They speak in such overlapping fragments that even words are incomplete '... one moment: some basic missed communi ...' goes one of John's full lines as written (6). As with *The Bridge*, our view of the pivotal academic course – the thing about which they argue – and of John's teaching, is partial, and not inspiring. She asks about his concept of 'virtual warehousing of the young', which he starts to explain but quickly dismisses ('It's just a course, it's just a book' [11–12]). Carol's frustration grows personal, which will be a key to the act. 'Nobody wants me,' she says, and John, adapting, eventually responds in a more familiar manner. But John does more than empathize: he theorizes, and his theory dooms him. He says, 'We can only interpret the behavior of others through the screen we ... (*The phone rings*)' (19). The call changes the subject to the complications of buying the house; Carol overhears that his personal life is some state of crisis because he allows it. She pursues the subject, and in what surely shapes up as a tragic flaw in the Mamet oeuvre, John further drops the professional mask – the 'Artificial Stricture, of "Teacher", and "Student",' John says (21). His strategy seems plain: to calm a distressed, ostracized student by declaring that he likes her, and by demonstrating that he is willing to work with her outside the institutional (or poker room) boundaries that she finds so un-navigable. He also reveals an unattractive pomposity in the process, trashing his bosses: 'They had people voting on me I wouldn't employ to wax my car' (23) – a misguided attempt to draw her into the kind of confidential kvetching that Moss and Aaranow might share, but that John and Carol cannot.

The moment John redirects the conversation to 'theory', Carol recoils, and the switch characterizes her as incurious and dumb. 'I want to know about my grade,' she says dully. A long pause follows, clearly demarcating a rift between them, and a disappointment that she detects: 'Did I upset you?' she asks (25). ('Presented alternately as a dunce and a zealot,' Rich noted accurately in his 1992 review, contrasting the dimension of John to the flatness of Carol.) John makes a friendly deal with Carol: he tells her that her grade is now an A, with the term only half over and the two of them starting fresh. Carol looks at her notes from John's lecture on hazing and justice; John unwittingly worsens things by telling Carol that part of his job is to provoke, which she interprets as 'to make me mad', and which he illustrates badly with an anecdote about how often the rich copulate (32).

The end of the act involves a tantalizing enigma: Carol begins to respond to John, and she starts to confess to something that may help us understand her better. Her preamble is simply 'I'm bad,' followed, after mild coaxing, by 'I have never told anyone this' and 'All of my life' – at which point the phone rings yet again and John erupts: he is being told he is losing the house. As he rants, though, he finally learns the calls have been a ruse to lure him home for a surprise party celebrating his tenure announcement. Carol's near-revelation of badness is dropped; like Levene's daughter, Carol's background (and, apparently, her present mental state) doesn't matter. Mamet's diamond-hard interest is not in the character, but in the action.

In the second act, John is talking – they are seated across from one another in the office – and he admits he loves teaching and 'performing' (43). He delivers a long monologue before they cut to the chase of the charges that have arisen, to our surprise, from that awkward first meeting. We hear Carol's distorted account, enumerated and deemed 'ludicrous' by John (47–8), and note a pronounced change in her now-confident character: 'What I "feel" is irrelevant,' she snaps when he asks, 'My God, are you so hurt?' (49). Pressing ahead with her interpretation of his harassment and sweeping away his explanations and defence, she declares with force, 'You. Do. Not. Have. The. Power ... Did you misuse it? *Someone* did. Are you part of that group? Yes. Yes' (50).

Would a professor charged with harassment meet alone again with the female student in his office? Carol says she has come as a favour, at his request, but the circumstances strain credulity (50). She is persuasive, charging John with holding his profession in low regard, arguing that his attitude demeans the students who come to him in pursuit of knowledge (52). But the conversation does not become an intellectual fencing match, and the interruptions continue to ratchet up tension as John makes still more mistakes, particularly when he tersely insists on the phone to his wife that 'I'm dealing with the complaint' (55) and, fatally, when he physically prevents Carol from leaving (57).

Assault charges have been filed, yet the adversaries are meeting privately in the office yet again. By now the semantic minefield is such that there is nowhere for John to safely step. He speaks of her 'accusations', and she cuts him off, insisting that the 'accusations' have been accepted by a committee as 'facts' (62). He uses the word 'indictment', and she tersely says, 'You will have to explain that word to me,' again illustrating her lack of intelligence and curiosity; surely a woman, even at twenty, who has surged so forcefully into legal combat will have taken on board this word, of all words. Evoking the renowned slur of *American Buffalo*, she says, 'You think I am a frightened, repressed, confused, I don't know, abandoned young thing of some doubtful sexuality, who wants, power and revenge' (68), a characterization he accepts. As she gets to the point of banning his book from the curriculum, his recognition is to declare her 'dangerous', at which point the phone rings and the formal rape charge surfaces – the first time that word has been used. Wrapping up a conversation, John calls his wife 'baby'; Carol forbids it, at which point John physically attacks her: 'You vicious little bitch. You think you can come in here with your political correctness and destroy my life?' (79). Carol's last line, the twice spoken 'Yes ... that's right,' is as tantalizing as the end of *Edmond*, though her embrace of a violent, dominated fate is more easily (though hardly incontrovertibly) understood as ironic.

In a sense, Mamet had become a sensation merchant, first with Madonna drawing inordinate attention starring in *Speed-the-Plow* and then with *Oleanna* grabbing headlines in the culture wars. Arthur Holmberg, who observes that Carol says 'no' 38 times in the first act, documents that Mamet (who directed the premiere) wanted 'big' performances from Macy and Pidgeon, telling them in rehearsal, 'It's got to be bigger than life, or the audience won't have a catharsis. "Don't call your wife baby" has got to be fucking huge. These moments drive the play, and they have got to be big. I've never worked on a play of this dimension before.'[38] By design, audiences and critics were sharply divided over *Oleanna*, starting with what it signified about Mamet's attitude toward women. A 1993 MLA Special Session on Mamet and Pinter 'essentially concluded, we think wrongly, that Mamet is a misogynist', Kane writes in the introduction to the 2001 *Gender & Genre: Essays on David Mamet*.

In *David Mamet's Oleanna*, David K. Sauer aggressively defends the play in Postmodern terms, arguing that the gaps in character and action effectively make the play about the audience and the individual perceptions and prejudices of its members. There is a stark contrast to be drawn, though, between the 'unstable realities' Sauer investigates and the direct politics of American dramatists Arthur Miller and Tony Kushner, who almost certainly would include communities and witnesses in an *Oleanna* of their own, representing the multi-vocal jostle and dimension of democracy. The Mamet of the 1980s foregoes multiple locations and communities, even sticking to single small rooms later in the expressly political *Romance* (2005), *November* (2008) and *Race* (2009). From *Buffalo* through to *Oleanna*, his exchanges typically are Spartan; he prefers groups of two and three.

There is no shortage of critics who see Mamet's parade of limited men and their difficulties with women as pro-feminist – an exposure of misunderstanding, failed language and resorts to violence, not a moral blindness or endorsement. Dorothy H. Jacobs, focusing on Levene's daughter in *Glengarry*, builds to a persuasive conclusion that the men in fact look quite bad as they fail to cope with women. Her argument could be made for many Mamet plays as she writes, 'In the imaginative recreation of a passive sit, in the hurried construction of a false identity, and in the halting invocation of a daughter, this community of men acknowledges the identity of Harriett Nyborg, recoils from the determined voice of Jenny Lingk, and momentarily goes mute at the mention of a female child. Something revelatory is gained.'[39]

Defending this aspect of Mamet's work requires substantial and sustained effort, though. Mamet's jolly essay 'True Stories of Bitches' cavalierly asserts that men's brawn is the ultimate trump card: 'People can say what they will, we men think, but if I get pushed just one little step further, why I might, I might just ___ (FILL IN THE BLANK) because she seems to have forgotten that I'M STRONGER THAN HER,'[40] a line frequently cited as evidence of a *he-just-doesn't-get-it* stance. Lindsay Crouse viewed Mamet's female characters as immature: 'They are just about to be born when the play ends,', she said.[41] *Playboy* asked Mamet about the violent/misogynist pattern, going back to *The Verdict* (the interviewers might have gone back further to *Lakeboat*, *Sexual Perversity* and *The Woods*); Mamet disputed any charge that his work 'incites' or 'supports' violence.[42] Steven Price's 'Disguise in Love' (*Gender and Genre*) closes with a splendid instance of the enigmatic quality Mamet perpetuated around gender in his work, citing a 1990 interview on BBC TV in which Mamet said, 'It's taken me a long time to figure out what I think it is that women actually want. And if you think I'm going to share it with your viewership, you're out of your mind.'[43]

In *Oleanna*, though, Mamet plainly stacked the deck. Even Debra Eisenstadt, who played Carol on tour and in the 1994 film, said, 'It's a little disconcerting that anyone would cheer when someone's getting beaten up on stage ... They don't like me.'[44] The linguistically precise and combative Mamet seemed to go out of his way to provoke yet again regarding the word that generated so much passion around *Oleanna* as he made the film. 'I had this play,' he said to the *New York Times* in 1994, 'and I wanted to rape it into a movie.'[45]

'It is "Oleanna" that manipulates, pretending to be an honest play about the indeterminacy of language and abuse of power, then assaulting us with its simplistic and dehumanizing denouement,' wrote Deborah Tannen, who compellingly viewed the play's first part as Pinteresque and the second as Kafkaesque, calling Carol 'a stereotype that audiences can join in hating'. Tannen found the cheers at the spectacle of the beating to be 'dangerous': 'Right now, we don't need a play that helps anyone feel good about a man beating a woman.'[46]

Conclusion

By the end of the 1980s Mamet was almost universally acknowledged as the country's leading dramatist as he coolly, almost cruelly sorted winners from losers, and his career seemed to expand with the same kind of thrilling, defiant energy that characterized his plays. No American dramatist was more profane, more jubilantly and intimidatingly slangy or more knowing, it seemed, about the ins and outs of American deal-making. As the decade progressed, possessing a ticket to a Mamet play meant possessing a ticket to a substantial cultural event.

The firestorm over *Oleanna*, though, and the universal embrace of the more politically in-tune *Angels in America*, emerging at the same time, retrospectively looks like the moment the increasingly narratively quirky and publicly combative Mamet ceded 'leading dramatist' status to Tony Kushner (with August Wilson's grand and popular cycle only beginning to make its mark). What remains inimitable and effective in Mamet's 1980s plays is the style – the showy linguistics and a nose for pared-down conflict in almost unmatched high relief – not the political content, which fully backfired on the playwright at either end of the decade. From the messy perplexity of *Edmond* to the ruthless but off-putting efficiency of *Oleanna*, Mamet honed his hungry, goal-focused characters' colourful vocabulary, the jabbing rhythm of their dialogue and his terse, suspenseful plotting; his storytelling facility catapulted him to the top of his profession, and toward a long career in Hollywood. So powerful were Mamet's verbal flamboyance and explosive climaxes that even when he wrote against the grain of cultural sensitivities, the punch of his speech, his nearly unmatched ability to crisply depict overt and subtle shifts of power, and his intuitive knack for entertaining gave his voice a prominence that few US dramatists have subsequently enjoyed.

4

David Henry Hwang: *FOB* (1980), *The Dance and the Railroad* (1981), *Family Devotions* (1981), *M. Butterfly* (1988)

William C. Boles

Introduction

During the early 1980s around the same time that August Wilson began writing *Jitney* – the first play in what would be a ten-play cycle documenting the African-American experience in the twentieth century – David Henry Hwang's first play, *FOB*, was being produced by Joseph Papp at New York's Public Theater. This imaginative, fresh and determined first-generation American born Chinese writer would go on to become the first Asian-American playwright to have a play premiere on Broadway. Like Wilson, who was interested in redefining the nature of the African-American experience, David Henry Hwang was providing a new theatrical focus on the Asian-American experience. In addition, like

Wilson, Hwang found himself creating a cycle of plays (in his case a trilogy) that ranged from the contemporary immigrant experience in California to the Chinese workers that built the transcontinental railroad in the mid-nineteenth century. Ensuing plays written during the 1980s found him exploring the West's fascination with Orientalism and the misunderstandings and misinterpretations that occur between Eastern and Western cultures, which, in some cases, can lead to fatal outcomes.

Starting in the early 1980s and continuing through to today, Hwang's plays have offered an eye-opening vision of what it means to be an Asian-American in the later part of the twentieth and the first part of the twenty-first century. And while the majority of his plays are tied to the Asian-American experience, they have never been limited to a specific ethnic audience. Like Wilson, Hwang's work appeals to a diverse population because of its inquiry into the complexity and richness of the American identity. For Hwang the 1980s have proven, so far, to be his most productive decade as a playwright, as he had six plays produced in New York – five of them at the Public Theater and the sixth, just after he turned 30, on Broadway, which was the internationally heralded *M. Butterfly*. Over his thirty-five-year-plus career, Hwang has become the most visible Asian-American in the theatre, and, through his works, he has challenged audiences to question political, social and economic relations between the East and West, ethnic stereotypes of Asians and the complex issues surrounding identity.

Born in California to two immigrant parents, Hwang and his siblings were raised with an eye toward being regular American kids rather than being raised as Chinese. Hwang admitted, 'My father has always been interested in discarding the past ... He's never much liked China, or the whole idea behind China or Chinese ways of thinking. He's always been much more attracted to American ways of thinking. He feels Americans are more open – they tell you what they think – and he's very much that way himself.'[1] To that end, the Hwang children never learned to speak Chinese, as their parents feared it would interfere with their study of English.

Dorothy, Hwang's mother, was a pianist, and as a child he followed her in music by playing the violin. However, not wanting to fit the stereotype of the Asian classical violinist, Hwang switched over to the electric violin, which he still plays. His father, Henry, a successful businessman and eventual bank president, wanted his son to be a business major in college. Hwang matriculated at Stanford University in 1975, where he foiled his father's plan by becoming an English major. Later deciding to be a playwright, Hwang shared a draft of a script with a creative writing professor, who informed the want-to-be writer that he needed to understand the genre better and recommended he read plays by Harold Pinter, Tom Stoppard and Sam Shepard to better his comprehension of the form. His immersion in these writers would become essential to his playwriting development. Not surprising, Hwang's decision to pursue writing did not please his father. 'To me,' Henry Hwang remarked, 'writing plays was not serious. It was not for lawyers or doctors. It was a pastime.'[2]

While still enrolled at Stanford, Hwang saw an ad in the *Los Angeles Times* announcing the opportunity to workshop with Sam Shepard. Hwang responded and was accepted. (It is worth noting, though, that only two participants actually applied and both were accepted.) While working with Sam Shepard as well as with Maria Irene Fornes, Hwang experienced an artistic epiphany that still drives his work today. Shepard and Fornes encouraged him 'to write from my unconsciousness, to transcend intellectualism and rationality'.[3] He admitted that before he started the workshop,

> I had simply wanted to be a playwright. But as I began to let my unconscious take over, surprising concerns began to emerge from my pen – East/West conflict, cultural fusion, immigration, assimilation. I hadn't thought that these issues mattered to me. I thought I was simply a kid who happened to have Chinese parents. It was the writing that taught me otherwise. That revealed me to myself. Its voice was my voice. One I had never known until I put pen to paper.[4]

During his time with Shepard and Fornes, he began working on what would become his first play, *FOB*, which stands for 'Fresh off the Boat'. When Henry Hwang saw the Stanford production of the play directed by his son, his objections over his David's career choice melted away. While watching the play, Henry admitted that 'I was so touched, so moved, that I was crying like a baby. It was about our lives, about how we came over.'[5]

Hwang submitted *FOB* to the Eugene O'Neill Festival in Connecticut, where it was one of 1,300 entries that year. His play, along with eleven others, was accepted to be developed during the summer of 1979. Newly graduated from Stanford, he travelled to the festival where he endlessly reworked the play, and, by the end of his residency, it had caught the attention of the Public Theater, which produced it the next year. Amazingly, in the span of a little over a year Hwang transformed from a student writer to a professionally produced and critically acclaimed New York playwright.

His initial success can be attributed to two of the most powerful men in the New York theatre in the 1980s. The first was producer Joseph Papp, who, upon seeing *FOB*, felt like he had found a kindred spirit in the recent Stanford graduate, despite differences in their Jewish- and Chinese-American identities. Papp admitted that the work 'reminded me of the "greenhorns," the Jews who came from Eastern Europe. Even though the cultures were strikingly different, it was the same notion. The principle of someone coming from the old country who didn't know how to behave himself was very much part of my own tradition.'[6] Papp would remain impressed with the young playwright's work of examining Chinese-American identity, proceeding to produce Hwang's first five plays.

The other powerful influence upon Hwang's career was more indirect. Frank Rich, drama critic for the *New York Times* in the 1980s, was perhaps the most powerful voice in the theatre, as a negative review from him could close a Broadway production. Rich, though, identified Hwang as a valuable and impressive theatrical voice and championed him throughout the decade. He provided insightful criticism and words of support for the developing writer's work, even when Hwang's works were an enigmatic experiment, like *Sound and Beauty*, or a failure, like *Rich Relations*. In Rich's perspective, even when Hwang's work was unsuccessful, he was still a valuable contributor to the theatrical landscape.[7]

However, there is another less discussed reason for Hwang's rapid movement from a Stanford student in one year to a produced Off-Broadway playwright the next. Hwang's big break occurred because of an 'affirmative action program'.[8] In 1979, Joseph Papp and the Public had engaged in 'yellow face casting', which is when a white actor is cast to play an Asian character. This casting decision prompted a major protest against the theatre and Papp. After meeting with the protestors, Papp hired actor David Oyama, one of the outspoken leaders, with the specific task of identifying producible Asian-American plays that would, in turn, require the casting of Asian-American actors. Oyama ended up bringing two plays to production at the Public. The first was *The Music Lessons* by Wakako Yamauchi, a Japanese-American author. One month later, Hwang's *FOB* premiered, which Oyama had discovered at the O'Neill Festival.[9] Like Oyama, one of Hwang's goals early in his career was to create roles for Asian-American actors, since there were so few to be found:

> One very important thing for me is to give Asian-American actors a chance to work and increase our visibility ... I know to some degree there's the feeling that Asian-Americans have made it economically in this country, but I think the acting profession is sort of a tell-tale sign that we aren't as fully accepted as we'd like to believe. Sometimes even the few roles that are written for Asian characters end up being played by Caucasians in yellow-face. I'd like to see Asian-Americans in plays which don't deal only with ethnic issues – because we don't spend all our time thinking about being Asian.[10]

Despite the fact that an Asian-American playwright was once again receiving attention from the New York theatre community (in 1972 Frank Chin's *Chickencoop Chinaman* was the first Asian-American play to be produced in New York), Hwang did not impress some fellow Asian-American theatrical professionals because he relied on white producers to have his work performed instead of making his way through the small in number but influential Asian-American theatre community, which was, essentially, represented by four main theatres, all of which were still in the early stages of existence. In fact, the first Asian-American theatre group, East West Players, was founded in 1967 in Los Angeles, a mere 13 years before Hwang achieved success with *FOB*. Three more theatres rounded out the important Asian-American theatre companies throughout the 1970s. These were the Asian American Theater Company in San Francisco, the Northwest Asian American Theatre in Seattle, and the Pan Asian Repertory Theatre in New York City. Unlike his Asian-American contemporaries, like Philip Kan Gotanda, whose first work *The Avocado Kid* (1979) was produced by East West Players, and Velina Hasu Houston, whose early plays were also produced by East West Players,¹¹ Hwang's failure to have his plays premiered at one of these four main theatres prompted some Asian-American theatre professionals to call his voice inauthentic. In addition, since his childhood was not embedded in a Chinese-American upbringing, they doubted his ability to provide an accurate voice of their ethnicity and experiences. One of Hwang's early literary idols, Frank Chin, whose work significantly inspired *FOB*, was one of the most vehement critics of the playwright, calling Hwang 'a white racist asshole'.¹² The questions surrounding Hwang's depiction of the Asian and Asian-American experience reached its zenith with the national and international attention received by *M. Butterfly*, as he became the first Asian-American playwright to have a play produced on Broadway. With the play's production, he had now become *the* literary, and, in turn, political representative voice for Asian-Americans, and in achieving such a lofty status it would be impossible for him to make everyone happy.

However, at the core of Hwang's depiction of being an Asian-American is the perspective of being perceived as an outsider and not belonging. Throughout his career, his plays have focused on the fact the Asian face is not automatically associated with the defined face of a citizen of the United States. Hwang told *New York Times* that 'Asians, more than any other ethnic group, more than blacks, are seen as "foreigners" in America', and, as a testament to his interpretation, he relayed that on some occasions he has been accosted on the street and told to return home to China.¹³ It is precisely this type of reaction faced by Asian-Americans that Hwang's plays continually combat, with the aim of educating his audience against the ingrained prejudice that an Asian face cannot be an American face.

FOB (1980)

FOB was the first in Hwang's three-part trilogy, called the Asian-American plays. Each play has a focus on the immigrant experience for Chinese nationals who are either just coming into the country or have been in the United States for a number of years. Scholar Stephen H. Sumida argues that Hwang's decision to focus his early plays on immigration placed him squarely within the larger conversation of contemporary Asian-American writers of the time, who were almost exclusively focused on exploring the immigrant experience.[14] In *FOB*, Dale, an ABC, 'American Born Chinese', plans to go on a double date with his cousin Grace, who arrived in the US when she was a young girl. Joining the group is Steve, an FOB, who has been sent to California by his wealthy Chinese parents to go to college. Dale, prejudiced against FOBs, is dismissive and rude to Steve, while Grace, only a decade removed from her own fresh off the boat experience, is more sympathetic. Dale and Steve battle for Grace's attention, including a stomach churning battle over who can survive the spiciest Chinese meal. Intermingled within the action are monologues about the difficult experiences of Chinese immigrants in making their way to and in the land of the Gold Mountain, the Chinese description of the US. By the play's end, the characters participate in a game of Story Telling and Grace and Steve take on the personas of two powerful mythological Chinese figures, Fa Mu Lan, a female warrior, and Gwan Gung, a Chinese god. The play ends with Grace and Steve, through the enacting of those roles, coming to an appreciated understanding of one another, while Dale, who has dismissed his Chinese ancestry and cannot appreciate or comprehend the stories conveyed by the myths from the old country, stands alone.

FOB would be the first of many Hwang plays to be based on an autobiographical event. In this case, Hwang was inspired by his own double date with his cousin, where the other male member of the group was a Hong Kong native, freshly arrived in the US, whose means of transportation was a limousine. Unlike the play, no competition ensued between the two males. Instead, they rode around town in the limo and then anticlimactically went to the movies. An additional point of inspiration stemmed from two of the most important Chinese-American writers from the 1970s: Chin, author of *Gee, Pop!* (1976), and Maxine Hong Kingston, author of *The Woman Warrior* (1976). Hwang drew the mythological figures of Gwan Gung and Fa Mu Lan from Chin and Kingston's works, respectively.[15] Hwang took those two figures and asked, 'What would happen if these two gods met in Torrance, California?'[16] Using Tom Stoppard's *Rosencrantz and Guildenstern Are Dead* (1966) as a template, he included the stories of Gwan Gung and Fa Mu Lan to contrast against the ethnic identity struggles of his college-aged characters. Finally, Henry Hwang, who would become the inspiration for many of the patriarchal figures in Hwang's early plays, was also an influence. Hwang revealed that 'A lot of the immigrant monologues in *FOB* are obviously things I heard at home. It was sort of a thrill for my father to see some of his own life material used in this stage production.'[17] *FOB* would be the first of many award-winning plays by Hwang, as it won an Obie for Best Play, and John Lone, who played Steve, received an Obie for Best Actor.

While affirmative action allowed Hwang's play to receive its initial production from Papp, Asian-American theatre expert Esther Kim Lee makes a compelling case as to why *FOB* ultimately became a success. One part was due to the gifted director Mako and the spirited performance of Lone (who had studied Chinese opera as a young man). Working together the two smoothed the initial rough juxtaposition between the play's use of Western theatrical narrative devices (learned from Shepard, Pinter and Stoppard) and the Eastern elements of Gwan Gung and Fa Mu Lan and Grace and Steve's Story Telling game. Essentially, Mako inserted Chinese opera elements into the production's ending, and Lone's experience with the genre allowed the play's disparate-seeming elements to mesh into a much more seamless and unified production than his earlier drafts had offered, an aspect that Hwang acknowledged when he directed the production in his residence hall at Stanford. He admitted that when it came to the play's final clash between the three characters, 'I went into sort of a ritualistic kind of Sam Shepardy vein where they were just a lot of triangular placements of the three characters with some sort of ritual movement. It wasn't specifically Chinese in any sense, although it could have been somewhat in the sense that it was archetypal enough that it could have been various cultures.'[18] Due to Mako and Lone's inclusion of Chinese opera elements, the play succeeded precisely because of its 'accessibility for both Asian-American and mainstream audiences.'[19] *FOB* examines the internal strife and fracturing that occurs within the Chinese-American community, specifically focusing on three college-age characters. Dale, who is the only character of the three born in the United States, has cast off his Chinese identity, refusing to acknowledge his heritage, even to the point of not knowing (or refusing to acknowledge) the Chinese words for the foods offered in Grace's parents' Chinese restaurant. Instead, he has embraced the materialist dogma of America, the pursuit of fast cars and Western cultural icons, like John Travolta and the Bee Gees. For him, to acknowledge his Chinese heritage is to go backwards. However, as much as he has embraced being American, the surrounding non-Asian community has not returned the affection. He finds himself constantly alone, wanting to be invited to his peers' homes, but not receiving any invitations. In turn, Dale turns that loneliness into hatred of FOBs, who prejudice others about the behaviour of Asian-Americans, spitting out the following in an opening instructional monologue about the characteristics that comprise an FOB: 'Clumsy, ugly, greasy FOB. Loud, stupid, four-eyed FOB. Big feet.'[20] Scholar James Moy argues that Dale's tirade against FOBs aligns him with those Westerners who oppressed his ethnic forebears, writing, 'The list of characteristics which Dale ascribes to the FOB bear a striking resemblance to the museum like list of fetishized aspects of difference employed by Anglo-American writers during the nineteenth century to theatrically stereotype the Chinese.'[21] Dale's words not only mirrored these earlier stereotypes but would also suggest the coming negative depictions of Asians in popular culture in the 1980s, best represented by John Hughes' *Sixteen Candles*, which features the Chinese foreign exchange student Long Duck Dong, who is presented as a pidgin English-speaking, drunk and horny high schooler, who hangs upside down from trees and destroys American automobiles.

In contrast to Dale's seeming comfortableness with his place in American culture, Grace, who came to America to rejoin her mother who emigrated without her, has struggled to find her place. She longed for acceptance at school, but found herself rejected by other students because she was placed back two grades because of her poor English skills. Later, she unsuccessfully attempted to blend in to white America by dying her hair blonde. She jealously covets the economic advantage Dale's father has had as the family's oldest son versus the struggle her mother has endured without familial economic support. In this regard, scholar Ban Wang notes a similarity between the cousins:

> Dale and Grace are both under the illusion that material abundance, blending into the American cultural ambiance, and a 'feel good' feeling about the self as consumer are key to a diasporic person. By absorbing all the airs and looks

of the cultural simulacrum, they seek to ease the distress of homelessness. Yet the superficial trappings cannot hide the anxiety of not belonging and not being accepted.[22]

However, unlike her cousin, she eventually has an epiphany and stops worrying about trying to find acceptance in and by the society around her, accepting her bifurcated identity. She studies Chinese history at college to better herself, while still working in her parents' restaurant and appreciating the cultural offerings of Southern California. Essentially, Grace blends both identities together for a more complete and fulfilling existence and, in turn, acquires a comfortableness with self that Dale fails to achieve.

Hwang's characterization of Steve, though, is deliberately crafted in response to the stereotype surrounding Chinese immigrants. Hwang said Steve 'is every Chinese immigrant subliminally attempting to gain empowerment – the antithesis of the coolie'.[23] When interacting with Grace, Steve's speaks immaculate English, but when he speaks with Dale, recognizing his bias and hatred of FOBs, he plays up the stereotype of the newly arrived immigrant with broken English patterns. As Dale interacts with Steve, he becomes more and more rude and insulting, telling Steve that once he has been in the United States he will never want to go back to China. However, over the course of the play through short monologues Steve embodies the voice of countless Chinese immigrants, relaying their stories of failed attempts to come to America as well as the successes and failures of Chinese workers in America hoping for a better life. At one point he takes on the voice of a struggling immigrant from 1914 who has been rejected numerous times in his attempts to enter the country: 'I come here five times – I raise lifetime fortune five times. Five times, I first come here, you say to me I am illegal, you return me on boat to fathers and uncles with no gold, no treasure, no fortune, no rice. I only to come to America – come to "Mountain of Gold"' (21–2). Steve's representation of the Chinese immigrants' path to the States foregrounds Dale's privileged existence, having been born into his father's success. Precisely because of his rejection of his heritage, he cannot see the struggles of his ethnicity, which are embodied through the stories and experiences of Steve and Grace. For this reason, the play ends with Steve and Grace making a connection forged by the myths of their forebears, represented through the story they enact between Fa Mu Lan and Gwan Gung. They recognize the deep-rooted history of China that they share in this small Chinese restaurant in a California town. Dale, because of his prejudice, fails to appreciate this ethnic bond and for that reason at the play's end, he is alone.

FOB provided Hwang with the template for his next two plays, as he examines the struggles to identify one's position and identity when entering a new country. Where does one's obligation reside? Is one a citizen of the new country? Or because of one's heritage and ethnicity, is there a stronger pull to one's country of origin? Ultimately, what defines the nature of one's identity? Is it ethnicity, place, citizenship, heritage or something else? For Hwang and his ensuing characters, it is a complicated question with no easy answers.

The Dance and the Railroad (1981)

The Dance and the Railroad, the second play in the Asian-American trilogy, is an extension of Steve's immigrant monologues in *FOB*, but now Hwang focuses on two Chinese workers on the transcontinental railroad in the 1860s. Hwang was inspired by a historical moment he had studied in college, when Chinese workers struck for shorter working hours and more wages. However, his interest was not on the dramatic wrangling around a negotiation table between hard-pressed workers and fat-cat American capitalists. Instead, the play examines the experience of two workers awaiting the results of the strike. Hwang acknowledged that his choice to use the strike as a narrative touch point was a response to stereotypes of Chinese immigrants from that time period. He explained that 'we tend to have this impression that they were really servile and weak – little coolies who were always being knocked down by big white men on horses'.[24] Instead, Hwang argues, 'These were strong and hardy and rebellious men who considered themselves warriors, adventurers or soldiers, and I think their resistance in this strike best typifies that attitude.'[25]

John Lone and Tzi Ma, both of whom acted in *FOB*, were cast as the two workers, and each character shares the name of the actor who originated the role because of how influential each performer was in shaping the nature of his character. Hwang even modelled the characters' speech patterns after Lone and Ma, bestowing upon the mid-nineteenth century characters a more contemporary linguistic edge. Hwang explained that 'the characters speak like twentieth-century urbanites – [as] a protest again the "pseudo-Chinese or broken English" that Asians usually speak in film or theater'.[26] As scholar Hsui-Chen Lin has noted, 'Asian-Americans are faced with a dilemma: the need to wage a war against pernicious stereotypes of Asian characters while striving to be recognized as part of America.'[27] Through *The Dance and the Railroad* Hwang reminded audiences of the important place Chinese-Americans played in a significant moment of American history, while also presenting the characters as sharing the same linguistic quirks and slang as the audience watching.

The play takes place on a mountainside overlooking the Chinese workers' camp and follows Lone and Ma's conversations during the strike. Every day after work, Lone ascends to the mountaintop to practise Chinese opera movements. Two years earlier he had been a promising opera performer until his parents sent him to America to make money to support his family. Now, he has grown disillusioned with his situation and hardened against his co-workers whom he views as dead men, having accepted their slave-like fate to the railroad owners. In contrast, Ma, recently arrived in America, fully embraces all aspects of his new home, from the gambling dice games he plays with his co-workers, who, unknown to him, are fleecing him of his money, to the wondrous warm snow that will come in the winter, according to the same men cheating him at dice. Despite his gullibility, he believes wholeheartedly in the American Dream of economic success and plans to return to his home village a rich man. In order to fill the empty hours of the strike, Ma has sought out Lone in hopes of some quick instruction about how to play Gwan Gung, the great Chinese god, in the Chinese opera. The majority of the play entails the training he undergoes by a sceptical Lone, who doubts his student's aptitude and fortitude for the task at hand.

Similar to *FOB*, where Dale's American identity is contrasted with Steve's newly arrived immigrant demeanour, Hwang explores the tension between the experienced, disillusioned Lone and Ma's excited, everything-is-awesome mindset. The contrasting philosophies become apparent when they discuss the strike. Ma does not share Lone's sentiment that their co-workers are 'dead men', precisely because they are on strike for better wages and hours. He tells Lone, 'These are the demands of live Chinamen, Lone. Dead men don't complain.'[28] When Lone later discovers that the strikers have won concessions from the railroad company, he is pleasantly surprised and shifts away from his negative attitude toward his co-workers as well as Ma. In celebration of the Chinese worker, Lone capitulates, informing Ma that he will train him to play Gwan Gung. However, Ma changes his mind, noting that while Gwan Gung's story has already been oft told, no opera has ever depicted his story. In a reflection of Ma's understanding of the American value of self-promotion, he insists that they perform an opera about his life. Ma and Lone then enact his story from his ignominious departure from his village to the torturous and deadly journey that all immigrants faced in coming to America across the Pacific, due to being packed tightly in unsafe boats.

> **Ma** We left with three hundred and three.
> **Lone** My family's depending on me.
> **Ma** So tell me, how many have died?
> **Lone** I'll be the last one alive.
> **Ma** That's not what I wanted to hear.
> **Lone** I'll find some fresh air in this hole.
> **Ma** I asked, how many have died.
> **Lone** Is that a crack in the side? (82)

Ma and Lone then proceed to capture, through dance, the daily battle of the railway workers against the mountain, attempting to craft tunnels through the unforgiving stone. In depicting the workers' struggles to defeat the mass of stone, Ma's dream of success begins to fade due to the repetitive brutality of the experience itself. In re-experiencing the harrowing nature of his story and, in particular, the backbreaking daily experience of chipping away at the immovable rock, Ma becomes disheartened about his position in life. Adding to his discouragement is the fact that not all of the demands of the Chinese worker were met. The workers compromised instead of beating back the railroad companies. He finally grasps that working for the railroad will not be a profitable and easy enterprise and, even more disheartening, returning home a rich man, who will be able to afford 20 wives, will be unlikely.

If he is to succeed, he will have to change his attitude. He tells Lone, 'I've got to change myself. Toughen up. Take no shit. Count my change. Learn to gamble. Learn to win. Learn to stare. Learn to deny. Learn to look at men with opaque eyes' (87). However, Lone, having seen the power of Chinese immigrants to defeat their Caucasian bosses, no longer views his colleagues as dead men, but instead sees them as warriors, like Gwan Gung. These immigrant workers are men with plans and steadfast negotiating skills. Their victory at the bargaining indicates that great potential exists for the Chinese to succeed in their new home in America. Hwang announces with *The Dance and the Railroad* that the travails of Chinese workers on the transcontinental railroad were not only an essential precursor to the successes earned by Chinese-Americans, but also a moment worth documenting as essential to the identity and role of contemporary Chinese-Americans in the United States.

Family Devotions (1981)

Family Devotions, the final work of the Asian-American trilogy of the immigrant experience, features a well-established Chinese-American family in California. Years removed from their immigration to the United States, the family has found monetary success. Unlike Hwang's two previous plays, this play focuses on three familial generations: the elder matriarchs, represented by the highly religious Ama and Popo; the middle-aged successful husband and wife pairs of Joanne, Ama's daughter, and Wilbur, her Japanese-American husband, and Hannah, Popo's daughter, and her husband Robert; and the younger generation of Jenny, Joanne and Wilbur's daughter, and Chester, the son of Hannah and Robert.

Hwang dedicated his third play to Sam Shepard, explaining, 'I started writing it at the Area Playwrights Workshop he was giving; the exercise was to create a set and then create the characters who lived in that set. That's where I wrote the first two or three pages of *Family Devotions* and then I just kept on writing.'[29] The religious element of the play, driven by Ama and Popo, stems from Hwang growing up in a highly religious family, which he likens to a 'weird Chinese American Baptist evangelical fusion'.[30] Like *FOB*, the narrative framework of the play stems from an autobiographical incident:

My extended family had a get-together at my uncle's house in Belair, with the tennis court in back, and we had [been] visiting my granduncle from the People's Republic of China who had not seen our family in twenty years. We decided that it was important to have a family devotion ceremony and confront him with his past, to see if he could be brought back to God. It seemed really odd, if I put myself in this guy's shoes, that he'd be coming out of the PRC after twenty years and end up in Belair with a bunch of Chinese-Americans playing tennis and trying to convert him to Christianity.[31]

The play takes place over one afternoon as the family prepares for the arrival of Di-gou, Ama and Popo's brother, whom they have not seen for many years. Before his arrival, Hwang introduces us to the rest of the family members. Ama and Popo define themselves and the family entirely through their worship of one ancestor, See-goh-poh, who was a successful missionary, converting countless worshippers to Christianity. As a child, Di-gou accompanied See-goh-poh on many of those missions, so their hope is that he still maintains his Christian faith despite his years in China. While religious, the next generation is more interested in its own financial successes as seen through the competitions between Wilbur and Robert to show off their wealth to one another, and when they do pray, personal success takes precedence over the greater good of humanity. Finally, the younger generation has no interest at all in religion and, stereotypically, only wants to distance itself from embarrassing, older family members. Jenny constantly escapes to her room to look at fashion magazines, and Chester prepares to move to Boston to play violin for the symphony. Of all the characters in Hwang's trilogy, the two households of Joanne and Hannah have achieved the greatest economic success, the kind Ma dreams about in *The Dance and the Railroad*, with their private tennis courts, investment portfolios and real estate deals, but with success has come a disconnect from their ancestral roots. Ama and Popo, who have not invested themselves in the pursuit of money and success, dismiss their sons-in-laws' pursuit of wealth but are unable to persuade their family members to possess the same level of worship of See-goh-poh. Chester and Jenny, similar to Dale and his inability to remember the names of Chinese food items, struggle to even remember the name of their great-uncle, calling him

'Dar-gwo', 'Dah-gim' and 'Doo-goo'.[32] As in *FOB*, Hwang depicts young adults being disconnected from their ethnic heritage, having been influenced by their parents to ignore their cultural identity.

After the arrival of their brother Di-gou, Ama and Popo hold a family devotion ceremony, where one professes one's belief in God. When Di-gou refuses to participate, his sisters tie him down and begin to attack him, hoping to beat Christianity back into him. Being restrained by his combative sisters, he takes spiritual possession of Chester, who begins to share the real story behind their worshipped ancestor See-goh-poh's conversions of scores of villagers to Christianity, none of which actually happened. Instead, her so-called first mission was an excuse to leave the village in order to give birth to an illegitimate child. Confronting the truth of their ancestor worship and the fact the entire basis of their existence was founded upon a lie, the sisters collapse to the floor dead. In describing the role that the two sisters' obsession with See-goh-poh has on the play's action, Hwang remarks, 'It's about the myths that grow up around a family history and how legends of past family members affect the lives of the living.'[33] Their error resides in their decision to beatify her to the exclusion of the rest of the ancestors and their own living family members. Their myopic view of See-goh-poh and her façade of Christian devotedness, in turn, influences the religious nature of their daughters, who have a shallow understanding of Christianity, especially as demonstrated by their religious devotion to the pursuit of wealth. In essence, Hwang argues, 'The play is about how Christianity alienates Asian-Americans from their root culture' of their familial ancestors.[34] By glorifying See-goh-poh exclusively, Ama and Popo disrespected all of their forebears, while the ensuing generations have no connection at all to their Asian relations, especially Chester and Jenny. They are a family that has become ignorant of their own history and lineage, much like Dale in *FOB*.

Despite the deaths of the sisters, who represent a narrow viewpoint in defining family and identity, and the material pursuits of the married couples, redemption for Chinese-Americans can still be found by looking to and at the family links to the old country. Di-gou teaches this concept to Chester in a conversation they have before the family devotion occurs. Using Chester's violin and its reflective varnish on the back, Di-gou instructs him, 'Look here. At your face. Study your face and you will see – the shape of your face is the shape of faces back many generations – across an ocean, in another soil' (126). Di-gou espouses that there is really little difference between Chester and his ancestors. Their facial features connect them together with an inescapable bond. While he might run away to Boston, he will still carry the features of his family with him wherever he goes. He can never escape the more visceral connection that exists between him and his immediate and extended family. He is, in other words, linked to China, while being invested in his American identity. In the last play of his Chinese-American trilogy, Hwang provides a sense of closure to the experiences of being Chinese and American. Just as Grace finds in *FOB* and Lone discovers in *The Dance and the Railroad*, Chester learns that he does not have to be exclusive in choosing one particular identity over the other. He does not have to be just Chinese. He does not just have to be American. There is room within the composition and make-up of the Asian character to be both, to be Chinese-American and to embrace one's place within both cultures.

M. Butterfly (1988)

M. Butterfly, the last play Hwang wrote in the 1980s, proved to be not only his most successful of the decade but also his entire career, winning him a Tony for Best Play and a nomination for the Pulitzer Prize. In addition, it was Hwang's top grossing play, earning $35 million on a $1.5 million investment. Unlike many of his previous works, *M. Butterfly* was not inspired by autobiography, but instead by a hard-to-believe news event from 1986. A French diplomat was convicted of treason when it was discovered that he had been having a twenty-year affair with a Chinese opera singer and never realized that *she* was actually a *he*. Hwang, whose earlier works explored the question of identity and the complexity of the relationship between East and West, was drawn to the story, remarking, 'I had the same reaction as everybody else – how could it have happened? But then on some level it seemed natural to me that it should have happened, that given the degree of misperception generally between East and West and between men and women, it seemed inevitable that a mistake of this magnitude would one day take place.'³⁵ When Hwang contemplated what it was that kept Bernard Boursicot, the French diplomat, in the relationship for twenty years, 'The answer came to me clearly: "He probably thought he had found Madame Butterfly".'³⁶ The Puccini opera became the framework for the play, as Gallimard, Hwang's version of the French diplomat, professes his envy of Pinkerton and his relationship with Cio-Cio San and looks to emulate the same type of relationship with Song, the play's version of Shi Pei Pu, the Chinese spy. The end result was a play that allowed Hwang 'to pull together various concerns that I have about racism, sexism and imperialism ... The story was like a perfect little jar that could hold all these different subjects.'³⁷

Hwang was inspired by the narrative form of Peter Shaffer's *Equus* (1973) and *Amadeus* (1979), where the main character narrates the play's action. In *M. Butterfly*, an imprisoned Gallimard reveals to the audience what led to his present state of incarceration, including his love for Puccini's opera and its romantic vision of an Eastern woman swooning for a Western man; his sexual difficulties as a youth and, later, as a man with forward Western women; his initial meetings with Song and eventual seduction of her; and the shocking discovery of Song as a man and spy. At points, though, Song disrupts Gallimard's narrative, as she provides details from her perspective, including her meetings with Comrade Chin, her Chinese handler, and his testimony before a French judge. (Song is referred to as a she, when she is dressed as a woman, and a he, when in between the second and third act he transforms into an Armani-suited man.) In a fantasy sequence, Gallimard finally confronts Song about their relationship and Song strips down to reveal his true sex to Gallimard, and in doing so Song completely destroys the illusion he had created for his lover. Realizing that he was actually playing the role of Cio-Cio San instead of Pinkerton in their love affair, Gallimard dons a kimono and make-up and commits suicide.

Hwang's earlier immigrant plays occurred on Western soil, allowing for an Eastern confusion with Western sensibilities. Here Hwang upends this narrative method by focusing on the West's confusion with the cultural, political and interpersonal elements of the East. Just as his Eastern characters experienced difficulty in adapting to and understanding the West, his Western characters equally struggle. Song highlights the West's problem in his testimony before the French judge, telling him, 'The West thinks of itself as masculine – big guns, bit industry, big money – so the East is feminine – weak, delicate, poor ... but good at art, and full of inscrutable wisdom – the feminine mystique' and in having this mindset that 'As soon as a Western man comes into contact with the East – he's already confused.'[38] Part of the defining difficulty between the two cultures resides in the West's monolithic perspective on the East. In short, the West believes that all Asians share the same characteristics and attributes, no matter if they come from China, Japan, Korea, Vietnam or any other Asian country. According to academic Rocio Davis, this is part of Gallimard's failure, as his *Madame Butterfly* 'fantasy merges the Orient into one indistinguishable mass, eliminating the differences among Chinese, Japanese, and Vietnamese'.[39] This monolithic mass is embedded in Gallimard's application of the behaviour of Cio-Cio San, a Japanese woman, to a Chinese woman. When he first meets Song after she has performed an aria from *Madame Butterfly*, he compliments her on her convincing performance of Puccini's tragic figure. She retorts, 'Convincing? As a Japanese woman? The Japanese used hundreds of our people for medical experiments during the war, you know. But I gather such an irony on you is lost' (17). The other Western characters share the same myopic view of the East, as seen by Gallimard's superior asking him to write a report on the Vietnamese for the Americans. His reason? Gallimard has a Chinese mistress; therefore, he must understand the Vietnamese as well. Gallimard sees nothing wrong in the request and states that 'The Orientals simply want to be associated with whoever shows the most strength and power ... Orientals will always submit to a greater force' (46). However, the most damning element of misunderstanding comes from the Western figures not appreciating the cultural aspects of their host country. If they had, all of them would have gleaned that female roles in the Chinese opera were played by men. Hwang's play challenges its Western audience to consider their own assumptions about the East and its citizens. He suggests that 'one of the more simple things the play's trying to say is that eventually one must look past all the cultural stereotyping we do of each other. West to East and East to West, and deal with each other just as humans if we're really to reach any point of true understanding.'[40]

In *M. Butterfly*, Hwang returns to the topic of male–female relationships that he explored in his earlier play *Sound and Beauty*, which is discussed in the conclusion, but this time with an interracial twist. Hwang suggests that perhaps one of the reasons his play was so successful was because it hit a similar nerve as the popular 1980s film *Fatal Attraction* (1987), which explores the darker and more violent nature of male–female coupling and, coincidentally, contains a lead male character with a similar fondness for *Madame Butterfly*. Hwang argues that perhaps *M. Butterfly* is 'the thinking man's *Fatal Attraction*. This movie touched a lot of things people were worried about, in terms of relationships between men and women: the way we don't understand one another; the way you can sleep with someone and they can turn on you; and, now, the underlying threat of Aids.'[41] His play, like the film, features a lead male with an inability to understand women. As a youth, Gallimard would look at pictures of naked women and be unable to attain an erection. He married his wife Helga out of a sense of convenience and when he has an affair with a Western graduate student, he finds her too masculine and explicit in her discussion of sex. Instead, he desires the unquestioned ability to dominate and be in control of the relationship, like Pinkerton does with Cio-Cio San. When Song invites him up to her apartment and admits that 'the forwardness of my actions makes my skin burn' (31), Gallimard finally acquires the position of dominance he desires, exclaiming, 'I felt for the first time that rush of power – the absolute power of a man' (32).

While the play is not autobiographical, Hwang has admitted that the behaviour of Gallimard and his expectations do not fall too far, at times, from his own experiences. Hwang explained that 'The really sexist things Gallimard says are things that I know on some level work in my own soul and color my relationships with women. Pleasure in giving pain to a woman is not that far removed, I think, from a lot of male experiences.'[42] However, while the play's beginning echoes *Madame Butterfly*'s depiction of stereotypical male dominance over the female, Hwang flips these expectations when Song's role as a spy and true sex are revealed. It then becomes clear that Song has been manipulating Gallimard, playing the role of a submissive Asian woman, resulting in, according to Douglas Kerr, 'the revenge of Butterfly'.[43] In turn, 'Song's submissiveness makes a conquest of Gallimard: it is an instrument of power.'[44]

Not all critics were as focused on the male–female nature of the play, since the true nature of Gallimard and Song's relationship is homosexual rather than heterosexual. James Moy was especially critical about the play's success in engaging audience members with issues of identity because 'most spectators are simply incredulous at how for twenty years Gallimard could have confused Song's rectum for a woman's vagina'.[45] If the audience is merely obsessed with the sexual logistics of the couple's relationship, then Hwang's deeper thematic elements can never be acknowledged and explored.

In his challenging of East–West and male–female relationships, Hwang relies on stereotypes. As scholar Josephine Lee argues, the play features a 'barrage of stereotypes – of heterosexuals and homosexuals, Orientals and cruel white men, divas, chauvinists, feminists, Communists, bureaucrats, socialites, and disco prowlers'.[46] Lee is not alone in her observations on this topic, as Hwang's use of stereotypes provoked, perhaps, the most discussion by academics on the play. Many of the scholars focus on Song Liling, whose characterization, they believe, reifies the negative stereotypes of Asians. Angela Pao has noted, 'Hwang ended up perpetuating the very stereotypes he intended to subvert.'[47] In short, *M. Butterfly* presented 'an exoticized view of East Asia as well as the perception that Asians are devious, manipulative, and cunning'.[48] Moy took umbrage with the stereotypical characterization of Song, who 'comes across as little more than a disfigured transvestite version of the infamous Chinese "dragon lady" prostitute stereotype',[49] while Hsiu-Chen Lin also saw problems with the depiction of Song, stating that 'Song's manipulation of Gallimard only changes his/her image from the helpless butterfly into the Dragon Lady, whose sexual perversion lures innocent white men into danger. Thus Song becomes, more than ever, a stereotypical threat to Western morality and security.'[50] In addition, male commentators argued that Hwang was merely continuing the 'effeminization of the Asian male' through Song's transvestite performance.[51] Williamson Chang argues that since the Asian male plays a female for the majority of the play, 'Asian males are again simply not there; they are *invisible*,'[52] especially when Song in his original male guise is rejected by Gallimard, who prefers his female version. Chang continues that 'While *M. Butterfly* results in a "victory" of sorts for the East, it does so by reaffirming the stereotypes that are used against Asians. Asians, particularly Asian women, are portrayed as cunning, shrewd, manipulative, and deceptive.'[53] Hwang acknowledges his use of stereotypes but counters that they are necessary in the larger context of the play, remarking, 'I'd like to think *Butterfly* says to an audience, "All right, we'll give you the Orientalia you seem to desire, but then we're also going to talk about why you're so attracted to this, and how that attachment to stereotypes blinds you to the truth of your own experience".'[54]

The play's ending suggests a reversal of the stereotypes, as Song acquires the Western role of Pinkerton, while Gallimard appropriates the Eastern role of Cio-Cio San. Lin acknowledges the complexity and multilayered nature of this reversal, which could be seen as upending stereotypes, but also as merely reifying them. She argues that 'With Song triumphant over the dead body of the eventually victimized Gallimard, the message the audience receives is not only "No. You are not supposed to see Asians as weaklings", but also "Yes. Playing up to the white male fantasy of the Oriental will still get you whatever you want".'[55] Ultimately, the play's reliance on stereotypes aids his Western audience in acclimatizing to this Eastern story, but its execution in the play has made it one of the most debated elements of Hwang's depiction and questioning of Asian identity. In other words, does Hwang subvert or reify the perception of Asians through his stereotypes? This question, though, did not end with *M. Butterfly*. It has continued with the works that followed, including his most recent work, *Kung Fu*, which premiered in 2014, about the career of Bruce Lee. Clearly, Hwang's plays show that there is no easy answer when it comes to Asian and Asian-American identities.

Despite the debate and the various positions posed, *M. Butterfly* is a powerful play and, as noted by Jon Rossini, 'a crucial document in shifting the critical discourse about the intersections of gender, ethnicity, sexuality, and power'.[56] In addition, its appearance in the waning years of the 1980s testifies to Hwang's increasing theatrical power and urgency and rapid development as a significant American playwright, as he explores the dichotomies of what it means to be of Asian ethnicity, while also questioning identity, immigration, familial relations and male–female relationships. *M. Butterfly*, then, becomes his representative work of the decade as it not only embodies his previous explorations in the plays produced by the Public Theater, but also encapsulates the confusions and misinterpretations between East and West that became predominant in the 1980s with the rise of Asia's economic fortunes and might, particularly in Japan.

Conclusion

During the 1980s, Hwang wrote two other plays, which were more experimental and did not gain the same critical notoriety as his Asian-American trilogy and *M. Butterfly*, but both would prove to be important touchstones for future successes and failures. After *Family Devotions*, Hwang's next work, *Sound and Beauty* (1983), comprised of two one-act plays, *The Sound of a Voice* and *The House of Sleeping Beauties*, was inspired by stories and films from Japan. Equally, he was interested in theatrically capturing the sparse and simple aesthetic of Japanese culture, noting that 'If you look at a Zen garden or a rock garden, there's a simplicity, an elegance that comes from placing just a few objects in a very particular way. *The Sound of a Voice* demonstrates this sparseness and stillness.'[57] Whereas his trilogy takes much of its structural and presentational foundation from Western influences, like Sam Shepard and Tom Stoppard, and then gradually adds in Eastern concepts toward the end of each play (the story telling in *FOB*, Ma's opera in *The Dance and the Railroad*, the possession of Chester in *Family Devotions*), *Sound and Beauty* stays entirely rooted in Eastern aesthetics. As scholar Robert Cooperman has noted, 'these plays show the playwright experimenting with a form which greatly interests him and with which he feels no compulsion to provide Western audiences with comfortable reference points'.[58] A simple plot description of the two pieces highlights the new territory Hwang was exploring.

In *The Sound of a Voice*, a hunter comes upon a home in the middle of the woods, days away from any other village. Living there is an older woman, rumoured by many to be a witch, whom the hunter has been hired to kill. During their conversations, he comes to realize that in many facets, including physically, she is stronger than he is, and at night her figure transforms from her older form to a younger, more attractive one. Enticed by her transformation, he stays, but the longer he remains, the more exhausted he becomes, as she siphons away his energy to fuel her magical transformations. Deciding not to kill her, he leaves, but he finds he is unable to be away from her and returns, only to discover that she has killed herself because of his abandonment of her. In *The House of the Sleeping Beauties*, Hwang turns the Japanese author

Yasunari Kawabata into the play's main character, an old man who arrives at a secret house where other old men come to slumber in a drugged state next to naked young women, who have also been drugged. Kawabata initially plans to write an exposé of the establishment, but through the encouragement of the old woman who runs the business, he becomes a repeat customer. Over the ensuing months, his relationship with the proprietress deepens, but he still publishes his profile. Realizing that he has physically and emotionally reached the end of his life (the drugged sleep allowed him to revisit moments from his life and make peace with his past), he kills himself by drinking a cup of poisoned tea. The owner, not having a future anymore due to his exposé, also drinks from the cup and kills herself, dying next to Kawabata.

Partly driving Hwang's interest in these two stories was his own struggles in his relationship with the opposite sex. During the process of writing *Sound and Beauty*, he admitted he was 'very pessimistic about the state of male–female relationships. I think there's a sense in it of an almost inherent mistrust between the man and the woman, which symbolizes the way, in general, we don't really know one another.'[59] By examining the dynamic of male and female relations through the spare, aesthetic lens of the plays' Eastern viewpoint, the interactions between his characters become the primary focus. However, despite the inherent communicative and emotional difficulties in male–female relationships, the characters search for the ever-elusive feeling of love, but, according to Hwang, 'love is impossible. The only alternative is death. If they're unable to love, they must die.'[60] *Sound and Beauty* was an experiment for Hwang as he stretched his voice and discovered a new topic to explore in terms of relationships, and this experimentation would prove to be crucially beneficial a few years later when he turned to *M. Butterfly*, which explored a similar dynamic as he aimed to expose the romantic complexities and power dynamics between men and women. Hwang would return to *Sound and Beauty* later in his career and adapt it into an opera with music by Philip Glass.

In the mid-1980s, Hwang found himself at a crossroads when it came to his identity as a playwright. He realized that he 'had exhausted what I wanted to say about what it meant to be an Asian living in this country, the whole ethnicity of that'.[61] In addition, he began to have doubts about the larger context of his value in the artistic world, as he had become, due to his success, the face and voice for all Asian-Americans when it came to the world of theatre.

> I was being put in a position for which I was not prepared ... At 23 or 24, I was asked to be some sort of spokesperson for Asian-Americans on various issues which I hadn't really thought out that well consciously. On the one hand, it was flattering. But on the other hand, growing up as a person of color, you're always ambivalent to a certain degree about your own ethnicity. You think it's great, but there is necessarily a certain amount of self-hatred, or confusion at least, which results from the fact that there's a role model in this society which is basically a Caucasian man, and you don't measure up to that.[62]

He admitted that he began to question the authenticity of his work. 'I began to wonder first of all if I was sort of creating Orientalia for the intelligentsia. I looked at my plays and some I liked and some I didn't. But the ones that seemed to be the most popular were the ones that had the oriental things in them, like gongs and dragons. So that was a bit of a problem.'[63] In addition, he felt that in the 1980s ethnic playwrights were being pigeonholed into pre-designated, ethnic boxes: 'It was no longer that I was a playwright per se, but that I was an Asian-American playwright, and my Asian-Americanness became the quality which defined me to the public.'[64] Not surprisingly, he found such compartmentalizing limiting. Not wanting to be part of a cultural ghetto of artistic expression, he argued, 'we should be able to claim a full franchise as American writers the same as other American writers have and be able to address any subjects that we want'.[65] Due to these concerns and a sense of exhaustion over the hectic pace that accompanied his success (four New York premieres in rapid succession), Hwang went through a dry period where nothing inspired him to write. Instead, he travelled extensively, whereby he ended up meeting and marrying his first wife. It was shortly after his marriage that he was inspired to return to his writing, producing *Rich Relations* (1986), which freed him from the weight of writing exclusively about Asian and Asian-American subject matter – for the first time (and only time so far) all of his characters were Caucasian.

Rich Relations, like *FOB* and *Family Devotions*, contains autobiographical elements (once again the patriarchal figure is based on his father, and Keith, like Chester in *Family Devotions*, is based on Hwang himself, who was an English teacher for one year) and is set in a hillside home overlooking Los Angeles. Picking up the theme of 1980s materialism again, Hwang's play centres on a successful and wealthy real estate agent, Hinson, who is obsessed with obtaining the most recent technological inventions, ranging from a television that doubles as a phone to spy pens, so he can eavesdrop on his employees, and his son Keith, who has left his East Coast teaching position under a cloud of controversy for sleeping with an underage student. As in *Family Devotions*, religion plays an important role but in this case the play was, according to Hwang, 'an attempt to talk about resurrection, which was what I felt had just happened to me' in terms of reawakening his passion for writing.[66] Resurrection is represented by many of the characters' actions and stories, but mainly through Hinson coming back to life after being pronounced dead when he was a young man. Embedded in the resurrection motif is Hwang's indictment of the hypocrisy of religion, as shown through Hinson's initial decision to become a pastor because of the prayers of his family to bring him back to life, but he quickly disowns the church and the belief in the power of prayer when he realizes he can make more money as a real estate baron. Critics were flummoxed by the uneven mix of religious commentary, farce, magical realism and statutory rape jokes. The *New York Times*, which had been a major supporter of Hwang's previous plays, perhaps summed up the reactions best in calling it 'stale' and 'wanly conceived'.[67] *Rich Relations* became Hwang's first flop, and looking back on the play, he acknowledged that there were issues with it, referring to it as 'problematical'.[68] Hwang attempted to rewrite the play and changed the characters from Caucasian to Asian-American, but to no avail. It still failed to captivate its audience. And yet, the flop was cathartic for Hwang, as he had only known success to that point. He credits the failure of *Rich Relations* as one of the reasons he was able to write *M. Butterfly*.

In total, Hwang had six plays produced in the decade of the 1980s, his most prolific time as a playwright. Over the ensuing decades his output would wane considerably with two full length plays produced in the 1990s, one being a failed Broadway production that closed in previews, *Face Value* (1993), and the other a much rewritten autobiographical play about his mother's family called *Golden Child* (1996). The 2000s offered only one new full length play, *Yellow Face* (2007), while the 2010s offered *Chinglish* (2011) and *Kung Fu*. From an initial glance it would appear that Hwang's subsequent output since the 1980s has failed to match his impressive collection of work from that decade. However, since the 1980s, Hwang's role in the performance world has broadened impressively, especially in the world of opera. He collaborated with Philip Glass for the first of many times in 1988 with *1000 Airplanes on the Roof*, and since that time he has written numerous librettos and worked with world renowned composers. Hwang is now recognized as the most produced librettists among living American writers. He has written screenplays, including one for *M. Butterfly* (1993), and has been involved in the world of musical theatre, having written the books for Disney's *Aida* (2000) and *Tarzan* (2006), as well as a complete revision of Rodgers and Hammerstein's *Flower Drum Song* (2001).

Despite his decreased production of plays since the 1980s, Hwang continues to be a significant voice not only on the stage but also behind the scenes. He has been a board member and playwright advisor at The Lark, a theatre lab based in New York that helps writers develop their plays, and recently he has taken a position as an Associate Professor of Playwriting at the School of the Arts at Columbia University. In addition, he travels around the country speaking to students in small classrooms and large auditoriums about his works, the nature of theatre and its importance to him and the world at large. Perhaps one of the most telling aspects of Hwang's commitment to not only the Asian-American experience and concept of identity but also to the integrity of the American theatre occurred a few years after the debut of *M. Butterfly*. Cameron Mackintosh's *Miss Saigon* (1989) had been a critical and financial hit in London, but in the musical Jonathan Pryce played the role of The Engineer in yellow face, including the taping down of his eyes to make him appear more Asian. When the production was scheduled to transfer to Broadway in 1991 with Pryce reprising his role, Hwang joined B. D. Wong, who played Song Liling in *M. Butterfly*, and won a Tony for his performance, in protesting against this act of yellow-face casting. Asian-Americans found themselves repeating history. Whereas the 1980s opened with a protest against yellow-face casting at the Public, now the start of the 1990s featured another protest against the same egregious act, but this time on Broadway. What had seemed to be a decade of great fortune and growth in American theatre for Asian-American writers and actors ended on a sour note. The racism and stereotypes still existed. While the protest was initially successful in having the production cancelled, *Miss Saigon* eventually opened, primarily because its $35 million advanced ticket sales and numerous jobs for ethnic performers trumped the protests of a group of minority actors, writers and performers. The dollar won out.[69] However, a decade and a half later, Hwang would have the final say on the issue of *Miss Saigon*, Asian-American identity and the persecution and racism of Asian faces in his Obie-winning *Yellow Face*.

While the 1980s introduced Hwang's challenge to his audience about its misconceptions about ethnicity and identity, that same passion and pursuit still continues today in his work, be it theatrical, operatic or musical. In turn, his success in the 1980s inspired other Asian-American writers and performers, who make up the third wave of Asian-American theatre professionals, including Diana Son, best known for *Stop Kiss* (1998). Since the 1980s, Hwang has maintained his stature as not only America's leading Asian-American playwright (he is the only one to have been produced on Broadway), but also as one of America's great writers for the stage.

5

Maria Irene Fornes: *The Danube* (1982), *Mud* (1983), *The Conduct of Life* (1985)

Gwendolyn Alker

Introduction

Maria Irene Fornes[1] is one of the most important and enduring, yet simultaneously under-acknowledged, theatre practitioners to emerge out of the Off-Off-Broadway theatre movement in New York City.[2] Perhaps the most influential American female dramatist of the twentieth century, Fornes was also a teacher of playwriting for a generation of Latina/o playwrights. Her work spanned many decades, from the 1960s and certainly until 1999, when the Signature Theatre in New York City devoted a season to the production of her work. While undoubtedly an important playwright of the 1980s (this chapter will focus on three of her most important plays of this period: *The Danube* (1982), *Mud* (1983) and *The Conduct of Life* (1985)), Fornes's work as a playwright emerged much earlier and in tandem with her role as a director and designer. Indeed, in a volume devoted to playwriting, Fornes's singular style compels one to ask how dramatic writing is shaped and shifted by the spatial and embodied considerations of a play in production.

Placing Fornes's work from the 1980s alongside other playwrights in this book – David Mamet, Henry Hwang and August Wilson – suggests a reckoning with identity politics in the theatrical communities of this decade. Unlike Hwang and Wilson, who, I would argue, embraced the growth of this movement, or David Mamet, who seemingly rejected identity politics, Fornes straddles the pros and cons of identity politics. As a woman, a lesbian and a Latina, Fornes should be a banner bearer for any crusade that tells the personal stories of under-represented peoples whose racial, gender, sexual or economic identities had previously precluded them from being canonized in volumes such as these. She has often been touted as the mother of Latino playwriting in the United States today.[3] Furthermore, Fornes is often heralded by feminist theatre scholars as an important voice in the growth of the women's theatre movement of the 1980s. Yet her relationship to the personal as political is infinitely more complex. Indeed, Fornes eschewed any labelling that might emphasize her as a minority, or any reading of her work that invoked her identity as a lens through which to analyse her plays.

As the only woman covered in this book, Fornes's complicated relationship with feminism sheds light on her relationship with identity politics. The 1980s can be seen as a decade in which feminist theatre came to the foreground in the United States – beginning with the success of Beth Henley's *Crimes of the Heart*, which opened in 1980, and culminating in the overwhelming reception of Wendy Wasserstein's *The Heidi Chronicles* in 1988. In these two plays, and in countless others during the 1980s, playwrights foregrounded the woman's experience and demonstrated considerable self-reflexivity on the role of the author as engine for the second wave feminism. For playwrights such as Wasserstein, Wilson and Hwang, playwriting and personal politics were often synonymous. Fornes, however, as a playwright, an immigrant and a lesbian, who was generally quiet but not overly secretive about her personal affairs, had a far more complicated relationship to feminism and race. The overwhelming critical outpouring about her work in the 1980s and 1990s was part of a larger move of inculcating theatre academics to the importance of women playwrights.[4] However, Fornes eschewed the use of such labels and was notorious about undermining critics who attempted to do so: 'As a writer, I am in an odd position in relation to feminism ... I feel myself as a woman in that I sense myself as a female organism, not as a woman in the way that society considers what I should do or think.'[5]

Looking at the body of her work from a feminist perspective, one can see that it is filled with enough contradictions to perplex even the most engaged Fornes scholar. Yet this does not discount the fact that Fornes created some of the most important feminist plays of the second wave feminist movement – *Fefu and Her Friends* (1977) and *Sarita* (1984), for example. Nor should it undermine the heavy political themes so prevalent in the plays themselves. Fornes, and her work, may be a type of double-edged sword with regard to feminism. Her work complicates questions of authorial agency and foreshadows the difficulties of identity politics that would develop in subsequent decades. For example, the story and (more significantly) the characters of *Fefu and Her Friends* demonstrate a central issue that led to a stall in the feminist movement of the mid-to-late 1980s: the perils and importance of cohesion among a diverse group of women. This same theme emerges, albeit in different ways, in *The Conduct of Life*, as will be discussed below. Ultimately, for Fornes, these questions of identity politics and agency were part and parcel of the creation of theatre, but her art was always written to express the story of an individual character rather than to have an individual character stand in for a larger political trope.

To understand the development and impact of her work as a woman, playwright, director and teacher, I must now turn to her more far-ranging biography. Born in Havana in 1930, Irene Fornes came to the United States in 1945 with her mother and siblings. Fornes trained as a painter early on, including with the abstract impressionist Hans Hofmann. By the early 1960s, she had settled in New York City's Greenwich Village and had begun writing in order to help Susan Sontag – with whom she was in a relationship at the time – cure a bout of writer's block.[6] In the early 1960s, Fornes joined the playwriting unit of the Actors Studio and thus came into contact with Lee Strasberg and his famous acting techniques to access emotional truth. She was not impressed with his work with actors; however, some of the sense memory exercises left an impression on her and later made their way into her development of characters and her teaching techniques. During this period, Fornes also worked with the Open Theater and, most influentially, the Judson Poets, where she composed her first well-known play, *Promenade* (1965). At Judson, she was allowed to write, design and even act in her own shows (see, for example, the script of *Vietnamese Wedding*, a piece of ritual with 'Irene' listed as one of the characters). Judson became her true artistic home partially because it nurtured her ability to be an interdisciplinary artist.

In 1968, *Molly's Dream* – a cowboy musical about love lost with some vampires on the side – was selected for workshop production at Tanglewood in western Massachusetts. Fornes asked to direct, but veteran member of the Actor's Studio, Bobby Lewis, instead chose a director with a very different vision of the play than her own. For Fornes, the customary splitting of the roles between playwright and director was problematic, and one that she has since compared to leaving your baby in the hands of another:

> It's as if you have a child, your own baby, and you take the baby to school and the baby is crying and the teacher says, 'Please, I'll take care of it. Make a note: at the end of the day you and I can talk about it.' You'd think this woman is crazy. I'm not going to leave my kid here with this insane person.[7]

Fornes struggled with this separation and subsequently insisted on directing the next workshopped production of *Molly's Dream* at New Dramatists in New York City later that same year. In retrospect, this challenge to her identity as a director may have shifted her relationship to writing plays, as did her belief that her work was becoming increasingly repetitive. After 1968, her writing came almost to a standstill. She took on managerial duties at the New York Theater Strategy from 1973 to 1979 and for almost a decade wrote only a few, currently unpublished, plays.

In 1977, Fornes returned to writing and directing her own work, beginning with the site-specific masterpiece *Fefu and Her Friends*, and continuing with a decade of unique, shape-shifting plays that combined sparse writing, creative genius and meticulous staging. *Fefu*, Fornes's most frequently read and anthologized play, and the one for which she won her third Obie Award, is usually given as an example of her feminist leanings. Yet Fornes talks about the characters not as political symbols, but as friends whom she felt close to. Such intimacy and compassion from the playwright towards her characters became a hallmark for all of her work from *Fefu* on.

In his recent publication *Maria Irene Fornes* (2013), Scott Cummings defines the 1980s as a 'period of fruition and one that secured [Fornes's] reputation as a major American playwright'.[8] By the beginning of the 1980s, she had already been recognized as a theatre artist with an enduring and revolutionary style, earning an Obie Award for Sustained Achievement in 1982. By the end of the decade, Fornes had written and directed 11 plays, including *Evelyn Brown* (1981), *Sarita* (1984), *Drowning* (1985), *Abingdon Square* (1987) and *What of the Night* (1989), which was short-listed for the Pulitzer Prize for Drama in 1990. *The Danube*, *Mud* and *The Conduct of Life* were some of her most often produced plays, with New York premieres for all three at the Theatre for a New City, one of a handful of theatres that gave Fornes important institutional support. Fornes went on to direct the premieres (and frequently the second production as well) of all subsequent plays that she wrote. The scripts would be changed up until or even after opening night; precise and unalterable stage directions would be added. As such, these plays must be understood as being written by Fornes the writer and composed by Fornes the director, who only fully understood her plays once she began staging them.[9]

Cummings labels *The Danube*, *Mud* and *The Conduct of Life*, alongside *Sarita*, as 'the PAJ plays'. Indeed, this compilation of plays, with a preface by Sontag, published in 1986 by PAJ Press, presented to many readers a first glimpse of Fornes's plays side by side. The publisher and founder of PAJ, Bonnie Marranca, became a staunch ally and supporter of Fornes's plays; in addition to the 1986 collection, she published a collection of her earlier plays, titled *Promenade and Other Plays* (1987), more recently a compilation of her Latino-themed plays, *Letters from Cuba and Other Plays* (2007), and finally *What of the Night: Selected Plays* (2008). Thus, PAJ has ensured that many of her plays are widely available, even as approximately forty of them remain unpublished. For Cummings, the publication of these first 'PAJ plays' exposed Fornes's work to a wider audience than her downtown New York circle, which had supported and nurtured her over the previous two decades. Her plays began to congeal; in the words of Sontag, 'Fornes's work has always been intelligent, often funny, never vulgar or cynical; both delicate and visceral. Now it is something more ... The plays have always been about wisdom: what it means to be wise. They are getting wiser.'[10]

With these PAJ plays, Fornes presented a clear challenge to the more linear and digestible style that was typical of American playwriting in the 1980s. Theatre critics such as Steven Drukman jested that 'entering into the world of Fornes means *not understanding*'[11] (emphasis in original). To which I would add that the academic impulse to codify specific themes in Fornes's work is un-Fornesian. Indeed, one of the causes of Fornes's proliferation of brilliant plays during the early 1980s was her decision, after her post-*Molly's Dream* writer's block, to make each play unique and different from the one before. Fornes remains enigmatic, and certainly less well known, perhaps due to this rejection of any formulaic standards – both in terms of theme and plot development.

Nonetheless, while finding a Fornesian aesthetic remains challenging, one can find a through line in her ability to allow her characters to develop their own stories and in her ability (as both a playwright and a director) to get out of their way. Such a process of playwriting as attentive passivity is discussed by the character Joseph in the opening lines of one of her later plays, *Letters from Cuba*: 'I think that's how poems get written. I think that's how difficult things get done. We can't really do them. We can't do difficult things. We can do easy things. But the difficult ones come to us by themselves. It's just that to learn to listen to them is difficult.'[12]

An examination of many of her plays also reveals additional elements that resonate with this metaphor of active listening. One such idea is Fornes's continued reliance on context over content. What I will call Fornes's 'environmentalism'[13] was an important and yet undervalued aspect of her work as an artist. The location of a theatrical workshop or early staging affected the creation of the plays that she directed, most notably when she decided to perform *Fefu* environmentally, using all of the various rooms at the New York Theater Strategy's Relativity Media Lab to simultaneously stage all of the scenes in Act Two of this play. In her description of this choice, it is exactly the ability to listen rather than fill the space that she found most inspiring:

When I worked with the actresses in those [four different] spaces it was one of the most beautiful directing experiences for me because I was sitting with them right in the room ... I would be sitting in a chair, and it was completely quiet. There was total silence. To me that silence was necessary. If I had at that point written down the stage directions that would have been forever binding, I would have said, 'It's important that the rooms be totally isolated so that there's no sound at all'.[14]

Fornes's work as director can also be found in her explicit stage directions which, when present, form a subtle link from her role as a playwright to her work as a director.

Fornes talked further about the merits of active listening in a 1994 interview about her directorial work: '[T]he director doesn't bring anything to [the work], he just tries not to miss anything that is in the play.'[15] As both a playwright and a director, the central role she occupied was as a midwife who reveals the artistry of the work itself.

The content of her plays was inevitably shaped by the contexts in which she researched, wrote and staged them. For example, Fornes often used so-called 'found objects' in the creation of her plays. She often found such objects in thrift stores, such as the ironing board that shaped Mae's manual tasks in *Mud*, or the eight dresses that morphed into the female characters in *Fefu*. 'We were at the flea market and I was looking for my set. (Also, you know, we had to put on these plays for hardly any money at all so when you find something cheap, then you write a play about that.)'[16] Fornes was also a consummate hoarder of materials, such as the letters from her brother that prompted *Letters from Cuba*. Much of the fraught sexuality of *Abingdon Square* emerges from the inclusion of found texts in Scene Six on the pollination of flowers. Such found objects appeared continuously, precisely placed at the centre of the story, often trumping the plot or the desire for a coherent product in befuddling ways. Here we may recall that Fornes was trained as a painter rather than as a playwright. The central placement of these objects in the story resonates with the idea of a still life painting where the story emerges out of objects placed carefully in scene, rather than as props used to embellish a pre-existing plot.

Fornes the writer was frequently in conversation with Fornes the director. While writing a play she sometimes rewrote the character list depending on who showed up to audition for a role. As Fornes the director put a script up on its feet, the playwright would change the lines or blocking all the way until opening night and beyond. She demanded that actor's pay attention to the silences within the scripts, crafting them into the language of the play. She also cultivated meaning from the spatial choices that her actors made and from the locations of the rehearsals or subsequent productions. And she pushed her actors to match her intensely emotionally lines with an equally strict physical presence. Sally Porterfield notes that Sheila Dabney, who won an Obie Award for her portrayal of Nena in *The Conduct of Life*, came to the physicality of a particularly difficult monologue through Fornes's direction to 'press into her finger with her fingernail' creating a sharp current that ran up her arms as she shelled beans in the kitchen.[17] While working with Fornes must have been challenging for actors, she was also admired and respected as an innovative theatre artist who crafted her plays differently than others and rarely appeared to be limited by the rules of the theatrical game.

The 1980s were also significant for Fornes as a teacher and as the beginning of what was to become a solid culture of Latino playwriting in the US. In 1981, Max Ferra, INTAR's artistic director, alongside Irene Fornes, founded INTAR's Hispanic Playwrights Lab. Fornes both co-initiated the programme and handpicked each subsequent member. She then led this Lab over the next decade, passing on her creative writing techniques here and in workshops she held at the Padua Hills Festival and elsewhere. Indeed, looking at the list of artists that Fornes trained over the years, one sees a veritable who's who of Latino playwrights: Migdalia Cruz, Nilo Cruz, Cherríe Moraga, Eduardo Machado and many others.

For Fornes, the Lab was also a personally prolific place where her plays, including *The Conduct of Life*, began as writing exercises that she both led and participated in. And while we don't have a record of how many of her plays began in her Lab, one has to believe that her teaching emerged from and came back to her own identity as a playwright. Her students, such as those included in the compendium *Conducting a Life: Reflections on the Theater of Maria Irene Fornes*, spoke with awe, sometimes tinged with fear, of her uncompromising ability to unlock what Fornes called the 'anatomy of inspiration'.[18] Thus, beyond the microcosm of Fornes's plays, one can locate Fornes during the 1980s as the pedagogical impetus of Latino playwriting that persists to this day.[19]

Fornes's engagement with environmental themes will guide my analysis *of The Danube*, a disturbingly quirky piece about the end of the world.

The Danube (1982)

If performance is repetition with difference, to invoke Richard Schechner's well-worn phrase from *Between Theatre and Anthropology*,[20] then perhaps *The Danube* can best be regarded as one of Fornes's more performative or even metatheatrical plays. Indeed, the repetition in this play, from pre-recorded Hungarian language tapes to scenes restaged with puppets, to puppet scenes restaged with humans, can be quite dizzying. Such repetition makes *The Danube* one of Fornes's more challenging works to comprehend, especially because such difficulties are rendered opaque with the simplicity and clarity of the dialogue. *The Danube* is set, at least in the beginning scenes, before the Second World War: 'The play starts in 1938. However, it soon departs from chronological realism.'[21] The characters include Paul Green, 'a well-meaning American' who is an acquaintance of Mr Sandor, 'a Hungarian bureaucrat', and soon thereafter a love interest to Sandor's daughter, Eve. A fourth actor plays a series of bit parts in the staged production – including a waiter and an associate of Mr Sandor. All are described as 'members of a well-mannered working class' (43) who reside in Budapest. *The Danube* tells a simple story of Paul falling in love with Eve, after his arrival in her country. This love affair is surrounded by Paul and Eve's relationship with her father, Mr Sandor, as well as various locations near the banks of the Danube, including a café, a garden and a sanatorium. The dialogue begins simply, even haltingly, as the first scene between Paul and Mr Sandor mimics and is intercut with the 'basic sentences' from the Hungarian language tape. They discuss the weather, the reason for Paul's visit and the eventual arrival and introduction of Eve. The scene winds on as Paul invites Eve to a movie, thus initiating their relationship alongside the mundane confidences of everyday life. As the play progresses, Eve and Paul's relationship slowly unwinds and is enveloped by an odd fragmentation of both the narrative and the world the characters inhabit. Scenes are repeated and lines are interrupted to the extent to which it becomes unclear if the seams of time still move forward at a steady pace.

Development, production and reception

In keeping with her fondness for found objects, the genesis for *The Danube* came from a Hungarian language record that Irene Fornes found in a thrift shop in downtown New York City. The playtext begins, as many of Fornes's plays do, with a lengthy author's note on the use of these tapes within the production: 'A tape which follows the language record convention is played where indicated in this script. Each sentence is heard in English, then in Hungarian, then there is enough blank tape for the actors to speak the same line' (42). What follows is a directorial suggestion on how the actors can and must respond naturalistically to this disembodied but central voice. Thus, once the play begins there are echoes with the recordings, the play of the actors' voices and the relationship between the two.

Inspiration for Irene Fornes, however, comes in many forms, and the more one hears about concrete moments of inspiration for each of her plays, the more one realizes that there are often multiple, even contradictory elements that initiate a play. In his account of the genesis of *The Danube*, Cummings does mention the language tapes as the impetus for writing the play. Then, in the same paragraph, he quotes Fornes saying, 'When the Theater for the New City asked me to do an antinuclear piece, I thought of how sorrowful I felt for the bygone era of that record.'[22] As such, Fornes suggests that the prompt from the Theater for a New City (TNC) was the reason for writing the play. Certainly the play engages with themes of nuclear holocaust, but in a manner that is abstract, even haunting. An earlier version of the play, entitled *You Can Swim in the Danube, but the Water is Too Cold*, had been performed at Padua Hills in 1982. The 1983 production at the TNC that Fornes mentions above ran as part of their Nuclear Freeze Festival. Here, the final image of the play was of a giant mushroom cloud. For the 1984 production at the American Place Theater, Fornes changed this final image to a 'brilliant white flash of light' (64), rendering the anti-nuclear message less direct and perhaps more consistent with the rest of the play. As this is the version that was published as part of the PAJ Play series, it can now be considered Fornes's preferred ending.

While Fornes's dialogue is usually compact, in *The Danube* it is even more abrupt and simple. For some, such as Frank Rich in his *New York Times* review of the 1984 American Place Theater production, such prose rendered the play 'deliberately lifeless'.[23] A more forgiving analysis of her use of found objects suggests that in this particular case the language tapes render clear the simple building blocks of the English language – remember that for Fornes, who came to English as a second language, everything was already in translation. Indeed, the play's strength is the contrast between the relative simplicity of the language and the plot (man meets woman in far-away country, they fall in love, things go awry) and the bizarre staging and unravelling of the environment of the play.

The Danube and environmentalism

The play script of *The Danube* must be read as the record of a production that played with the influence and eventual breakdown of its environment. It is difficult to say how Fornes directed this play, as we do not have extensive notes on her process. There remain a few production stills and the descriptions of some of the cast and crew. What we do have, as in all of Fornes's plays, are the extensive stage directions. As noted above, one such stage direction, added in a later version of the play, does suggest a nuclear disaster at the end of the play. Yet the creeping presence of the corrosive environment exists as early as the end of the first scene when smoke seeps from the stage floor and, more overtly in the middle of Scene Three, where Eve faints, suggesting the beginning of an invasive illness that overcomes her throughout the play. Production photos of Mr Sandor and Paul Green (presumably from Scene Ten) show them with goggles and splotches of ash on their costumes, all implying that the nuclear or other contaminant was woven into the fabric of the play before the ending gives a narrative explanation. This is in keeping with Fornes's tendency to play out themes through the visual eye of a director rather than through a more linear narrative as a playwright.

Scholars Bill Worthen and Una Chaudhuri have utilized *The Danube* as a pre-eminent example of Fornes's engagement with the environment, albeit in differing ways. For Worthen, Fornes plays 'share a common impulse: to explore the operation of the mise-en-scène on the process of dramatic action ... [Her] plays suspend the identification between the drama and its staging.'[24] Chaudhuri suggests that *The Danube* 'produces a topography, a special conjuncture of language and place, and tests this topography against traditional theatrical meaning'.[25] Both scholars therefore note Fornes's care toward the location of the story and its subsequent staging, as well as a disjuncture between story and location that defies the common narrative of more traditional American plays. I would unpack this notion of disjuncture by suggesting that Fornes as director, with an eye toward visual frames that happen from moment to moment, often trumps the sequential development of story, bringing about the bizarre incongruence of the timeline in some of her plays such as *The Danube*. But taken as one piece, the story of *The Danube* suggests the general omnipresence of the character's context and specific inescapability of an environmental apocalypse.

Thinking more generally about environmental theatre as a genre, one of Fornes's greatest contributions to this conversation was her recalibration of the relationship between play script and environmental staging. Certainly Fornes staged all of her plays with a hyperawareness of the location in which they would be staged. We see a similar focus on context determining content in *Mud* – both *Mud* and *The Danube* demonstrate how location was both a practical matter and a source for content. Environmental theatre in the 1970s and 1980s cannot be divorced from the downtown New York City avant-garde, concretized by Richard Schechner in his 1973 text of the same name. In Schechner's formulations, however, environmental theatre existed, among others reasons, to challenge the pre-eminent role of the playwright and the ensuing script's authority. With Fornes, as both the author and the director of these environmentally staged plays, a new relationship to script emerged. Here the environmental staging infiltrated both the scripts, which were revised endlessly until opening night and even beyond, and the staging, as the locations she scouted out as director often returned to influence the script. Thus, Fornes challenged previous notions of environmental theatre by not dismissing the centrality of the script and the authority of the playwright, but instead encouraging the playwright to write with a more refined awareness of environmental staging. Unlike Schechner, however, Fornes never wrote down her ideas on environmental staging and its impact on her larger body of work. Thus, we must look for hints of her philosophy in the dialogue and stage directions. If one reads the plays alongside the histories of their design, direction and staging that do exist, this narrative unfolds as an important counter-narrative to Schechner's anti-textual and anti-playwright stance.

Mud (1983)

Similar to *The Danube* (also foreshadowing *Conduct*), *Mud* is about three people whose individual desires brutishly conflict, both with each other and the world that envelops them. Indeed, a theme of Fornes's middle work is this notion of entrapment that emerges within personal relationships as well as through the characters' relationship to an insidious environment that is both unseen and omnipresent. Here, the subtlest yet pervasive entrapment is the 'mud' of the play's title. Feminist scholars usually connect the notion of entrapment in *Mud* to the experience of Mae, the only female in this play and arguably the protagonist of the dramatic action. Yet for Fornes, this entrapment affects all of the characters in a manner that is more environmental than political.

Development, production and reception

Mud was first developed as a workshop in 1983 at Padua Hills, where Fornes noted that the red mud of the California hillside became an important set piece in her design.[26] The play was further developed and moved to New York City, where it debuted later that year at the Theatre for a New City and helped earn Fornes another Obie for writing and directing. Here, the literal mud of the hillside near Padua morphed into the filth of the characters' interior landscape. As usual, Fornes directed both of these productions as well as the ones at the Omaha Magic Theatre in 1983 and the New City Theatre in Seattle in 1990. David Esbjornson also directed *Mud* as part of the Signature season devoted to Fornes in 1999.

Most critics would agree that the three characters of the play are held together by Mae's desire to escape from the poverty, filth and inhuman conditions in which they dwell. The critiques of Mae's role in this threesome soon diverge. She can be seen as the driving force of the play, as a woman who has a desire to reclaim her agency or as a backbiting man hater. Fornes has spoken eloquently on the critical reception of Mae as a character and *Mud* as a play:

> I have often been told that in *Mud* I have written a play about a woman's subservience ... but [t]hese people are too poor to indulge in bizarre ego games. They have a reality to deal with, which is poverty ... To understand *Mud* as being about Mae's oppression and my more recent play *The Conduct of Life* about the subjugation of Latin American women is to limit the perception of those plays to a single minded perspective. It is submitting your theatergoing activity to an imaginary regime or discipline that has little to do with the plays.[27]

Fornes's decision to focus on class over gender is echoed in many of her other statements. As such, she demonstrates a prescience regarding the challenges to second wave feminism that emerged later in the decade; with the birth of third wave feminism, class and race came to frequently trump gender. Second wave feminism was critiqued for only focusing on the label of male or female while not acknowledging the complicated ways that social context must also be included.

Mae as a complicated character

Fornes presented another version of Mae's feminist double bind in an interview with Allen Frame:

> When I did a shorter version of [*Mud*] at the Padua Hills Playwrights Festival last year there was a critic who said I treated men like pigs. And I was shocked by that because first of all I think these three people are wonderful ... [Mae's] more self-centered, more ambitious, in a way harder than they are ... that critic is anticipating that I'm going to write a play that has a feminist point of view, maybe because I wrote *Fefu* ... I think *Mud* is a feminist play ... because the central character is

a woman ... The subject matter is ... [a] mind that is *opening* ... and she would do anything in the world to find the light.[28]

Here we see Fornes's nuanced response to the feminist politics of the 1980s. Sidestepping the possibility that feminist theory can produce a complex interpretation of individual characters, Fornes instead wages a larger critique on identity politics as an all-encompassing frame. In these quotes, she rejects using a feminist lens as an overdetermining and overly simplistic force to explicate her plays.

The reality of Mae as a character must emerge through a close reading of her presence and interactions with the other characters throughout the play. The first scene opens on Mae and Lloyd, two young adults who have been living together since childhood, but who are not siblings. In this opening scene, Mae is lacerating Lloyd about his filthy habits, and Lloyd, in turn, demonstrates a stark sexual aggression toward Mae and a propensity for bestiality with the pig who clearly wallows nearby outside in the mud: '(*She irons.*) I'm going to die in a hospital. In white sheets. You hear? ... I'm going to die clean. I'm going to school and I'm learning things. You're stupid. I'm not. When I finish school I'm leaving. You hear that? You can stay in the mud.'[29]

Mae later describes her relationship with Lloyd to Henry, the only other character in the play: 'He's always been here, since he was little. My dad brought him in ... We are like animals who grow up together and mate. We were mates till you came here, but not since then' (28). The tension between Lloyd and Mae escalates as she turns to Henry, who is older than them both, but who is only slightly better educated. Mae's attraction to Henry emerges due to the intellectual mentoring she thinks he can offer. She invites him to live with them, over the objections of Lloyd, only to find out that Henry's intellectual acumen barely outpaces her own. Through each brief, terse scene, we see Mae's hopes for escape and enlightenment fade through a series of tragic yet quotidian events. Towards the beginning of Act Two, we learn, rather obliquely, that Henry has suffered some type of accident, perhaps a stroke, and that he is now incapacitated. Mae is now further trapped, as she commits to taking care of both these men – the one who had initially trapped her in the mud, and the one who failed her as she tried to escape.

Cummings argues that Mae manifests a character type found frequently in Fornes's plays: 'When *Mud* premiered in 1983 Mae became the most pronounced manifestation of the Fornes Innocent to date ... In Fornes, to become a speaking subject is to make oneself visible, present, alive.'[30] She becomes exemplary among characters such as Leopold from *Tango Palace*, Leticia from *Conduct*, and perhaps all of the characters from *The Danube*, who emerge from humble beginnings but who share a desire to better themselves. This desire to command and wield language is perhaps most eloquently demonstrated as Mae reads from a textbook in Scene Six. Fornes describes her reading as 'inspired' even as the simplicity of the language resonates with the terse dialogue throughout:

> **Mae** The starfish is an animal, not a fish. He is called a fish because he lives in the water. The starfish cannot live out of the water ... Starfish eat old and dead sea animals. They keep the water clean. The starfish has five arms like a star. That is why it is called a starfish ... A starfish's eye cannot see. But they can tell if it is night or day.[31]

Seemingly dropped in like one of Fornes's ubiquitous found objects, the starfish of this monologue returns at the end of the play. Here, Mae finally decides to leave both men, 'to look for a better place to be ... Just a place where the two of you are not sucking my blood.' She exits with Lloyd running after her and the paralyzed Henry left alone onstage. We hear the sound of gunfire, and then Lloyd returns carrying Mae's dying body. Her last lines conclude the play: 'Like the starfish, I live in the dark and my eyes see only a faint light. It is faint and yet it consumes me. I long for it. I thirst for it. I would die for it. Lloyd, I am dying' (40).

Mae's death ends the play, but the narrative as a whole depicts Mae as a complex character – one who strives and fails to grow as a human being, while demonstrating the real flaws of her character. Fornes continually pushed to have Mae read as a complex and flawed human being in a network of relationships, rather than as a singular female protagonist framed against a backdrop of male characters. While this may have made her an outlier in this decade where feminist playwriting was gaining force as its own genre, it has given her credibility and staying power as a playwright who can be continually read through themes of race, gender and politics, but whose work was never contained or created for these themes alone.

The Conduct of Life (1985)

The script of *The Conduct of Life* begins with an obsessive description of the staging of the play. Fornes dictates, 'The floor is divided into four horizontal planes. Downstage is the living room, which is about ten feet deep. Center stage, eighteen inches high, is the dining room, which is about ten feet deep. Further upstage, eighteen inches high, is a hallway which is about four feet deep. At each end of the hallway there is a door' (67). As with the openings of many of Fornes's plays, she continues for almost a full page, with minute and detailed instructions on all of the entrances and exits, scenic rules and a prop list that would render any prop master overwhelmed. In such moments, we see not only the playwright's influence as a director, her predisposition towards visual thinking, but also her inclination towards predetermining any future production of her play.

Development, production and reception

In an introduction to a late publication of the script, Fornes states that an image of Nena, one of the four characters in the play, first inspired the creation of *Conduct*. Fornes discovered Nena, a character whose role and importance changes with time, while working alongside her students in the INTAR Playwrights Lab: 'I saw a girl – a mulatto girl – wearing a little pink slip and a soldier who was wearing an undershirt, military breeches and boots. They were in a hotel room, and she was being sweet to him. I think I wrote what was happening rather than dialogue. The girl's boyfriend had been arrested and she had met and seduced this captain to see whether through him she could get her boyfriend freed.'[32] The level of Nena's agency presented in this version of events differs radically from the play that Fornes subsequently wrote.

While *Conduct* is rarely seen as one of Fornes's environmental pieces, the subsequent development of the play suggests otherwise. An earlier production, workshopped at the California Institute of the Arts in the summer of 1984 as part of the annual Padua Hills Playwrights Festival, was developed due to the space that she encountered: Fornes chose to stage certain scenes on a platform overlooking an expansive plain with a distant road. Other scenes, including one of the characters being harassed and kidnapped by thugs in a car, were played on this road below. Thus, the earlier inspiration for the piece came together through the development of short, visual vignettes, while the bulk of the text was written later for the New York City premiere at the TNC in 1985. The staging of the TNC production placed domestic spaces next to a cellar and a warehouse, which, as the characters move from these separate spaces into each other's worlds, slowly erodes any sense of safety or privacy that the characters have.

Response to *The Conduct of Life* from both the academic and theatrical communities has been strong. The original production at the TNC won an Obie for best new play of 1985. *Conduct* continues to be one of Fornes's most frequently staged plays, and has been published no fewer than eight times in various volumes and anthologies, in both English and Spanish.

A feminist re-reading of *Conduct*

The plot of *The Conduct of Life* ostensibly follows Orlando, 'an army lieutenant at the start of the play. A lieutenant commander soon after.'[33] The audience first sees him in Scene One as he does jumping jacks 'for as long as can be endured' (68); Orlando then goes on to give himself a rousing, rather grotesque locker room talk on how he will climb the ranks of the military while not letting his sexual passions interfere. From here, we learn that Orlando is married to Leticia, a woman ten years his elder, and lives in a house with Leticia and their maid Olimpia, a staunch yet simple-minded housekeeper. Through nineteen quick, episodic scenes, we see Orlando struggling to become the master of the domestic space that is controlled by these two women.

By the third scene, we see that Orlando's affections and brutality, in equal measure, are focused on Nena, a young girl of twelve, who he has kidnapped off the street and now holds and forcibly rapes in a warehouse. Throughout the course of the play, Orlando brings Nena into his home, eventually introducing her to Olimpia and finally Leticia, eroding the power dynamic that tenuously exists in the life of these women from three different social spheres. Simultaneous to this domestic drama of abuse and invasion, it is suggested that Orlando is making his way through the ranks of the military in the unidentified 'Latin America country' (70) where the play takes place. He is clearly being trained and instructed as a torturer, and is eventually no longer able to separate his work life from his home. His brutality increases, eventually turned not only on Nena but on his wife.

From a feminist perspective, however, Orlando's plot differs from what this play may actually be about. While the spine of the script follows Orlando's moral devolution, it is the two women as well as Nena who animate the soul of the play. Ultimately, I would argue that Nena, perhaps like Julia in *Fefu*, is both the genesis and the ethical centre of this play, even as she is granted little voice or subjectivity by the adults around her. Nena's name, of course, is a Spanish diminutive for 'little girl', and she only speaks in two scenes of the play – once in Scene Three, where we are quickly and horrifically introduced to her relationship with Orlando; and in Scene Fifteen, where she has emerged from the dungeon to Olimpia's kitchen. Nena's monologue that follows is one of the most astonishing in Fornes's canon:

> He comes downstairs when I'm sleeping and I hear him coming and it frightens me ... He touches himself and he touches his stomach and his breasts and his behind. He puts his fingers in my parts and he keeps reciting. Then he turns me on my stomach and puts himself inside me. And he says I belong to him. (*There is a pause.*) I want to conduct each day of my life in the best possible way. I should value the things I have. And I should value all those who are near me. And I should value the kindness that others bestow upon me. And if someone should treat me unkindly, I should not blind myself with rage, but I should see them and receive them, since maybe they are in worse pain than me. (*Lights fade to black.*) (84–5)[34]

The critical response to Nena as a character, and this monologue as a flashpoint for the politics of the play, has diverged widely.

Worthen, for instance, argues that Nena's words reinforce her own subjugation and objectification by Orlando.[35] Yet Fornes's use of Nena's own line as the title of the play suggests that these words rise above the political and personal swamp of the characters' lives and set this monologue apart. Indeed, while Nena has the least verbal presence in the play, she is the character who leads her life with the most dignity.

It is specifically because Fornes is sensitive to the inability of these characters to do anything differently in this void of moral and ethical inequity that Nena's words do something as a staged *gestus* of verbal transcendence.[36] Fornes once spoke of the inability of the female characters in *Conduct* to create substantive change:

> I don't think everybody there is supporting the system. What are they going to do? Olimpia has a job. She has to survive. You think she's going to say, 'You son of a bitch. I'm not going to work in this house anymore. I'm going to go out and starve.' We can do that in this country ... But not in other places. So you cannot say, if you don't fight it, you're with it.[37]

Notably, this is one of the few moments in which Fornes talks about Latin America directly in any of the secondary literature. And she reveals a keen sense of differentiation between the values of *Conduct*'s location and those of her naturalized homeland, the United States.

Elsewhere, Worthen has also suggested that with *The Conduct of Life*, Fornes 'replaces the "objective" and objectifying relations of masculine vision with the "fluid boundaries" characteristic of feminist epistemologies'.[38] Perhaps in light of this statement, one could argue that there is both an objective plot, running alongside the time frame that Orlando so clearly lays out for himself at the beginning of the play, and a more intimate, atemporal plot of these three women as their lives intersect. This latter storyline seems to take place in a differing time frame, much like the odd sequencing of the women's meeting in *Fefu*, or the mundane storyline of domesticity in *Evelyn Brown*. One can look at the other longest monologue in the play, Olimpia's defence of her actions to her employer, Leticia, in Scene Four, as existing on this different timeline of feminine domesticity:

Olimpia (*In a mumble.*) ... You can't just ask me to do what you want me to do, and interrupt what I'm doing. I don't stop from the time I wake up in the morning to the time I go to sleep ... I wash ... I get the milk and the bread from outside and I put them on the counter. I open the icebox. I put one bottle in and take the butter out.[39]

These lines are followed by an immaculate account of every action that she undertakes in this home. The extremely long monologue is followed by a debate about dinner and procuring groceries that becomes a subtle power play between these two women. Not only does the monologue shift the audience's consideration of domestic tasks, it literally slows us down to contemplate the time and space of the house through the eyes of the servant, whose perspective contrasts starkly with that of her master and mistress.

Conduct has the relationship between these three women at its heart. But these relationships are in no way free from the sexism, misogyny and class bias that undergirds and runs throughout the play. As Fornes is a complicated feminist, we cannot expect the male protagonist to entrap while the upper-class woman liberates. The third female character here – and the one ostensibly in charge of the domestic sphere – is Leticia. In Leticia, similarly to Mae in *Mud*, we see a woman striving to educate and improve herself, even as her inability to see the realities around her leads her to cruel actions and a disregard for those who are abused by her husband. We also see a woman whose love for her husband exists alongside his mounting cruelty. In Scene Fourteen, Orlando tells Leticia that he is bringing Nena into the house: 'She's going to be a servant here.' Leticia's response seems to focus more on herself; she complains that she 'can't stand' Nena's screams (82) and forbids her husband from bringing in his mistress. Yet two scenes later, when Nena's path finally crosses with Leticia's, the interaction is written thus: '*Leticia enters and sits center at the table. Nena starts to get up. Olimpia signals her to be still. Leticia is not concerned with them*' (86). A troubling stage direction indeed.

It is the ending that confirms the centrality of Nena and Leticia's interactions, albeit in no clear way. In the ultimate fracturing of the public and private, Orlando accuses Leticia of taking a lover in front of the two other women, and, when she denies these accusations, submits her to the same mental and physical torture that he has perfected in his profession. He extracts a confession from his wife that, as in all cases of torture, may or may not be true. The scene climaxes as he demands to know,

> Was he tender to you! (*She doesn't answer. He puts his hand inside her blouse. She lets out an excruciating scream. He lets her go ... She goes to the telephone table, opens the drawer, takes a gun and shoots Orlando. Orlando falls dead. Nena rushes to downstage of the table. Leticia is disconcerted, then puts the revolver in Nena's hand and steps away from her.)* **Leticia** Please ... (88)

As with the ending of *Fefu and Her Friends*, the violence at the end of the play is framed by the inconclusiveness of what will happen next. Some have suggested that Leticia is asking Nena to shoot her so that she may die with her husband. Others have suggested an ending less charitable to Leticia, and one that Fornes validated in her second publication of the script in 1987.[40] Here, Fornes clarifies some of these questions by adding a key line to the stage directions:

> *Leticia is disconcerted, then puts the revolver in Nena's hand, hoping she will take the blame. Leticia steps away from Nena.*
> **Leticia** Please ...
> *Nena is in a state of terror and numb acceptance. She looks at the gun. Then, up. The lights fade.*'[41] (emphasis added)

The possibility that Leticia is bringing Nena to her own level vanishes in this revised scenario. Here, we see Leticia, out of shock and perhaps due to her ingrained class bias, condemning Nena to take the blame for the vengeance she has committed. Yet while this ending eradicates some of the myriad options for a feminist camaraderie amongst the characters onstage, there are still openings here. As Linda Kintz states, the ending still 'holds the possibility of a very different ending'.[42] We do not know what Nena's response will be, nor do we know what will occur when the outer world comes crashing into this intimate nightmare. What Fornes has done with her addition of this stage direction, however, is ended any possibility of a utopian feminist interpretation of the relationship between these three women at the end of the play. Yet, I would add, she has not curtailed the possibility that a feminist impulse should emerge from the audience members watching the play.

Conclusion

While certain themes have been introduced above, the most central way of entering into Fornes's world remains a careful reading of the plays. While these three plays give insights into Fornes's middle period, the Beckettian *Tango Palace* (1963) or the maniacal monologue that is *Dr. Kheal* (1968) are fine examples of her early work. Certainly her most well known play, *Fefu and Her Friends*, is worth the quizzical response it often brings; while *Abingdon Square*, a melancholic mediation on love, or the sprawling *What of the Night*, which can be read as Fornes's answer to Tony Kushner's apocalyptic *Angels in America*, are exemplary mature works.

Through a close reading of these and her other plays, Cummings describes the following reoccurring elements:

> characters imbued with a pre-cognitive innocence and often caught up in a thwarted romance; a sequence of short, often fragmented scenes that present a dramatic landscape more than a plot; a deepening mystery that envelops the action with metaphorical import; a pared-down language that is lyrical in its simplicity and often opens up into song; the inclusion of found or borrowed textual material; and an ironic relationship between the characters' situation and the manner of its presentation.[43]

To this I have added the use of found objects beyond the textual; the development of gritty, tough and eventually trapped characters; a nimble relationship to environmentalism; Fornes's playtexts that are visibly influenced by her work as a director; and a manifestation of and challenge to the prevailing identity politics of the time. Most importantly, Fornes was committed to creating good art.

Fornes wrote characters that were fully realized and rich, but that did not necessarily map onto her own experiences as a Latina and a lesbian living in the United States in the late twentieth century. As Stephen Bottoms notes in an essay comparing the violence of *Conduct* to the foreign policy debacles of Abu Ghraib, in this, one of the few plays that harkens back to a Latin American context, there is a denial of affinity to the characters based on the author's own ethnicity. Bottoms suggests that in Fornes's style, insight and brilliance come from her ability to continually position herself as a keen observer – or, to quote Fornes's own words, as someone 'looking through a window'[44] into the lives of those around us. Thus, while we can situate her oeuvre within the impact of the identity politics of this decade, Fornes's relationship with the movement remains complex. Rather than an insider, as her own identity might allow her to be, she chooses to identify as one who remains outside, and who comments on society from afar. True, there are feminist implications to *Conduct* and *Mud* as plays where violence is mapped onto the bodies of female characters in deep and profound ways.[45] Yet the characters refuse to act as mouthpieces for Fornes's own personal politics. Instead, Mae, Leticia, Nena, Olimpia and the many other female characters created by Fornes stand as complex individuals whose racial, class, gendered and even sexed selves reveal themselves only tangentially within the larger worlds of the plays they inhabit.

While Fornes herself would not recommend reading her characters through the lens of her own autobiography, one has to wonder about the paradoxes in her work of the 1980s. In these years in which she achieved such openness and freedom in her own artistic life, many of her characters struggled with their own imprisonment, whether psychologically, spatially or in terms of their relationships. Again and again throughout her career, Fornes defied the ghettoization of her own identity as an artist and as a human being. Yet she did not attain mainstream success in the ways that other artists of her theatrical cohort did (such as Sam Shepard). Perhaps, as a woman who broke through many barriers while others remained steadfast, it makes sense that Fornes wrote and directed with such humanity, tenderness and yet ultimately distance about others who faced similar or even worse barriers of class, environment or gender.

There can be no simple formula for understanding Fornes's work. Indeed, while talking about teaching playwriting she said, 'people who teach the use of formulas are actually preventing and impeding learning'.[46] Fornes can be best understood as someone who was ahead of her time. She lived fully in the interstitial places between identities: as both a playwright and a director; as a theatre artist who was trained as a visual artist; as an insider in the New York downtown theatre scene and as a self professed outsider; and as a feminist who predicted that second wave feminism would soon be critiqued for denying the complexity of the individual experience. And while she earned nine Obie Awards, wrote over fifty plays and has influenced a generation of playwrights, Fornes, the playwright, remains an enigma. This is because, as Steven Drukman notes, 'she reinvents the Fornés play each time she writes one. No major playwright who has lasted so long can make the same claim.'[47]

6

August Wilson: *Ma Rainey's Black Bottom* (1984), *Fences* (1987), *Joe Turner's Come and Gone* (1984)

Sandra G. Shannon

Introduction

The 1980s marked the introduction of poet-turned-playwright August Wilson to the world stage with three plays that he penned in relatively rapid succession: *Ma Rainey's Black Bottom* (1982), *Fences* (1983) and *Joe Turner's Come and Gone* (1984). Midst a decade dominated by white male power and privilege, August Wilson committed to writing not just these three plays, but a cycle of ten plays chronicling the African-American experience in the twentieth century. In an era so dominated by the crass Republican politics of Ronald Reagan, August Wilson adopted a cultural nationalist agenda that stood in bold contrast with its focus upon the 'unique particulars' of Africans in America. He proclaimed this mission in an essay published in the spring of 2000, well before he wrote his final so-called 'bookend plays' – *Gem of the Ocean* and *Radio Golf*:

I wanted to present the unique particulars of black American culture ... to place this culture onstage in all its richness and fullness and to demonstrate its ability to sustain us in all areas of human life and endeavor and through profound moments of our history in which the larger society has thought less of us than we have thought of ourselves.[1]

Wilson would go on to populate these race plays with characters whom he referred to as 'sons and daughters of newly freed African slaves'[2] – transplants to a hostile North, where many either perish or harbour deep-seated psychological wounds as a result of a cultural disconnect and the lingering trauma of slavery.

Wilson's decade-specific, sociologically accurate renderings of *Joe Turner's Come and Gone* (set in 1911), *Ma Rainey's Black Bottom* (set in 1927) and *Fences* (set in 1957) may, at first, seem alien to a generation of African-Americans divorced from their past and living in the immediacy of the 1980s. Still, all three underscore the playwright's commentary on how African-Americans' past and present are more so undeniably intertwined than at odds – that is, according to Wilson scholar Harry Elam, Wilson realizes that history is not 'a static fact, but as malleable perceptions open to interpretation, as a place to envision the past as it ought to have been in order to understand the present and to achieve a future they desire'.[3]

August Wilson grew up in a low-income Pittsburgh area known among its residents as the Hill District. Named Frederick 'Freddy' August Kittel at birth, he was the fourth child and first son of Daisy Wilson, a black domestic worker and daughter of Southern sharecroppers, and Frederick A. (Fritz) Kittel, a white German immigrant baker whom his son recalled to be a 'wine drinker – Muscatel by the gallon' – and couldn't keep a job.[4] August Wilson, as he would later rename himself during one of the most volatile and restless decades in American history, recast himself in a calculated effort to disown his wayward father's European heritage and to affirm his mother's ties to the South and to her African-American racial and cultural identity: 'The only father–son experience Wilson remembers,' according to John Lahr, 'was being taken downtown by Fritz in a blizzard to get a pair of Gene Autry cowboy boots.'[5]

Wilson was a native of an ethnically mixed, predominately African-American neighbourhood, one of the poorest, most beleaguered areas of Pittsburgh. Memories of his childhood not only included an emotionally and physically distant father, but also the squalid living conditions he and his siblings faced in the cold-water flat behind Bella's Market on Bedford Avenue. Known to residents as simply The Hill, the 1.4-square-mile cluster of neighbourhoods perched above downtown Pittsburgh was home to jazz greats like Stanley Turrentine and Art Blakey and was once the home of the Negro National League baseball team that fielded Satchel Paige, Josh Gibson and James 'Cool Papa' Bell. Harlem Renaissance poet Claude McKay called the Hill District 'the crossroads of the world', referring to The Hill's heyday between 1930 and 1950. But the political and social change that followed pitched The Hill into a downward spiral. Once vibrant businesses deteriorated into crumbling shells. Corners that once hummed with commerce became sites for drug transactions, and boarded up buildings provided cover for addicts and the homeless. The Hill underwent monumental changes from nearly two decades of urban renewal and the devastation from the riots, in 1968, ignited by the assassination of Martin Luther King, Jr. A once-vibrant, culturally rich and diverse community was rapidly descending into blight, isolation and dislocation.

Despite these bleak circumstances, Wilson and his family thrived in this notorious section of Pittsburgh under the watchful care of Daisy Wilson, who saw to it that her children were well fed, clothed and schooled. As her first-born son after a succession of older sisters, Freddie was the favourite – and, for a time, the only son – in the Kittel household. As such, his mother eagerly thrust upon him the mantle of responsibility, fully expecting that he would build upon the confidence she bestowed upon him later and pursue a career as a lawyer. She began grooming her favourite son early for success, teaching him how to read at four, entrusting him with the care of his siblings and regularly sending him off on personal errands. Due, in large part, to the grounding he received from Daisy Wilson while under the watchful care of elderly men from his neighbourhood, August was able to navigate his way through the troubling circumstances of his boyhood in Pittsburgh and set himself on a trajectory that would open up new opportunities for the fledgling poet.

Wilson's big break on the long road to becoming a 'serious' playwright came in the form of an invitation from Claude Purdy, a former Pittsburgh resident, theatre director and friend, to visit the Twin Cities. After a decade of writing poetry and fostering art and education in Pittsburgh, Wilson accepted Purdy's call to work with him at an African-American theatre company in St. Paul, Minnesota. In an interesting twist of fate, playwriting became Wilson's day job as well, when the Science Museum of Minnesota hired him to write short plays for its anthropology section. At 33, Wilson had pulled up his Pittsburgh roots and replanted them in a cold, white, alien city – only to gain renewed appreciation for the landscape and the people he left behind. 'I left Pittsburgh but Pittsburgh never left me. It was being in St. Paul, being away from the environment I was most familiar with, that I began hearing the voices.'[6]

Wilson's evolution into a first-rate playwright continued when – upon the advice of playwright, poet, social activist and professor Robert Lee 'Rob' Penny – he submitted a play script to be workshopped at the Eugene O'Neill Theater Center. That play was *Jitney*, which became the first of his early attempts to become a 'serious' playwright. He recalled, 'I sat down to write it and the characters just talked to me. In fact, they were talking so fast that I couldn't get it all down.'[7] Set among jitney drivers and numbers runners in an unlicensed taxi station on the Hill, *Jitney* evoked the rhythms of the life he knew in Pittsburgh. But the play was not an immediate success. Though he did get it staged at the Allegheny Repertory Theatre in Pittsburgh, Wilson tried and failed twice to bring *Jitney* to the highly competitive summer development workshops at the Eugene O'Neill Theater Center's National Playwright's Conference in Waterford, Connecticut. In 1982, he set the play aside and tried again – this time successfully – with *Ma Rainey's Black Bottom*. From that moment, the curtains opened wide for August Wilson.

The O'Neill workshop brought Wilson together with Lloyd Richards, Dean of the Yale School of Drama and Artistic Director of the Yale Repertory Theatre, who, twenty-five years earlier, had directed Lorraine Hansberry's groundbreaking African-American drama, *A Raisin in the Sun*, on Broadway. The veteran director took the neophyte playwright under his wing, teaching him dramaturgy and stagecraft and introducing him to a powerful network of theatre practitioners and financiers. Their theatrical partnership would bring Wilson's first six published plays to regional and Broadway stages and formed the basis of an historic partnership.

In a remarkable run over the next two decades, Wilson had ten plays produced – nine of which made their way to Broadway

– winning the author a Tony, two Pulitzer Prizes and the National Humanities Medal from President Bill Clinton. His plays, alternately called the 'American Century Cycle' or the 'Pittsburgh Cycle', include *Gem of the Ocean* (set in 1904, first produced in 2003); *Joe Turner's Come and Gone* (set in 1911, first produced in 1986); *Ma Rainey's Black Bottom* (set in 1927, first produced in 1982); *The Piano Lesson* (set in 1936, first produced in 1986); *Seven Guitars* (set in 1948, first produced in 1995); *Fences* (set in 1957, first produced in 1983); *Two Trains Running* (set in 1969, first produced in 1990); *Jitney* (set in 1977, first produced in 1982; revised and restaged in 1996); *King Hedley II* (set in 1985, first produced in 1999); and *Radio Golf* (set in 1997, first produced in 2005).

Over the course of some 25 years – beginning in the mid-1980s – Wilson steadily honed his playwriting skills to become a major American playwright. In this span, he wrote and staged a series of ten plays – each, in its own way, chronicling some aspect of African-American life in the twentieth century. While each play has its own autonomous storyline, collectively, the ten plays that make up the now-completed 'Pittsburgh Cycle' or 'American Century Cycle' boast a much more sweeping narrative – one that chronicles the African-American presence from post-Civil War America to the Clinton years. The epic storyline traces the struggles of 'sons and daughters of newly freed African slaves'[8] through several watershed moments in history to the threshold of the twenty-first century, complete with various measures of both triumph and tragedy.

With the exception of *Ma Rainey's Black Bottom*, which is set in a Chicago recording studio, all of the ten plays in August Wilson's decade-by-decade twentieth-century cycle take place in Pittsburgh's Hill District. And while it is, for the most part, a continuing saga of a community, culture and people, the characters, families, settings and the plays' ultimate focus change from one play to the next. Though each is set in a significant watershed moment in history, none of the plays owes allegiance to any concomitant historical events. History, in fact, serves as backdrop to Wilson's plays, usurped only by the stories of the triumphs and tragedies of his characters. As such, the cycle plays depict changes in their attitudes and circumstances, their sometimes questionable courses of action, threats to their cultural memory, and the struggle to survive with dignity. According to Wilson, 'I was trying to focus on what I felt were the most important issues confronting black Americans for [each] decade, so ultimately they could stand as a record of black experience over the past hundred years presented in the form of dramatic literature.'[9]

Once Wilson accepted the mantle of a 'serious playwright' in the mid-1980s, he, just as seriously, began to define the principles that would guide his work. To simplify matters, he coined a series of alliterative terms to convey the influences that are most prevalent in his playwriting: the Blues, Romare Bearden, Amiri Baraka and Jorge Luis Borges. 'My four B's', as he referred to them, were his essential artistic, political and spiritual influences. As early as 1987, Wilson had already conceptualized a blues-driven aesthetic that would inform each play. In an interview with David Savran that same year, he revealed his rationale:

> Blacks do not have a history of writing – things in Africa were passed on orally. In that tradition you orally pass on your entire philosophy, your ideas and attitudes about life. Most of them were passed along in blues. You have to make the philosophy interesting musically and lyrically, so that someone will want to repeat it, to teach it to someone else as soon as they've heard it. If you don't make it interesting, the information dies. I began to view blues as the African American's response to the world before he started writing down this stuff.[10]

August Wilson traces the source of his artistic vision to 1965, the year he was introduced to the blues. Perhaps it was providence that led him to purchase a three-dollar record player and to discover among some old 78s he had bought Bessie Smith's 'Nobody Can Bake a Sweet Jelly Roll Like Mine'. As he listened to the record, he was mesmerized by the emotions that Smith's sassy delivery stirred in him. The effect on the twenty-year-old Wilson was profound; he had discovered the universal language of the blues. He had tapped into a non-verbal means of understanding the gamut of emotions locked up inside him.

Evidence of the impact of the blues upon Wilson is manifested both implicitly and explicitly in plays such as *Ma Rainey's Black Bottom*, *Seven Guitars* and *Fences*. In *Ma Rainey's Black Bottom*, its influence is on multiple levels. The play is not just about the blues recording industry. If regarded as a blues composition presented as a play, *Ma Rainey's Black Bottom* becomes infinitely more understandable. Like a blues song or jazz rendition, the play is a slow-building, repetitious, unpredictable ride on an emotional roller coaster. Ma does not appear until well into Act One, yet the goings-on during the pre-rehearsal session are analogous to a lengthy musical prelude leading up to the vocal accompaniment. Levee's recurring complaints against Ma and the other band members function as the refrain to this blues play; and the competing stories of Ma and her band echo the interwoven improvisations of blues and jazz performers. Corresponding to the emotion-charged lyrics of the blues song are the characters' tortured testimonies of survival. Both Ma and Levee, though constantly at odds with each other in the play, turn inward to reveal the source of their private pain.

Collagist and fellow Pittsburgh native Romare Bearden, who participated in the Great Migration as a young boy, influenced August Wilson's thinking as an artist on multiple levels. At thirty-two, Wilson was introduced to the work of the world-famous artist. He saw Bearden's work as expressing visually what blues lyrics stirred inside of him. In a foreword to a study on Bearden, Wilson writes,

> What for me had been so difficult, Bearden made seem so simple, so easy. What I saw was black life presented on its own terms, on a grand and epic scale, with all its richness and fullness, in a language that was vibrant and which, made attendant to everyday life, ennobled it, affirmed its value, and exalted its presence. It was the art of a large and generous spirit that defined not only the character of black American life, but also its conscience.[11]

For Wilson, Bearden and the blues are provocative means of communicating the otherwise incommunicable triumphs and tragedies of African-American life: 'In Bearden I found my artistic mentor and sought, and still aspire to make my plays the equal of his canvas.'[12]

Bearden's imprint is especially noteworthy in *Joe Turner's Come and Gone* (originally titled *Mill Hand's Lunch Bucket*) and *The Piano Lesson*. In his collages, Bearden, who also spent some of his formative years in Pittsburgh, took disparate objects from the everyday world – photos, print, fabric and wood – to create compositional portraits of black life and experience. His collages, while carefully and intricately designed, appear improvisational, akin to jazz. Wilson reimagined Bearden's technique for the stage as well as finding direct inspiration in the work. Bearden's *Mill Hand's Lunch Bucket* (1978) planted the seed for *Joe Turner's Come and Gone*, just as Wilson's *The Piano Lesson* grew out of Bearden's collage of the same name. Bearden's imagery infuses the sets, lighting and blocking of Wilson's plays.

The inspiration that Wilson derived from black playwright Amiri Baraka resulted from his fascination with his politically charged poetry and his collection of one-act revolutionary plays. Baraka awakened in Wilson a sense of social awareness and provided another means of affirming his own racial identity. Baraka used his writings to accuse and attack, to boldly dramatize black power and identity in the face of being defined by white society. 'Amiri Baraka has said that when you look in the mirror, you should see your God,' Wilson told Bill Moyers. 'If you don't, you have somebody else's God.'[13]

Finally, the complexly structured stories of Argentine fiction writer Jorge Luis Borges also contributed to Wilson's approach to drama. In particular, he was intrigued by Borges' non-linear style of starting his narrative at the end and then going back to trace the path that brought the character to that juncture. Though Wilson employs this technique sparingly in his work, Borges opened his eyes to the structural possibilities of storytelling. Joan Herrington also notes that, like Borges, Wilson takes ordinary characters on a journey that often leads them to a mystical or metaphysical release.

One must know that the above list of conveniently alliterative influences upon Wilson's work is certainly not exhaustive, for his American Century Cycle also reveals a noticeable number of other competing influences that weighed heavily upon his consciousness and found their way into his writing. For example, essayist, activist and public intellectual James Baldwin, whom he often cited, figures prominently in his developing aesthetic. Christian and African belief systems often collide as do Old and New World views, past and present, and the written and imagined historical records. As playwright and – arguably – as prophet, Wilson stood at the crossroad negotiating the way forward.

Ma Rainey's Black Bottom (1984)

Not before finally coming to grips with repeated negative assessments of his writing from O'Neill Center officials and from a close circle of well-intentioned friends in the profession did Wilson turn his full attention toward writing *Ma Rainey's Black Bottom*, a bluesy play set in 1920s Chicago. His efforts paid off, for the play that featured a day in the life of real life blues legend Gertrude Pridgett 'Ma' Rainey (1886–1939) reaped significant praise from mainstream theatre critics and went on to garner him the type of critical attention reserved for 'serious' playwrights. On the advice of then-director Lloyd Richards, Wilson dodged offers from several producers to convert the play into a musical – as was the case with much of Broadway during the mid-1980s. He insisted that *Ma Rainey* was to be a play in the traditional sense; he was not swayed by the prospect of huge profits from ticket sales.

In effect, *Ma Rainey's Black Bottom* must be credited for introducing Wilson to America! Following the play's April 1984 opening at the Yale Repertory Theatre, critics heaped both guarded and unrestrained praise upon it for its riveting storyline, crisp dialogue and superb acting. Samuel Friedman, who saw the play as part of a tradition established by writers and public personas such as Ralph Ellison, Langston Hughes, Richard Wright, Amiri Baraka and Louis Armstrong, wrote in the *New York Times*, 'Wilson has made the blues a metaphor, or, more precisely, several metaphors for black life.'[14] The play met similar praise during its October 1984 Broadway run. Richard Christiansen, for example, writing in the *Chicago Tribune*, noted reflections of Lorraine Hansberry's *A Raisin in the Sun*, Amiri Baraka's *Dutchman*, James Baldwin's *Blues for Mr. Charlie* and Charles Fuller's *A Soldier's Play*.[15]

Not all critics found *Ma Rainey's Black Bottom* praiseworthy, however. Added to the faction who seemed resentful that the play was not a musical were those who took Wilson to task for blurring the lines between the main character and supporting cast members. To them, the play's title not only suggested that the performance would entail a generous helping of her blues tunes but also that she would remain at centre stage. In the January 1985 edition of *Saturday Review*, theatre critic Stanley Kaufman seemed none too pleased and argued that the play's central flaw is that it 'is split figuratively, just as the set is split literally'.¹⁶ Robert Isaacs of the *Waterbury Republican* could not contain that he was disappointed that the play was not about Ma Rainey,¹⁷ and John Fisher of the *Buck County Courier Times* roundly criticized Wilson for what he saw as imbalance in beefy portrayals of Toledo and Levee and limited development of Ma Rainey.¹⁸ In fact, the chorus of dissatisfaction among many who saw the play's spring 1984 premiere in New Haven made its way through to Wilson even as he basked in accolades from others. He would later revisit these concerns in *Fences*.

Despite this measurable degree of dissension, the overall success of *Ma Rainey's Black Bottom* proclaimed Wilson's arrival upon the American theatre scene, yet one can easily surmise that, were it not for his perseverance and good fortune, the initial script for *Ma Rainey* may have never come across the desk of Artistic Director of Yale Repertory Theater and Dean of Yale School of Drama Lloyd Richards in 1982. In fact, Richards was so taken by the play that he selected it for a staged reading at the National Playwrights Conference during that summer. These settings gave Richards the opportunity to candidly convince Wilson to address some of the play's most glaring weaknesses and remaining challenges. For example, the workshops revealed that several decisions must be made about the play's structure. Should the playwright employ actors who double as musicians or resort to pre-recorded music? Should Wilson de-emphasize competing plot lines between Ma and her band members or write two separate plays? Further, were it not for Richards's advice and Wilson's refusal to turn *Ma Rainey's Black Bottom* into a musical, the play that would ultimately launch his career may have taken what would have been a much more profitable but less artistically noteworthy course.

The play that pays homage to a host of abused and forgotten blues players is based upon an imaginary day in the life of real-life legendary blues woman Gertrude Pridgett 'Ma' Rainey (1886–1939) and a host of sharply drawn and intriguingly lifelike portrayals of her fictional band members, her nephew, her lover, two white promoters and an arresting police officer. The plot evolves out of a stalled rehearsal session during which 'Ma's band' warms up and engages in light banter before her anticipated arrival at the recording session. When the flustered and belligerent Ma Rainey finally shows up in the dingy space in the company of an arresting officer, she further angers the two white promoters on hand who are anxious to get on with the recording session, despite her series of antics. Meanwhile, her crew of black male musicians waiting for Ma in the basement band room argue over trifles and amuse each other with bouts of dozens and pseudo-philosophical commentary. Their conversations, which slip from tense exchanges about the correct spelling of 'music' to an existential discussion of black history, gradually intensify and unexpectedly erupt when a misplaced foot leads to murder. The self-made philosopher and pianist Toledo inadvertently steps on the new Florsheim shoes of the sulking trumpeter Levee, who – having been recently duped by the same white promoters out of several of his original songs – takes out his disdain on the piano player, the only literate one among them.

Ma Rainey's Black Bottom not only became Wilson's ticket to the Great White Way, but the play also distinguished itself by exposing deep chasms that existed between the white power brokers and the powerless black minority in pre-Depression era America. Wilson frames this binary in terms of a historically familiar power dynamic between the colonizers and the colonized or between the ruling class and the proletariat or – as described it in a 2012 presidential campaign slogan – between the 99 per cent and the 1 per cent. That is to say, in this chilly Chicago recording studio, those who wield power, money, equipment, access to heat and overall control of the space trump those who hold the very means of production. While Ma's band is comprised of musicians who are excellent in their own right, they are powerless, stunted and essentially emasculated in their role as mere back-up for Ma Rainey and as 'boys' to Sturdyvant and Irvin. Similarly, while Ma's presence brings gravitas and assurance of brisk record sales to the session, she, too, is regarded as no more than a commodity. The power she wields over her band becomes relative when considered in the larger capitalist scheme at work here.

Ma Rainey's Black Bottom plays out what seems to be the inevitable result of pent-up black rage in America in the early years of the twentieth century when the seething trumpet player Levee stabs and kills the piano player Toledo for mistakenly stepping on his shoe. As evidence in the play strongly suggests, this impetuous act is directly related to Levee's frustration over being duped out of songs that he secretly wrote and shared with one of the white promoters at the session who made light of his creative genius but predictably kept the lyrics. In a scene that is eerily reminiscent of the callous murder perpetrated by Richard Wright's troubled protagonist in *Native Son* (1940) – who, in one instance, inexplicably rapes his 'girlfriend' and, in another, bludgeons her to death and tosses her body out of a widow – Levee snaps and thrusts his knife into a fellow black musician – clearly a substitute target for his anger.

While the play's 1920s setting may have afforded the 1980s audience some distance, its gritty display of heartless greed and ruthless predatory tactics so typical of the burgeoning and unregulated blues and jazz industry at that time paralleled similar economic and racial divisions that flourished during the Reagan era.[19] As such, the play collapses six decades as it re-enacts a troubling yet familiar narrative. 'Greed is good', according to fictional tycoon Gordon Gekko at the close of Oliver Stone's popular 1987 film *Wall Street*. In this now infamous line, actor Michael Douglass, who portrayed the unscrupulous financier, captures what many cultural historians regard as the zeitgeist of the decade dubbed the 'Reagan era', yet it could also easily suffice as the subtitle for *Ma Rainey's Black Bottom*. In this regard, the manipulative and predatory business transactions that take place in the band room between corporate reps in the guise of white promoters Sturdyvant and Irvin and the group of disenfranchised black musicians Levee, Slow Drag, Cutler, Toledo and, of course, Ma Rainey force the past to be in conversation with the present.

In fact, *Ma Rainey's Black Bottom* charts a clear causal relationship between the actions of those who are completely cut off from the American Dream and those who resort to inexplicably violent acts to protest against this exclusion. In this regard, the play can be seen as a case study, for it captures the plight of marginalized and disenfranchised African-American musicians during the Jazz Age/Harlem Renaissance era of America's cultural history. Barred from access to the American Dream, a group of talented band members resort to essentially 'pimping' their music for a capitalist-driven 1920s music recording industry. The blues then become their source of cultural identity and solace for them and the object of greed for Sturdyvant and Irvin.

Ma Rainey's Black Bottom has its origins in *The Homecoming* (1976),[20] an earlier work by Wilson in which he exposes the underhand tactics of white blues scouts who preyed upon illiterate

Southern black musicians who, all too often, possessed neither business savvy nor street smarts to fend off human predators. This relatively unknown early play explores the mystery surrounding Blind Lemon Jefferson's[21] death through the guise of Wilson's fictitious alter ego, Blind Willie Johnson, whose life and death in the play parallel that of the real singer. While Wilson's *The Homecoming* turns the tables on a couple of unscrupulous white recruiters and offers vengeance for the prey upon black musicians, *Ma Rainey's Black Bottom* assesses the long-term psychological toll of institutional racism upon the oppressed. Although temporarily suppressed, as the play suggests, the damaging effects of racism, exclusion and marginalization inevitably erupt in displays of irrational acts and misdirected violence.

As he does in the majority of his Century plays, Wilson juxtaposes the past and the present, according to Harry Elam, author of *The Past as Present in the Drama of August Wilson*, in an effort to 'recreate and reevaluate the choices that blacks have made in the past by refracting them through the lens of the present' (xv). As such, *Ma Rainey*'s exposé on the plight of African-American bluesmen and blueswomen in the predatory racist and sexist environment that saw the commodification of their music is shown through the lens of the 1980s economic realities. No doubt contemporary audiences could see just how illusive the American Dream was, not just for black musicians in pre-Depression era America but for many African-Americans as well. Also communicated through the stories of this group of justifiably irritable black musicians is a continuing narrative of oppression and marginalization that spans across 60 years and continues to be relevant.

Fences (1987)

During its 1987 Broadway run at the 46th Street Theatre, August Wilson's *Fences* broke the record for non-musical plays by grossing $11 million during its first year in New York. It went on to garner four Tony Awards, including Best Play, and to earn the prestigious New York Drama Critics' Circle Award. It also captured the John Gassner Outer Critics' Circle Award and ultimately the Pulitzer Prize.

Apart from the commercial success of *Fences*, its importance may be determined by what the play reveals about the changing American psyche in the late 1980s as the country grappled with long-standing constructs of race, class and gender. As a popular non-musical Broadway play of the late 1980s that featured an entire cast of African-Americans, *Fences* signalled a shift in America's theatrical taste. That shift also involved risk-taking by producers who gradually began to financially back African-American plays other than popular cash cow musicals. Just as its predecessor *Ma Rainey's Black Bottom* proved in 1984, Broadway audiences and, by extension, Americans were more willing to gaze through the window of African-American experience and see aspects of their own diverse cultures.

Wilson wrote *Fences* in 1983 as an antidote to concerns expressed by critics about the obscure focus and unwieldiness of *Ma Rainey's Black Bottom*. This 1950s play, then, grew out of the playwright's determination to prove that he could raise a single character to a much grander scale. Initially he had no plans to write this riveting domestic drama, which ultimately won more honours than any play in Broadway history. In fact, having already completed *Ma Rainey* and *Jitney*, he had intended to follow his own strategy, which was next to write *Joe Turner's Come and Gone* and then go on to complete *The Piano Lesson*. But Wilson listened to the advice of his circle of theatre professionals who encouraged him to bring some variety to the then well-populated, talkative cast of characters that had become so familiar. As a means of motivating the playwright to try his skills in other directions, they challenged him to write 'a more conventional play with one main character and others supporting him'[22] as successfully as he had drawn the enigmatic one-dimensional figures of his earlier plays.

At the centre of Wilson's play for the 1950s is the towering, tragic figure of Troy Maxson, a roaring lion of a black man and one of American theatre's most indelible characters since Willy Loman and Stanley Kowalski. *Fences* revolves around a once-great Negro League ballplayer, Troy, who grapples with the mid-century changing racial landscape and who is caught between his furious resentment of the opportunities denied him and the prospects tentatively opening for his son, Cory, in the decade of Jackie Robinson and *Brown v. Board of Education*. As in other Wilson plays, such as *The Piano Lesson* and *Radio Golf*, a generational family battle reveals the psychological toll that racism has exacted on characters who still struggle to partake of some portion of the American Dream.

The play opens as garbage man, husband, father, friend and disgruntled baseball player Troy Maxson and Jim Bono, his close friend of thirty years, make their way home to celebrate the end of another gruelling week of hard labour. For eight hours a day, they bend, stoop and hoist and toss canned refuse into the waiting mouth of a huge trash compactor. As Troy has done each Friday evening, he hands over his weekly pay cheque to his wife, Rose, who manages their home. As they come onto the set, Troy and Jim Bono tease each other and look forward to another weekend away from the mental and physical pressures of their jobs.

But, for Troy, putting the pressures of his job behind him is not an easy task. Because he continues to witness the blatant discrimination on his job and in other aspects of his daily existence, he harbours a deep-seated disgust for the racism of his country and fumes over the fact that all of his co-workers who lift garbage cans are black, and all who drive the trucks are white. But garbage collecting is one of the few professions now open to Troy. Although a top-notch baseball player during the Negro League's heyday, by 1957 he is too old to play on a desegregated Major League team.

These feelings of being passed over change Troy into a man obsessed with extorting from life an equal measure of what was robbed from him. Despite a seemingly loving and passionate relationship with his wife, Troy finds the 'big-legged Florida gal' Alberta irresistible. He strikes up a physical relationship with her – one that produces their baby daughter, Raynelle. After Alberta dies in childbirth, Troy is left to raise the baby girl but finds that his only recourse is to plead with Rose to care for the motherless infant. Rose accepts this responsibility heroically, but at the same time, erects an emotional fence between Troy and her. The effects of Troy's massive ego extend to his son Cory as well. In one of the play's many tense moments, father and son clash over the boy's plans to become a football player. When Cory is convinced by high school coaches that he has a future in football, he pre-emptively quits his after-school job at the local A&P. Troy, however, has other plans for his son's future and secretly sabotages an offer for an athletic scholarship from an interested recruiter. As expected, Troy and Cory have a major argument during which father and son come to blows and exchange harsh words. It becomes clear that Troy encounters more opposition from Cory than he has ever faced from any member of his family. Troy's brain-damaged brother, Gabriel, always worries that Troy is angry at him; Lyons, Troy's son from a previous marriage, avoids confrontation and visits his father only when he wants a small loan; and Rose exists as a mere shadow in Troy's presence until she learns that he has impregnated his mistress Alberta. However, throughout the play, Cory dislikes his father's tactics and is not afraid to express his dissatisfaction, whether verbally, in the form of snide remarks, or physically, in a brief wrestling match.

Fences ends in the 1960s, a decade that brought significant changes for African-Americans. The final scene takes place during preparations for Troy's funeral. It seems that one of his favourite concocted stories about doing battle with the Grim Reaper has finally caught up with him. As Death encroaches during a practice batting sessions in his yard, Troy – never one to succumb to fate – assumes the familiar batter's stance and, in one last showdown, it seems, welcomes his familiar foe. Previously alienated, the family members respond to Troy's death by tightening their communal bonds at this solemn occasion, and Rose gently convinces her prodigal son Cory to tear down the fences that have long existed between him and his father. Cory returns home upon news of his father's death, but he is, at first, adamant about not attending Troy's funeral. Still smarting from Troy's words and actions against him in the past – as well as his dad's sins against his mother – Cory has to be convinced to put the past aside and step out from his father's shadow.

Deemed a generational play, *Fences* presents a portrait of three generations of black men whose roots converge in a brutish sharecropper of the Reconstruction era. As a direct descendant of the elder Maxson, Troy is a pivotal force. He is a 53-year-old garbage collector of the late 1950s who still can recall ugly images of life under the iron rule of a frustrated, defeated dirt farmer of the early 1900s. At the same time, Troy tries the best way he knows how to direct the course of his own son's life away from the depressing state of victimhood that so damaged both his father and grandfather. *Fences* typifies Wilson's belief that 'you should start making connections to your parents and your grandparents and working backwards. We're not in Africa anymore, and we're not going back to Africa. You have to understand your parents and understand your grandparents.'[23] Apparently, Wilson sees wisdom in promoting the values of one's African kin, but argues, first, for an acknowledgement of the compromised lives of living ancestors.

In 1987, August Wilson sat for a revealing interview with Theatre Communications Group host David Savran, during which he outlined the need to sustain intergenerational connections between both young and old African-Americans. This belief manifests as a major theme in *Fences*.

> First of all, we're like our parents. The things we are taught early in life, how to respond to the world, our sense of morality – everything, we get from them. Now you can take that legacy and do with it anything you want to do. It's in your hands. Cory is Troy's son. How can he be Troy's son without sharing Troy's values? I was trying to get at why Troy made the choices he made, how they have influenced his values and how he attempts to pass those along to his son. Each generation gives the succeeding generation what they think they need. One question in the play is 'Are the tools we are given sufficient to compete in a world that is different from the one our parents knew?' I think they are – it's just that we have to do different things with the tools. That's all Troy has to give.[24]

Wilson's comments provide a more liberal and enlightening context for audiences and readers of *Fences* to process the crude relationships between the three generations of Maxson men. The fact that Troy endures the ugly politics of his own workplace in order to keep the steady pay cheque, for example, must be weighed against his infidelity and devious tactics against Cory, Rose and Gabriel. Judged also within this new framework, the actions of Troy's father become less of an indication of an inherently evil man and more of a potentially good man who has been beaten down by the circumstances of his life and times. When viewed through generational and historical lenses, therefore, Troy's father is more likely to enlist empathy rather than scorn for his decision not to give in to the 'walking blues' and remain with his family, even as he endured backbreaking labour while employed by his merciless white proprietor, Mr Lubin.

Despite his poor relationship with his father, Troy's bloodline dictates that he will inherit both admirable and objectionable features. Most notably, it appears that Troy advances a similarly strong work ethic along with a serious regard for responsibility to his own family. Although Troy's father does much to disgust him (driving his mother away with sheer cruelty, sexually assaulting Troy's girl, punching him unconscious when confronted, and denying food to his children), Troy is still able to boast, 'he felt a responsibility toward us. Maybe he ain't treated us the way I felt he should have ... but without that responsibility, he could have walked off and left us ... made his own way' (1.4.51).

Just as Troy is able to do, Cory eventually brings himself to accept and put to use certain life lessons that his father somehow manages to impart. To be sure, Cory does not see anything worthy of emulation in Troy until he faces the profound final ritual marking his father's death, and when he is subjected to Rose's compassionate appeal for a truce in their longtime feud, he indicates a change of heart. In the wake of his mother's emotional speech, evidence suggests that her words have had an impact upon Cory in his sudden pivot to his baby sister Raynelle whom he urges to finish getting dressed for their father's funeral. Though subtle, Cory's gestures indicate his acceptance of the generational torch passed on to him by Troy. This redemptive moment in the play is an epiphanic moment for Cory, who signals that he accepts the mantle from his father in moving the Maxson family forward.

While Wilson's larger motive in writing *Fences* may have been to redeem himself among his harshest critics by creating a three-dimensionally, fully drawn character, the play also confirms his adeptness at portraying the realities of African-American women during the 1950s. Toward that end, Rose Maxson – whose character was brought to the Broadway stage by veteran actresses Mary Alice and Viola Davis – at first seems to epitomize the familiar Cult of Domesticity.[25] As the play progresses, however, she begins to gradually break free of prescribed roles to find her own voice. To be sure, African-American women in the 1950s, such as Rose, had few options upon reaching adulthood. Seldom did these choices extend beyond marriage, motherhood and domesticity. Money spent then toward their education was considered an unwise investment, especially because few jobs awaited them that required more than the ability to cook, clean and cater to the service demands of a white world. Moreover, the prevailing climate of anti-intellectualism cautioned women against seeking education attainment which might prevent them from being good wives and homemakers to potential husbands.

Rose lingers half in the shadows during the entire first act of *Fences*, speaking largely in reaction to her husband's exaggerated stories about himself. However, when she finally discovers her voice, she violates one of the key tenets of this ideology: she – not Troy – sets the conditions of her marriage, two of which is that she will accept and raise Troy and Alberta's baby girl and that she will no longer share the marriage bed with him. For much of the play, she was the predictable image of temperance, before suddenly becoming a woman able to stand up to an egoistic husband: 'I been standing with you! I been right here with you, Troy. I got a life too. I gave eighteen years of my life to stand in the same spot with you. Don't you think I ever wanted other things? Don't you think I had dreams and hopes?' (2.1.70–1). In this one impassioned scene, Rose's entire history rushes forward out of nearly two decades of dormancy. She summons up her own means of empowerment outside of her husband's overbearing influence.

In an effort to breathe more life into a singular character, Wilson stretched his dramatic skills to create a complex character that is, on the one hand, brutish, conniving and domineering, yet, on the other hand, pensive, sensitive and lovable. In doing so, he silenced those critics who doubted his dramatic range. This character (who was brought to life on the Broadway stage by veteran actors James Earl Jones and Bill Dee Williams) represents a large number of black men in his day who were caught between expectations of being responsible in a white-controlled world and the innate desire to pursue their own desires and ambitions. Wilson's success at fashioning just such a character is an indicator of his capability to move beyond what some saw as shallow characterizations in *Ma Rainey's Black Bottom* and *Jitney*. Clive Barnes, theatre critic for the *New York Post*, offers a testament that he was transfixed during the play's 26 March 1987 Broadway opening: 'Once in a rare while, you come across a play – or a movie or a novel – that seems to break away from the confines of art into a dense, complex realization of reality. A veil has been torn aside, the artist has disappeared into a transparency. We look with our own eyes, feel with our own hearts.'[26]

When all of Troy's fears and insecurities associated with being a black man in 1957 join forces with demons of his past, a bluesman of tragic proportion is born. As a result, Troy Maxson can hold his own among protagonists such as Arthur Miller's Willie Loman, Lorraine Hansberry's Walter Lee Younger and William Shakespeare's Hamlet. Not only did Wilson find his way through to the ending of *Fences*, but along the way, he managed to avoid becoming a slave to conventions or rules. *Fences* does adhere to recognizable aspects of Western drama, yet it also bears the unmistakable stamp of Wilson's Africanist inspired creative intuition, which frequently operates outside the box of Aristotelian conventions about drama. *Fences*, which now stands as one of August Wilson's two Pulitzer Prize-winning works, represents a marriage of his art, his politics, his life and his dramatic vision for honest depictions of the African-American experience during the 1950s. The play has since become an *American* classic, extending its reach beyond the printed page to stage and, most recently, to the big screen.[27]

Joe Turner's Come and Gone (1984)

The mid-1980s was, quite conceivably, the busiest and most productive time in Wilson's career as a playwright. Having been thrust into sudden notoriety with the success of *Ma Rainey's Black Bottom*, he worked steadily to avoid the stigma of being a 'one-play playwright'. Under Lloyd Richard's gentle command, he revised early drafts, wrote new ones and shepherded several of his best known plays – including *The Piano Lesson* and *Two Trains Running* – on a familiar trek that began with a staged reading at the Eugene O'Neill Theater Center and that moved on to the Yale Repertory Theatre, to regional theatres and ultimately on to Broadway. *Joe Turner's Come and Gone*, set in 1911 during America's era of Reconstruction, is a product of this busy period. Originally titled *Mill Hands Lunch Bucket* after a Romare Bearden collage and retitled *Joe Turner's Come and Gone*, the play is the first to be set in Wilson's native Pittsburgh and the second in his ten-play series.

Joe Turner's Come and Gone underscores collateral damage suffered by Africans in America as a result of massive displacement and subsequent cultural fragmentation – that is, according to Wilson, the lingering emotional and psychological effects associated with the slave era of the seventeenth and eighteenth centuries and, later, during the Great Migration at the turn of the twentieth century. The play's time frame strategically encompasses these two historical eras – both of which are responsible for the largest dispersal, separation and splintering of the African-American population in history. Wilson finds dramatic conflict in the cultural fragmentation or in the dissolution of families and communities and the devaluation of their culture that came in the wake of the mass relocation of newly Americanized Africans following the Civil War. He was motivated by a desire to convey the profound and lasting impact of these two periods of flux upon the African-American psyche and set out to do so in epic fashion. Toward this end, his characters are made into archetypes; what they say, do, believe and espouse speak not just for their individual characters but for an entire race of people.

Herald Loomis, the play's protagonist, is reminiscent of the Ulysses archetype in his monumental quest to return home or – as expressed by this former ward of Joe Turner – to find his 'starting place'.[28] As the play opens, Loomis and his young daughter Zonia come upon a boarding house where he seeks clues as to the whereabouts of his estranged wife, Martha. Seven years earlier, Loomis had been forcefully kidnapped and made to become one of the numerous farmhands of legendary Joe Turner, who notoriously tricked freed black men into extended periods of forced labour in a scheme not entirely unlike slavery. Finally released after seven years of hard labour, Loomis tries to locate his family, only to find his wife Martha and their daughter Zonia evicted and long gone from the meagre tenant farmer's dwelling where he had left them. He tracks down little Zonia at his mother-in-law's house, but wages a long and tiring search for his wife, who has taken up with a distant church.

With the assistance of the notorious People Finder, Rutherford Selig, Martha Pentecost (formerly Martha Loomis) eventually finds her way to the boarding house shortly after her estranged husband and abandoned daughter have been evicted. Yet when the family does finally meet, only a partial reunion takes place. Martha reclaims her daughter, but she cannot accept the heathen Loomis, whose harrowing experiences in captivity have hardened him against Christianity. To coax him away from what she sees as his life of sin, she offers up a passionate plea that he be 'washed in the blood of the lamb'. Loomis, having finally 'found his song' – that is, his place in the world – responds by slashing his chest in a profoundly sacrilegious gesture to, in effect, denounce her God and affirm self: 'I don't need nobody to bleed for me! I can bleed for myself' (2.5.93).

Tensions between a religion that was forced upon Africans upon coming to America and their own belief systems that survived the Middle Passage drive the conflict of *Joe Turner's Come and Gone* and reveal deep fissures within both the boarding house community and Loomis's own marriage. By juxtaposing aspects of African spiritualism and various customs that survived the Middle Passage with a drastically different set of rituals, customs and religious beliefs, *Joe Turner* captures the essence of cultural strangulation to which Africans were subjected. No doubt informed by Wilson's own oft-repeated belief that 'God does not hear the prayers of blacks,'[29] the play presents a searing indictment against New World Christianity and a seeming approbation of man's penchant for self-determination. The friction between the slave owner's Christianity and African spirituality create sparks that draw attention to the play's overriding message about the dangers – and the essential impossibility – of completely erasing aspects of one's culture and replacing them with those of another. Bynum Walker, the resident voodoo man in the Holly boarding house, best captures the reaction against cultural erasure for the sake of unity: 'I'm a Binder of What Clings,' he notes. 'You got to find out if they cling first. You can't bind what don't cling' (1.1.10).

An extension of this reaction in each of Wilson's plays is the cynical regard for Christianity as a positive force in the lives of his African-American men. In Loomis's case, a dollar bill given to a so-called 'People Finder' substitutes for what might have been a fervent prayer for God's assistance. Moreover, displays of religious devotion are met with biting cynicism and blasphemy. For example, during a scene in which the doubting Loomis and the saved Martha finally confront each other, he reveals that Jesus Christ, to him, has become no more than a 'Great big old white man' (2.5.92).

Joe Turner dramatizes the contradictions and controversies that have historically surrounded religion and spiritualism among African-Americans. Wilson's oft-professed belief that 'God does not hear the prayers of blacks'[30] channels the sentiments of many African-Americans who, through the generations, have rejected Christianity as the slave masters' tool to annihilate all memory of African practices and traditions and replace them with a white man's religion that promotes docility and subjugation. Yet the profound influence of Christian churches, clergy and teachings is undeniable. Churches have historically served as African-Americans' political and social community base. They were the driving force behind the civil rights movement. 'The church is probably the most important institution in the black community,' Wilson explained in an interview with journalist Bill Moyers. 'There's no question of that. But it's an overlay of African religions onto the Christian religion.'[31] Earlier, he explained to theatre scholar David Savran, 'Blacks have taken Christianity and bent it to serve their African-ness. In Africa there's ancestor worship, among kinds of religious practices. That's given blacks, particularly southern blacks, the ideas of ghosts, magic and superstition ... Relating to the spirit worlds is very much a part of African and Afro-American culture.'[32]

Herald Loomis, a former member of Joe Turner's chain gang and one-time deacon in the Christian church, flatly rebuffs his wife's religious fervour by brandishing a knife and drawing his own blood in an act that mirrors Jesus Christ's crucifixion. His dramatic self-inflicted wounding, coupled with his abrupt phallic showdown with God – 'Why God got to be so big. Why he got to be bigger than me? How much big do you want?' (1.4.52) – suggest the extent to which Loomis wants no part of this new and alien religion. Indeed, the derisive tone of his comments as well as his outright challenge to God's omnipotence coupled with his willingness to draw his own blood in the final scene of the play reflect a level of exasperation that is relatively new to African-American theatre.

To best convey the long-term collateral damage suffered by a population of Africans forcefully removed from their homeland and displaced as slaves in America, Wilson turned to a mixture of metaphysical and naturalistic elements to cast this historical moment in epic fashion. While the main storyline of *Joe Turner's Come and Gone* is a spin-off of real-life kidnappings conducted by the infamous plantation owner Joe Turner, the legendary brother of Tennessean governor Pete Turner, Wilson stretches its premise to signify the immeasurable toll that the slave enterprise took and continues to exact from Africans in America. In this regard, the restless vagrant Herald Loomis typifies to the alienation and cultural fragmentation that impacted on this transplanted population during both slavery and the Great Migration to the North.

While just beginning to become accustomed to the bittersweet freedom afforded by the Emancipation Proclamation, Loomis – like many freedmen during post-emancipation America – is again enslaved. This time, however, he is nabbed and put to work by the legendary white Tennessean, Joe Turner. According to Wilson,

> the seven years Loomis is with Joe Turner, seven years in which his world is torn asunder and his life is turned upside down, can in fact represent the four hundred years of slavery, of being taken out of Africa and brought to America. At some point someone says, 'Okay, you're free.' What do you do? Who are you, first of all, and what do you do now that you are free, which is Loomis's question. He says, 'I must reconnect and reassemble myself.' But when he goes to the place where he lived, his life is no longer there. His wife and daughter aren't there. He is, in effect, a foreigner to the place. So he goes off on a search. He searches for a woman to say goodbye and to find a world that contains his image, because there's nothing about the world that he finds himself in that speaks to the thing that's beating inside his chest?[33]

The intersecting narratives of slavery in America and Herald Loomis's kidnapping ordeal are acted out by characters whose roles also approximate rarely explored realities within the African-American community during the early twentirth century when the slave experience was not so far removed from their consciousness. To this end, the resident voodoo man Bynum Walker – more so than the psychologically traumatized Herald Loomis or the business-minded People Finder – personifies this memory albeit amid suspicion and ridicule. Bynum is, at once, a spiritual shaman imbued with the rituals and memory of Africa but whose odd behaviour earns him the reputation among the boarding house tenants as a slightly off-balanced yet tolerable tenant.

Wilson began writing *Joe Turner's Come and Gone* at a point in the 1980s when the concept of post-blackness had begun to gain traction among artists and intellectuals who argued that art should no longer be encumbered by the politics of race and who sought to produce works that reflected more universalities rather than differences.[34] According to American writer, music journalist, cultural critic and television personality Toure, 'Post-black is ... about people who are rooted in blackness but not constrained by it. They want to be black. They want to deal with the black tradition, and the black community, and black tropes. But they also want the freedom to do other things. Blackness is not necessarily the entirety of who they are.'[35]

Although the 1980s saw black artists in the vanguard of a movement loosely termed 'post-black', they faced significant opposition from a contingent of unwavering Afrocentrists and cultural nationalists in their midst who were products of the 1960s cultural nationalist mindset, such as Molefi Asante, Cornell West, Amiri Baraka and, of course, August Wilson, who boasted of having been 'fired in the kiln of the Black Power movement'.[36] That August Wilson would write what is arguably his 'blackest' play during this ideologically tense climate of the post-black era put him in opposition to those who would rather have downplayed race in favour of what they believed to be a colour-blind society.

Despite his unwavering stance as a cultural nationalist, Wilson encountered detractors from among pragmatic-minded African-American actors who worried less about colour-blind casting than they did about landing a role that offered them a decent pay cheque. During the late 1980s and early 1990s, while at the height of his campaign, Wilson seemed taken aback by fellow African-Americans in the profession who challenged his aesthetic position. He recalled a conversation with one such actor who schooled him on the unintended collateral damage that he feared may come of Wilson's demands: 'Man, let me explain something to you. I appreciate what you're doing by wanting a black director, but we've been out here for fifteen years telling these people it don't matter if we're black or not. We're trying to get a job directing *LA Law*, and we've been telling them it don't matter.'[37]

While the figurative gauntlet that Wilson threw down during his 1980s and 1990s campaign against colour-blind casting and directing meant little to a certain segment of the African-American theatre community, four years after his death in 2005, more than a few African-American veteran actors and directors of his plays were more than willing to defend his cause. When white director Bartlett

Sher secured permission from Wilson's estate to stage a Broadway production of *Joe Turner's Come and Gone* in spring 2009, he ignited a media firestorm that was fuelled by those who knew well and remembered the controversial position that Wilson had taken up years ago. As I noted in the Introduction to *August Wilson and Black Aesthetics*, actor Charles Dutton and directors Marion McClinton and Kenny Leon, for example, expressed deep concerns that 'one of the most defining concepts of Wilson's career as an African-American artist and as a disciple of the 1960s who boasts having been "fired in the kiln" of the "Black Power" movement had been completely ignored less than five years after his death' and concluded that giving Sher control of Wilson's 'blackest' play was 'an affront to August Wilson's self-defining articulation of black aesthetic'.[38]

Joe Turner's Come and Gone, then, resonates on multiple levels: historically, culturally, aesthetically and personally. Reflected in the ideological differences between Herald and Martha Loomis, for example, is a similar kind of marital conflict that drove a wedge between Wilson and his first wife Brenda Burton, who was of the Muslim faith. Likewise, one can discern parallels between Herald Loomis's quest for 'his song' or his 'starting place' upon his release from seven years of servitude and Wilson's own existentialist struggles to find his cultural and racial affinities, despite being an essentially rudderless young black man growing up without the benefit of a dependable father. When pressed in interviews, Wilson often singled out *Joe Turner's Come and Gone* as his favourite play. It stands to reason, therefore, that his fondness for this second play in his American Century Cycle has as much to do with the autobiographical imprint that it bears of his own personal journey as it does the masterful use of metaphor as a substitute for the lingering trauma of slavery. As I argue in 'The Role of Memory in August Wilson's Four-Hundred-Year Autobiography', 'In recreating this record of the past, Wilson, as autobiographer, is at once author and subject.'[39] Reflections of the playwright's own story emerge in *Joe Turner's* focus upon marital tensions, the social pariah's quest for identity within an alien environment, the obligations of fatherhood, and religious and spiritual ambivalence. As such, this play supports Wilson's assertion that writing the Cycle plays was, for him, tantamount to writing a 'four-hundred-year-old autobiography'. That is, in rewriting the history of African-Americans, he discovered his own.

According to Lloyd Richards – who directed *Joe Turner's Come and Gone* at the Yale Repertory Theatre in April 1986 and, later, in March 1988 at New York's Ethel Barrymore Theatre – this play 'took you deeply into a place where you had never been before' and 'made you work'.[40] In order to fully resonate, *Joe Turner* requires of its audiences a significant level of knowledge about slavery's deep and lasting imprint upon contemporary African-Americans. Steeped in archetypal implications, this play draws upon metaphysical images, symbols and rituals that hearken back to the hull of a Middle Passage ship, to Joe Turner's chain gain, to the tobacco and cotton fields of the South and to the painstaking journey to the North. The play brings to the fore recognizable landscapes drawn from what Wilson terms 'blood memory'[41] or shared consciousness among members of the African diaspora based upon their common origins. According to Wilson, this profound level of group 'understanding' lies dormant in every African in America.

Many early audiences and theatre critics alike found the premise of *Joe Turner* too allusive – this, despite Wilson's often expressed efforts to make the characters in this play immediately recognizable as Africans. By all measures, on that front, however, he failed; the play suffered stinging reviews and a relatively short Broadway run. Wilson was both surprised and saddened that large segments of both African-American and white audiences did not see evidence of this onstage. In a 1987 interview, he told Savran:

> I have found tremendous resistance to that. I talked with an audience at Yale Rep after Joe Turner and I actually lost my temper. I said, 'How many recognize these people as Africans?' There were two hundred people sitting there and about eight raised their hands. I'm very curious as to why they refuse – I have to say it's a refusal because it's so obvious. So many people blocked that, wanting to recognize them as black Americans. I was really surprised to find that.[42]

Despite what was then and now a difficult play for both audiences and critics alike, within the limitations of this play's structure, Wilson managed to convey in epic fashion separation, migration and reunion of African-American people. As such, this play bears the mark of classic theatre and remains one of Wilson's most complex, most profound and most instructive statements about the odyssey of Africans in America from the decks of slave ships and cotton fields to Ivy League campuses and corporate boardrooms.

August Wilson is now celebrated as one of a small select group of major American dramatists. There is something particularly remarkable and noteworthy about this playwright's self-described commitment to write ten plays and about his determination to make good on this herculean effort, even as his health was failing him. It was not long after he completed the last play, *Radio Golf*, in spring 2005 that news of Wilson's cancer diagnosis spread. He died in October of the same year shortly after completing what we now know as the 'American Century Cycle'. Perhaps there is no better indication of the enduring as well as endearing nature of this Cycle than the recent finale of a twenty-plus-year journey of Wilson's signature play *Fences* from the page to the stage, culminating in a late 2016 big screen premiere starring Viola Davis and Denzel Washington. Similar watershed moments that underscore Wilson's stature are the 2015 release of *The Ground On Which I Stand*, an American Masters documentary on his life, and the 2017 Broadway premiere of *Jitney*, the very last play in the Century Cycle to be so honoured. Moreover, with the imminent rollout of HBO productions of the remaining nine plays – under the able supervision of Denzel Washington – August Wilson's place in American theatre history will be sealed.

Afterword

Sandra G. Shannon

David Mamet

One reviewer described David Mamet's post-1980s work as a 'downward spiral' and argued that the playwright 'has been on a steady downhill slide for nearly two decades, bottoming out with his labored period piece *Boston Marriage*, in 1999, and his brutally unfunny political farce *November*'.[1] Many, like *Time* magazine reporter Richard Zoglin, concede that Mamet's reputation as a playwright rests not upon the overall body of his work but upon a set of plays routinely regarded by theatre historians and critics as masterpieces. These include *American Buffalo* (1975), *Glengarry Glen Ross* (1983) and *Edmond* (1982). Truth be told, Mamet's impact has indeed dwindled since his peak influence with these 1980s dramas, and, many like Zoglin believe that his career has become idiosyncratic. Mamet now debuts his plays directly on Broadway rather than in regional theatres, and, lately, they do not filter into the theatrical bloodstream as staples of regional company programming.

Despite the inevitable comparisons to what is, arguably, his best work, Mamet's post-1980 years have been nothing less than prolific. Buoyed by the momentum of his early success, he has written another dozen or so plays including *The Old Neighborhood* (1997), *Boston Marriage* (1999), *November* (2008) and *Race* (2009). His reputation remains intact and influential enough to attract major actors to plays that continue to be mounted on Broadway – both in revivals such as *Glengarry Glen Ross* in 2012 (starring Al Pacino) and in seriously flawed new works, such as the short-lived *China*

Doll in 2015 (again, starring Pacino) and, in 2012, *The Anarchist* (starring Patti Lupone and Debra Winger), a performance that critics dismissed as an 'instant flop'. In addition, he has also maintained a very busy career as screenwriter, film director and nonfiction author. For example, he created the 2006–9 CBS TV series *The Unit*, based on Eric L. Haney's book *Inside Delta Force*.

Fortunately, less than flattering assessments of Mamet's recent dramatic output are – for those who care to or can remember – often overshadowed by his enduring reputation in the 1980s for the hard-boiled plots and dialogue of *Glengarry Glen Ross* and for the wicked satire of *Speed-the-Plow*. In retrospect, Mamet's Machiavellian prototypes and high-stakes dramas seem more relevant now than ever, especially given the current political climate in an America once again fraught with unchecked power brokers who have perfected 'the art of the deal'. His Pulitzer-winning *Glengarry Glen Ross* with its heartless ethos and crystal depiction of cold-blooded salesmen at work (revisited for comic effect in *Speed-the-Plow*) and the terse, profane, jargon-filled 'Mamet-speak' of his predatory workplace characters summon a foreboding sense of déjà vu. How prophetic is it that David Mamet is to be remembered for adding substantially to America's archetypes of businessmen and con men at work, and to the portrait of America as a Darwinian jungle?

David Henry Hwang

In total, David Henry Hwang had six plays produced in the decade of the 1980s, his most prolific time as a playwright in his career. Ironically, *M. Butterfly*, arguably his most acclaimed work of this era, in effect, defined him but, at the same time, paved the way for him to pursue a host of other career opportunities, including work in opera, film and the musical theatre. For instance, he wrote lyrics for the world renowned composer Philip Glass and penned an original script, *Golden Gate*, which was produced in 1994 by American Playhouse. Throughout the 1990s, Hwang continued to write for the stage, including short plays for the famed Humana Festival at the Actors Theatre of Louisville and *Golden Child*, which received its world premiere in 1996 at South Coast Repertory. *Golden Child*, Hwang's second Broadway venture, won the 1997 Obie Award for its Off-Broadway production and gave Hwang his second Tony nomination.

In the new millennium, Hwang had successive Broadway achievements. The first was *Aida* (based upon the opera by Giuseppe Verdi). In 2000, the Disney Theatrical Group reached out to Hwang and invited him to help write *Aida* the musical, along with Robert Falls. An earlier draft of *Aida* had failed in regional theatre tryouts. Hwang and Falls rewrote a significant portion of the book by Linda Woolverton, and *Aida* (also known as *Elton John and Tim Rice's Aida*) opened in 2000 to commercial success. Hwang's second successful undertaking in the new decade was a radical revision of Richard Rodgers, Oscar Hammerstein II and Joseph Fields's musical *Flower Drum Song*, which originally opened on Broadway in 1958. Forty-four years later, in 2002, this musical returned to Broadway with a plot significantly revised by playwright Hwang, while retaining the Chinatown setting and the inter-generational and immigrant themes and emphasizing the romantic relationships. Hwang's version of *Flower Drum Song*, which simultaneously honored the original version and offered a bolder, more modern rethinking, won him his third Tony nomination. The 2002 revival of the play was finally produced with an all-Asian cast of actor-singers. The original production had cast many non-Asians in leading roles, including Caucasians and an African-American.

Beyond the 1980s, Hwang has continued to work steadily in the world of opera and musical theatre; he has written for children's theatre as well, co-writing the English language libretto for an operatic adaptation of Lewis Carroll's *Alice in Wonderland*, with music (and part of the libretto) by the Korean composer Unsuk Chin, which received its world premiere at the Bavarian State Opera in 2007. Since 2010, Hwang has worked on a theatrical commission for the Oregon Shakespeare Festival and Arena Stage, a musical version of Aimee Mann's album *The Forgotten Arm* with Mann and Paul Bryant and screenplays for DreamWorks Animation and directors Justin Lin and Jonathan Caouette. In 2013, a production of *Yellow Face* premiered on YouTube, while 2014 saw the premiere of two new Hwang plays. The first, *Kung Fu*, about the life of Bruce Lee, premiered as part of Hwang's residency at the Signature Theatre Off-Broadway. The second 2014 play was *Cain and Abel*, which was one of many plays included in *The Mysteries* or retellings of Bible stories. In the autumn of 2016, the San Francisco Opera premiered *Dream of the Red Chamber*, an opera by Hwang and Bright Sheng based on the eighteenth-century Chinese novel.

Hwang continues to be a significant voice not only on the stage but also behind the scenes. He has been a board member and playwright advisor at The Lark, a theatre lab based in New York that helps writers develop their plays, and recently he has taken a position as an Associate Professor of Playwriting at the School of the Arts at Columbia University. In addition, he travels around the country speaking to students in small classrooms and large auditoriums about his works, the nature of theatre and its importance to him and the world at large. Hilton Als of the *New Yorker* has described Hwang as 'the most successful Chinese-American playwright this country has produced'.[2]

Maria Irene Fornes

A key way to view Latina plays today is through the foundational frame of playwright and teacher Maria Irene Fornes. Fornes has trained a generation of theatre artists and transformed American theatre in the 1980s. In some circles, she is as hallowed for her playwriting pedagogy as she is for her plays. During her 40-year career, she developed a series of playwriting exercises and a method of presentation that included Yoga postures and meditation techniques designed to guide her playwriting students in what she described as 'learning how to create life'. While these luminaries have drawn scholarly attention to the INTAR lab and to themselves, scant regard has been given to countless others influenced by Fornes whom she taught in venues outside of INTAR, away from New York City – places such as the Bay Area Playwrights Festival, West Coast Playwrights, Latin American Writers' Workshop (a non-exclusive, diverse entity) and the Padua Hills Playwrights' Workshop and Festival, many of which have been abandoned or morphed into other organizations.

Fornes's plays have been kept alive by colleges and Latino theatres like INTAR, where she taught for many years. They have been kept alive in the minds, souls and words of the many playwrights who cite her as a major influence. And they have been kept alive by the many artists and critics who marvelled at them throughout the 1960s, 1970s and 1980s. But, in a sad irony, the resurgence of energy around her writing may owe something to her fight with Alzheimer's and the recent struggles of her family members and close friends to save her life.

Fornes's work continued to evolve past the 1980s.[3] Beyond the works discussed earlier, she wrote *Abingdon Square* (1987), in which protagonist Marion is trapped between her need for her older husband and her desire for a younger man. First produced by the Women's Project in New York City, it won Fornes another Obie Award. The following year she edited *What of the Night?* (1988) from four previously completed or in-the-works one-acts. This lengthy play, one her most complicated and profound, was shortlisted for the Pulitzer Prize. A somewhat darker play than Kushner's *Angels*, it can be seen as her apocalyptic response to the social crisis of AIDS that swept through New York City in the 1980s. Other notable works from her later period include an operetta with music by Robert Ashley – *Manual for a Desperate Crossing/Balseros* (1997) – which finally saw Fornes turn to the crisis of Cuban immigration through the story of yet another triangular love affair; *The Summer in Gossensass* (1997), a meta play interrogating Fornes's fascination with Ibsen; and *Letters from Cuba* (2000). Overall, her later plays became longer and more introspective, even as she continued with the ramifications of intimate relationships and challenged any consistency of form.

In total, Fornes has won nine Obie Awards, including one for Sustained Achievement in theatre in 1982. She has received a Distinguished Artist Award from the NEA, grants from the Rockefeller and Guggenheim foundations and taught in numerous universities throughout the United States and Latin America. Perhaps the strongest tribute to her work, Fornes's plays were the focus of the Signature Theatre's 1999–2000 season. During this season she also directed the premiere of *Letters from Cuba* (2000), Fornes's first play to confront her Cuban heritage in a notably personal way. Here she used personal letters from her older brother Cuco (who had remained in Cuba) as source material for this somewhat surreal, yet very personal story of a Cuban dancer who had moved to New York City. PAJ more recently published a compilation of her Latino-themed plays, titled *Letters from Cuba and Other Plays* (2007). In retrospect, *Letters* was the last play written and directed by Fornes before the onset of Alzheimer's.

While, at this writing, Fornes is still alive, her current memory loss has prevented her from writing any plays since 2001. Michelle Memran's documentary film, *The Rest I Make Up*, interrogates Fornes's legacy in the light of her descent into amnesia.

Fornes radically challenged and shaped the Off-Broadway scene in New York City, making it both interdisciplinary and environmental. She also originated and shaped (by being both exemplary and by mentoring a new generation of writers) a culture of Latina/o playwriting in the United States that continues to thrive to this very day. Her notable students include Cherríe Moraga, Migdalia Cruz, Eduardo Machado, Caridad Svich, Nilo Cruz and others. She also systematized a playwriting technique that is taught by many of her students in the top dramatic writing programmes across the US. Anne García Romero's recently published book, *The Fornes Frame*, highlights the impact of her teaching on Latino playwrights.

Fornes has to her credit a long list of plays that secure her place among the greatest and most prolific American playwrights of the 1980s. In addition to the plays discussed earlier, she has the following to her credit: *Abingdon Square* (1987); *Hunger, What of the Night?* (1988); *Nadine, Springtime, Lust, Oscar and Bertha, Terra Incognita* (1991); *Enter the Night* (1993); *Ibsen and the Actress* (1995); *Manual for a Desperate Crossing/ Balseros, The Summer in Gossensass* (1997); *The Audition* (1998); and *Letters from Cuba* (2000).

August Wilson

Over the span of more than two decades, August Wilson earned the respect of the American theatre community by, against unimaginable odds, fulfilling his mission to write what is now known as the American Century Cycle – that is, ten plays that chronicle the experiences of African-Americans in each decade of the twentieth century. Beginning in mid to late 1980s, Wilson wrote a succession of riveting, award-winning plays that would ultimately place him among America's premier playwrights. Even before his all-to-sudden death in October 2005, his resounding achievements in the realm of theatre had forged him a place in the canon of American letters. In fact, the consensus in many circles was that he was poised to receive the Nobel Prize for Literature pending completion of his historic undertaking. This recognition would have been the logical next step, as the Pulitzer Prize Committee had already twice voted to award Wilson its top honour for the startling realism and classic resonance captured in *Fences* in 1987 and in *The Piano Lesson* in 1990. Further attesting to the calibre of his work is an array of other awards ranging from the New York Drama Critics' Circle and Drama Desk Awards to the coveted Tony Award.

Without question, the 1980s was August Wilson's most prolific decade, for these were his formative years as a playwright when he received much needed affirmation for his writing, when he increased his confidence as a playwright and when he ultimately found his artistic voice. From 1980 to 1989, he wrote the unpublished and unproduced *Fullerton Street*, which was based on the fight between boxers Joe Louis and Billy Conn, and in relatively hasty succession he turned out *Fences, Joe Turner's Come and Gone, Ma Rainey's Black Bottom* and *The Piano Lesson*. From 1990 to his death in 2005, he worked steadily, adding to this already impressive list of plays by writing the remaining six to complete his magnum opus: *Two Trains Running, Seven Guitars, Jitney* (revised in 1996), *King Hedley, II, Gem of the Ocean* and *Radio Golf*.

For Wilson, the fifteen-year span between the 1980s when he came into his own as a playwright and 2005 when he completed *Radio Golf*, the last American Century Cycle play in 2005 – mere months before his death – was filled with awards and accolades that affirmed his standing as a premiere American playwright. In 1990, for example, his play *The Piano Lesson* earned him the New York Drama Critics' Circle Award and his second Pulitzer Prize award. He also took time out in 1990 between a very hectic writing schedule to marry costume designer Constanza Romero, while *Two Trains Running* made its way around the country's regional theatre circuit on its way to Broadway. In 1996, Wilson was awarded the New York Drama Critics' Circle Award for *Seven Guitars* and the William Inge Award for Achievement in the American Theatre at the William Inge Theatre Festival in Independence, Kansas.

While honours continued to be bestowed upon Wilson's work in 1996, he found himself in the middle of a hotly contested issue about African-American aesthetics. On 26 June he took up this issue in a provocative speech, 'The Ground On Which I Stand', presented at the 11th Biennial Theatre Communications Group Conference at Princeton University. Regarded by many as his manifesto, this speech set off a controversy about race and American drama that led to a highly publicized January 1997 Town Hall debate with Robert Brustein about the best way to preserve African-American identity in American theatre.

In 1999, August Wilson was awarded the National Humanities Medal by president Bill Clinton, and in 2000 he brought home another New York Drama Critics' Circle Award – this time for *Jitney*. In 2002 he tried his hand at writing and acting in *How I Learned What I Learned*, a well-received and often-staged one-man show made up of episodes from his early life in Pittsburgh's Hill District. This theatrical memoir includes stories about his first few jobs, a stint in jail, his lifelong friends and his encounters with racism, music and love as a young poet in the Hill District. In 2003 he received the Heinz Award in Arts and Humanities and in 2004 the Freedom of Speech Award at the Comedy Arts Festival in Aspen, Colorado. Later in this same year, 2004, he was awarded the Chicago Tribune Literary Prize for Lifetime Achievement.

Although Wilson's death in October 2005 came at the zenith of his career, he left a body of work that lives on. The enduring importance of his legacy can be seen in a number of high profile gestures. On 16 October 2005, fourteen days after death, Broadway's Virginia Theater was renamed the August Wilson Theater in his honour; its marquis bears a facsimile of the playwright's original signature. In 2007 the Theatre Communications Group packaged and published all ten of Wilson's plays in the handsomely bound *The August Wilson Century Cycle* –complete with solid endorsements from luminaries ranging from Toni Morrison and Phylicia Rashad to Samuel Freedman and Frank Rich. September 2009 marked the opening of Pittsburgh's August Wilson Center, whose naming and programming honour the playwright's life and legacy and serve as the city's local venue for cultural programmes. In 2015, American Masters partnered with noted director Sam Pollard and PBS stations throughout the country in making *August Wilson: The Ground On Which I Stand*, a definitive documentary on the life of the playwright. Moreover, visitors will find fascinating memorabilia from the set of Wilson's *The Piano Lesson* on display in Washington, DC's National Museum of African American History and Culture, which opened in September 2016.

Equally high-profile gestures that occurred in the 2000s continued to further acknowledge Wilson's place among great American playwrights. In the autumn of 2013, for example, close to 100 theatre artists from across the globe convened at the Greene Space at WNYC in Lower Manhattan to record, for the very first time, all ten plays in *August Wilson's American Century Cycle*. Dr Indira Etwaroo, Executive Producer, in partnership with the August Wilson Estate, led by Constanza Romero, Wilson's widow, brought together many long-time Wilson collaborators and interpreters, including Tony Award-winner Ruben Santiago-Hudson, the project's Artistic Director, and Associate Director and Tony Award nominee Stephen McKinley Henderson.

Beginning Sunday, 26 April 2015, with the first two plays – *Gem of the Ocean* and *Joe Turner's Come and Gone* – the Greene Space released an audio recording of a live dramatic reading of *August Wilson's American Century Cycle*, as well as videos and photographs.

Also, since Wilson's death, *Ma Rainey's Black Bottom* and *Fences* have enjoyed Broadway revivals in 2010 and 2016 respectively. The first Broadway revival of *Fences* opened at the Cort Theatre on 26 April 2010 under the direction of Kenny Leon and starring Denzel Washington (Troy Maxson) and Viola Davis (Rose). During the autumn of 2016, actress Phylicia Rashad directed *Ma Rainey's Black Bottom* at the Mark Taper Forum in Los Angeles. On 19 January 2017, *Jitney* – the last play in Wilson's American Century Cycle to open on Broadway – did so to rave reviews at the Samuel Friedman Theatre. Directed by Wilson's long-time friend and protégé, actor Ruben Santiago-Hudson, and starring veteran actor Anthony Chisholm, this performance represented a milestone of historic relevance, for it placed the lone hold-out *Jitney* in the company of the other nine other plays in the Cycle to headline in a Broadway theatre.

In 2013 the National Park Service placed the childhood home of August Wilson, at 1727 Bedford Avenue in the Hill District, on the National Register of Historic Places. Pennsylvania also declared the house a historic landmark in 2007. It is also a city-designated historic building and deemed a historic landmark by the American Historical Society, thus making it eligible for grant funding to enable much needed repairs to the building's exterior structure; renovations to the building and grounds located on this modest parcel of land are underway to restore this site that figures so prominently in the formative years of the playwright. Other fundraising efforts to secure this property are in progress.

Other noticeable ways of honouring Wilson's legacy can be seen in the frequency with which his plays are staged throughout the world, the steady increase in scholarship on his work and the increased accessibility of his plays made possible by publishers such as the Theatre Communications Group, the New American Library, Dutton, Plume and Overlook Press. This ease of access has made Wilson's most popularly known plays (*Fences*, *The Piano Lesson*, *Ma Rainey's Black Bottom* and *Joe Turner's Come and Gone*) more available to an increasingly interested reading audience.

On Christmas Day 2016, after more than 20 years of setbacks, haggling and delays, Wilson's 1950s play *Fences* opened to much fanfare in theatres across the country. In many ways, this much beloved play that was converted to film represents a triumph for Wilson, who, for years, famously held out for a black director. His reward for holding out is Denzel Washington, who accepted the role of director and created an Oscar-worthy contender in the process. In the early 1990s, Wilson dug his heels in and ignited a firestorm with his unrelenting demands that only a culturally sensitive black director be allowed to translate his 1950s play for a film audience. And now, like a Phoenix, *Fences* will arise to introduce the Maxson family to a new generation of theatregoers and readers alike. What is most apparent with each new iteration of Wilson's work is that his place in American theatre history has been solidified.

Documents

Ronald Reagan's Berlin Wall speech

In 1987, President Ronald Reagan issued an historic call for an end to communism: 'Mr. Gorbachev, Tear Down This Wall!' In a moment that would later define his presidency, Ronald Reagan delivered an impassioned speech at the Berlin Wall in the west of the city. His resounding plea to General Secretary Gorbachev to 'tear down this wall' became a touchstone of his presidency. This barrier was built by communists in August 1961 to keep Germans from escaping communist-dominated East Berlin into democratic West Berlin. The wall stood as a stark symbol of the decades-old Cold War between the United States and Soviet Russia in which the two politically opposed superpowers continually wrestled for dominance, stopping just short of actual warfare. The following is an excerpt from one of President Reagan's most notable addresses.

In the 1950s, Khrushchev predicted: 'We will bury you'. But in the West today, we see a free world that has achieved a level of prosperity and well-being unprecedented in all human history. In the Communist world, we see failure, technological backwardness, declining standards of health, even want of the most basic kind – too little food. Even today, the Soviet Union still cannot feed itself. After these four decades, then, there stands before the entire world one great and inescapable conclusion: Freedom leads to prosperity. Freedom replaces the ancient hatreds among the nations with comity and peace. Freedom is the victor.

And now the Soviets themselves may, in a limited way, be coming to understand the importance of freedom. We hear much from Moscow about a new policy of reform and openness. Some political prisoners have been released. Certain foreign news broadcasts are no longer being jammed. Some economic enterprises have been permitted to operate with greater freedom from state control.

Are these the beginnings of profound changes in the Soviet state? Or are they token gestures, intended to raise false hopes in the West, or to strengthen the Soviet system without changing it? We welcome change and openness; for we believe that freedom and security go together, that the advance of human liberty can only strengthen the cause of world peace. There is one sign the Soviets can make that would be unmistakable, that would advance dramatically the cause of freedom and peace.

General Secretary Gorbachev, if you seek peace, if you seek prosperity for the Soviet Union and Eastern Europe, if you seek liberalization: Come here to this gate! Mr. Gorbachev, open this gate! Mr. Gorbachev, tear down this wall!

I understand the fear of war and the pain of division that afflict this continent – and I pledge to you my country's efforts to help overcome these burdens. To be sure, we in the West must resist Soviet expansion. So we must maintain defenses of unassailable strength. Yet we seek peace; so we must strive to reduce arms on both sides.[1]

The onset of the AIDS epidemic

In June 1981, the US Centers for Disease Control and Prevention (CDC) published a Morbidity and Mortality Weekly Report (MMWR), *describing cases of a rare lung infection called* Pneumocystis carinii pneumonia *(PCP) that was detected in five young, previously healthy, gay men in Los Angeles, California. All of the men had other unusual infections as well, indicating that their immune systems had been compromised. Two died apparently from related complications. This edition of the* MMWR *marked the first official reporting of what later became known as the AIDS epidemic. A key portion of this report follows.*

Epidemiologic notes and reports

Pneumocystis pneumonia – Los Angeles

In the period October 1980–May 1981, 5 young men, all active homosexuals, were treated for biopsy-confirmed Pneumocystis carinii pneumonia at 3 different hospitals in Los Angeles, California. Two of the patients died. All 5 patients had laboratory-confirmed previous or current cytomegalovirus (CMV) infection and candidal mucosal infection. Case reports of these patients follow.

Patient 1: A previously healthy 33-year-old man developed P. carinii pneumonia and oral mucosal candidiasis in March 1981 after a 2-month history of fever associated with elevated liver enzymes, leukopenia, and CMV viruria. The serum complement-fixation CMV titer in October 1980 was 256; in May 1981 it was 32.* The patient's condition deteriorated despite courses of treatment with trimethoprim-sulfamethoxazole (TMP/SMX), pentamidine, and acyclovir. He died May 3, and postmortem examination showed residual P. carinii and CMV pneumonia, but no evidence of neoplasia.

Patient 2: A previously healthy 30-year-old man developed P. carinii pneumonia in April 1981 after a 5-month history of fever each day and of elevated liver-function tests, CMV viruria, and documented seroconversion to CMV, i.e., an acute-phase titer of 16 and a convalescent-phase titer of 28* in anticomplement immunofluorescence tests. Other features of his illness included leukopenia and mucosal candidiasis. His pneumonia responded to a course of intravenous TMP/SMX, but, as of the latest reports, he continues to have a fever each day.

Patient 3: A 30-year-old man was well until January 1981 when he developed esophageal and oral candidiasis that responded to Amphotericin B treatment. He was hospitalized in February 1981 for P. carinii pneumonia that responded to TMP/SMX. His esophageal candidiasis recurred after the pneumonia was diagnosed, and he was again given Amphotericin B. The CMV complement-fixation titer in March 1981 was 8. Material from an esophageal biopsy was positive for CMV.

Patient 4: A 29-year-old man developed P. carinii pneumonia in February 1981. He had had Hodgkins disease 3 years earlier, but had been successfully treated with radiation therapy alone. He did not improve after being given intravenous TMP/SMX and corticosteroids and died in March. Postmortem examination showed no evidence of Hodgkins disease, but P. carinii and CMV were found in lung tissue.

Patient 5: A previously healthy 36-year-old man with clinically diagnosed CMV infection in September 1980 was seen in April 1981 because of a 4-month history of fever, dyspnea, and cough. On admission he was found to have P. carinii pneumonia, oral candidiasis, and CMV retinitis. A complement-fixation CMV titer in April 1981 was 128. The patient has been treated with 2 short courses of TMP/SMX that have been limited because of a sulfa-induced neutropenia. He is being treated for candidiasis with topical nystatin.

The diagnosis of Pneumocystis pneumonia was confirmed for all 5 patients ante mortem by closed or open lung biopsy. The patients did not know each other and had no known common contacts or knowledge of sexual partners who had had similar illnesses. Two of the 5 reported having frequent homosexual contacts with various partners. All 5 reported using inhalant drugs, and 1 reported parenteral drug abuse. Three patients had profoundly depressed in vitro proliferative responses to mitogens and antigens. Lymphocyte studies were not performed on the other 2 patients.

Reported by MS Gottlieb, MD, HM Schanker, MD, PT Fan, MD, A Saxon, MD, JD Weisman, DO, Div of Clinical Immunology-Allergy; Dept of Medicine, UCLA School of Medicine; I Pozalski, MD, Cedars-Mt. Siani Hospital, Los Angeles; Field services Div, Epidemiology Program Office, CDC.[2]

David Mamet

From Matthew Roudane

Matthew Roudane conducted this interview with David Mamet in December 1984. The focus of his line of questioning is the foundational aspects of Mamet's art. Following are several revealing excerpts.

Roudane: The myth of the American Dream seems central to your artistic vision. In *American Buffalo*, *The Water Engine*, *Lakeboat*, *Mr. Happiness*, *A Life in the Theatre*, and *Glengarry Glen Ross*, a whole cultural as well as spiritual dimension of the American Dream myth is present. Could you comment on why this myth engages you so much?

Mamet: It interests me because the national culture is founded very much on the idea of strive and succeed. Instead of rising *with* the masses, one should rise *from* the masses. Your extremity is my opportunity. That's what forms the basis of our economic life, and this is what forms the rest of our lives. That American myth: the idea of something out of nothing. And this also affects the spirit of the individual. It's very divisive. One feels one can only succeed at the cost of someone else. Economic life in America is a lottery. Everyone's got an equal chance, but only one guy is going to get to the top. 'The more I have the less you have.' So one can only succeed at the cost of, the failure of another, which is what a lot of my plays – *American Buffalo* and *Glengarry Glen Ross* – are about. That's what Acting President Reagan's whole campaign is about. In *Glengarry Glen Ross* it's the Cadillac, the steak-knives, or nothing. In this play it's obvious that these fellows are put in fear for their lives and livelihood; for them it's the same thing. They have to succeed at the cost of each other. As Thorstein Veblen in *Theory of the Leisure Class* says, sharp practice inevitably shades over into fraud. Once someone has no vested interest in behaving in an ethical manner and the only bounds on his behavior are supposedly his innate sense of fair play, then fair play becomes an outdated concept: 'But wait a second! Why should I control my sense of fair play when the other person may not control his sense of fair play? So hurray for me and to hell with you ...

... **Roudane:** I think one of your major contributions to the stage is your 'language': clearly you have an ear for the sounds, sense, and rhythms of street language. Could you discuss the role of language in your plays?

Mamet: It's poetic language. It's not an attempt to capture language as much as it is an attempt to create language. We see this in various periods in the evolution of American drama. And when it's good, to the most extent it's called realism. All realism means is that the language strikes a responsive chord. The language in my plays is not realistic but poetic. The words sometimes have a musical quality to them. It's language which is tailor-made for the stage. People don't always talk the way my characters do in real life, although they may use some of the same words. Think of Odets, Wilder. That stuff is not realistic; it is poetic. Or Philip Barry: you might say some part of his genius was to capture the way a certain class of people spoke. He didn't know how those people spoke, but he was creating a poetic impression, creating that reality. It's not a matter, in *Lakeboat* or *Sexual Perversity in Chicago* or *Edmond* or my other plays, of my 'interpretation' of how these people talk. It is an illusion. It's like when Gertrude Stein said to Picasso, 'That portrait doesn't look like me.' Picasso said, 'It will.' It's an illusion. Juvenile delinquents *acted* like Marlon Brando in *The Wild One*, right? It wasn't the other way around. It was life imitating art! So in this sense my plays don't mirror what's going on in the streets. It's something different. As Oscar Wilde said, life imitates art! We didn't have those big pea-soup fogs until somebody described them.

Roudane: Despite your social exposures of human folly, one could argue that you're a playwright concerned with existentialist themes. That is, you seem fixed on objectifying certain crimes of the heart: the failure to communicate authentically with the self and the other. Possible? What do you think?

Mamet: Concerning ourselves with the individual's soul is certainly the fit province of drama. I really never understood what existentialism meant. I've tried a whole long time. It has something to do with sleeping with Simone de Beauvoir, but other than that I'm kind of lost. But I suppose my plays are about the individual's inner spirit. I think that's what it's about. The purpose of the theatre, to me, is to examine the paradox between the fact that everyone tries to do well but that few, if any, succeed. The theatre concerns metaphysics, our relationship to God and ethics or our relationships to each other.

Roudane: Whereas many contemporary playwrights create antimimetic plays, you seem to re-work a more classic, Ibsenesque dramatic form: the well-made play. Could you discuss the dramatic form of your work?

Mamet: I'm sure *trying* to do the well-made play. It is the hardest thing to do. I like this form because it's the structure imitating human perception. It is not just something made up out of old cloth. This is the way we perceive a play: with a clear beginning, a middle, and an end. So when one wants to best utilize the theatre, one would try to structure a play in a way that is congruent with the way the mind perceives it. Everybody wants to hear a story with a beginning, middle, and end. The only people who don't tell stories that way are playwrights! Finally, that's all that theatre is: story-telling. The theatre's no different from gossip, from dirty jokes, from what Uncle Max did on his fishing trip; it's just telling stories in that particular way in which one tells stories in the theatre. Look at *Sexual Perversity in Chicago* or *The Duck Variations*. To me, recognizing the story-telling dimension of playwriting is a beginning of a mark of maturity. That's why I embrace it. Nobody in the audience wants to hear a joke without the punch line. Nobody wants to hear how *feelingly* a guy can tell a joke. But we would like to find out what happened to the farmer's daughter. That's what Ibsen did.

Roudane: Has your cinema work – the screenplays for *The Postman Always Rings Twice* and *The Verdict* – helped your playwriting technique?

Mamet: My work in Hollywood has helped me very much. The good movie has to be written very clearly. The action has to be very clear. You can't take time out to digress to the highways and the byways of what might happen. You've got to tell the story. And I am trying to do this in my plays. I mean I wrote a lot of plays about feeling slices of interesting life. Nothing wrong with that – I just didn't know any better. I'm talking about my earlier plays; *Lakeboat*, for example, and others with those episodic glimpses of humanity. Those were fine, but now I am trying to do something different.

Roudane: What's the effect of Hollywood and mass media on the theatre today?

Mamet: It ain't good but it doesn't make any difference. They're flooding the market with trash. The taste and the need for a real theatrical experience, which is an experience in which the audience can come to commune, not so much with the actors but with themselves and what they know to be true, just increases. Everyone's pallet has been dulled to an extraordinary degree by the mass media. But that's just the way it is. Television, of course, isn't an art form. It might be, but nobody's figured out how to make it so. It's not even a question of doing good work on television, which happens once in a while. It's that nobody seems to understand the essential nature of the media. I certainly don't.

Roudane: How might you answer the charge that your plays tend always to focus on the negative, cynical side of experience?

Mamet: I've never heard that charge, so I say that's interesting. But it's easy to cheer people up if you lie to them. Very easy. Acting President Reagan says he's not going to raise taxes; of course he's going to raise taxes, he has to raise taxes. Although it's easy to cheer people up by lying to them, in my plays I'm not interested in doing that; I'm not a doctor, I'm a writer.[3]

'David Mamet's Master Class Memo to the Writers of *The Unit*'

David Mamet's long and eclectic writing career straddled several genres; movies and television were among them. In his role as Executive Producer of the cancelled CBS drama series The Unit *(which ran from 7 March 2006 to 10 May 2009), he critiqued what he deemed to be show's greatest flaws: its writers' inability to discern differences between dramatic and non-dramatic writing. Mamet authored the following widely circulated retrospective to the show's staffers disparaging their use of stilted dialogue. In the piece titled 'David Mamet's Master Class Memo to the Writers of* The Unit', *the characteristically forthright writer made the case for what makes good television and implored screenwriters to avoid mistaking expository writing for what he characterizes as authentic 'drama'. (Mamet's original memo is written in all-caps though the tone of this communique is not angry.)*

TO THE WRITERS OF *THE UNIT*, GREETINGS.

AS WE LEARN HOW TO WRITE THIS SHOW, A RECURRING PROBLEM BECOMES CLEAR. THE PROBLEM IS THIS: TO DIFFERENTIATE BETWEEN DRAMA AND NON-DRAMA. LET ME BREAK-IT-DOWN-NOW ...

QUESTION: WHAT IS DRAMA? DRAMA, AGAIN, IS THE QUEST OF THE HERO TO OVERCOME THOSE THINGS WHICH PREVENT HIM FROM ACHIEVING A SPECIFIC, ACUTE GOAL.

SO: WE, THE WRITERS, MUST ASK OURSELVES OF EVERY SCENE THESE THREE QUESTIONS.

1) WHO WANTS WHAT?

2) WHAT HAPPENS IF HER DON't GET IT?

3) WHY NOW?

THE ANSWERS TO THESE QUESTIONS ARE LITMUS PAPER. APPLY THEM, AND THEIR ANSWER WILL TELL YOU IF THE SCENE IS DRAMATIC OR NOT. IF THE SCENE IS NOT DRAMATICALLY WRITTEN, IT WILL NOT BE DRAMATICALLY ACTED ...

THE JOB OF THE DRAMATIST IS TO MAKE THE AUDIENCE WONDER WHAT HAPPENS NEXT. NOT TO EXPLAIN TO THEM WHAT JUST HAPPENED, OR TO*SUGGEST* TO THEM WHAT HAPPENS NEXT ...

HOW DOES ONE STRIKE THE BALANCE BETWEEN WITHHOLDING AND VOUCHSAFING INFORMATION? THAT IS THE ESSENTIAL TASK OF THE DRAMATIST. AND THE ABILITY TO DOTHAT IS WHAT SEPARATES YOU FROM THE LESSER SPECIES IN THEIR BLUE SUITS.

FIGURE IT OUT ...

THIS IS A NEW SKILL. NO ONE DOES IT NATURALLY. YOU CAN TRAIN YOURSELVES TO DO IT, BUT YOU NEED TO START.

I CLOSE WITH THE ONE THOUGHT: LOOK AT THE SCENE AND ASK YOURSELF 'IS IT DRAMATIC? IS IT ESSENTIAL? DOES IT ADVANCE THE PLOT?'

ANSWER TRUTHFULLY.

IF THE ANSWER IS 'NO' WRITE IT AGAIN OR THROW IT OUT. IF YOU'VE GOT ANY QUESTIONS, CALL ME UP.

LOVE, DAVE MAMET

SANTA MONICA 19 OCTO 05[4]

David Henry Hwang

David Henry Hwang's papers are housed at Stanford University. The following three samples of early drafts of M. Butterfly are published courtesy of Stanford University Libraries, Department of Special Collections, The David Henry Hwang Papers, M0636. In addition, these draft samples are published courtesy of David Henry Hwang.

Sample 1

Act 1, Scene 11:
Summary of the scene from the final version:
Marc and Gallimard discuss Isabelle, who was Gallimard's first sexual experience. In addition, more is revealed about Gallimard's naiveté when it comes to sex.

Summary of this early draft:
Marc and Gallimard discuss Gallimard's sexual relationship with Florette. Like the final version, this draft reveals more information about Gallimard's naiveté when it comes to sex. However, what makes this scene distinctive is that in the early drafts of the play Gallimard's wife's name is Florette (her name changes to Helga in later versions). This scene provides more background to their married relationship than exists in the final play script and also suggests a reason for their inability to have a child.
Material from all the samples that ended up in the final version of M. Butterfly *is in* **bold**.

Scene Eleven
<u>The French Embassy. Beijing. 1960.</u>
Gallimard moves towards a desk.

GALLIMARD
I determined to try an experiment. In 'Madame Butterfly,' Cio-Cio San fears that the Western man who catches a butterfly will pierce its heart with a needle, then leave it to perish. I began to wonder: had I, too, caught a butterfly who would writhe on a needle?

> (Marc enters, dressed as a BUREAUCRAT, holding
> a stack of papers. As Gallimard speaks, Marc
> hands papers to him, who peruses, then signs,
> stamps, or rejects them.)

GALLIMARD
Over the next five weeks, I immersed myself in my work. **I stopped going to the opera, I didn't phone or write her.** You might think that such a separation would depress me. No – I woke up each morning giddy as a schoolboy. I worked like a dynamo. My wife

was blissful in our marriage. I knew this little flower was waiting for me to call, and, as I wickedly refused to do so, I felt for the first time that rush of power – the absolute power of a man.

(Marc continues acting as the Bureaucrat, but he now speaks as himself. Gallimard continues without looking at him.)

MARC

Rene! It's me!

GALLIMARD

Marc – I hear your voice everywhere, now. Even in the midst of work.

MARC

That's because I'm watching you – all the time.

GALLIMARD

You were always the most popular guy in school.

MARC

Well, there's no guarantee of failure in life like happiness in high school. Somehow, I knew I'd end up in the suburbs working for Renault and you'd be in [the] Orient picking exotic women off the trees.

(*pause*)

You've come a long way from Florette, huh?

GALLIMARD

Oh, don't make fun. She was my first experience.

MARC

Yes, and given her dimensions, it's a wonder you ever went back for seconds.

GALLIMARD

She was a nice girl.

MARC

I'm sure she was nicer with her clothes on.

GALLIMARD

She was a virgin, you know.

MARC

I never imagined otherwise.

GALLIMARD

She trusted me. Never more than one night, I remember, about six months after we first slept together. For no reason, she burst out crying. I didn't know what was going on. She said, she had a terrible thing to confess, and I would hate her for it. A year before we'd met, she'd become pregnant. By a farmer boy near her parents' country home. A doctor had taken care of it. She said, 'Now you hate me, don't you?' She'd been crying so long, her breath had gone sour.

MARC

You mean, for all that, she wasn't even a virgin?

GALLIMARD

Huh? No, listen! That was the moment I liked her best. I said, 'Of course, I forgive you.' She looked ... so grateful. She let me take her to bed again, and she said, 'Rene, you made me a woman.'

MARC

But you didn't.

GALLIMARD

What do you mean?

MARC

I mean, she wasn't a virgin.

GALLIMARD

Yes, she was. She said so.

MARC
But, then she took it back.

GALLIMARD
No, she didn't. She said I made her a woman.

MARC
Rene, can you add two and two? That abortion stuff – that was code – for 'Just kidding, Charlie!'

GALLIMARD
Wait. Isn't it possible for someone to get pregnant and still be a virgin? Didn't I read someplace, in some science book – ?

MARC
It must've been science fiction.

GALLIMARD
I mean, can't you just be petting or something? And the guys' thing gets too close to – didn't they tell us you could a girl pregnant that way?

MARC
What? You think the little spermy-guys jump off a girl's leg, then make a wild dash for the canal? Rene – someone has to be there to plant the flag!

(*pause*)

GALLIMARD
So you're saying, technically, she wasn't a virgin.

MARC
All virgins are technical! She wasn't a virgin at all!

GALLIMARD
I think that's a very cynical attitude. You never liked her much, did you?

MARC

Rene, trust me. I know virgins.

GALLIMARD

Yeah?

MARC

Yeah. I have had a lot of virgins.

GALLIMARD

You have?

MARC

Well, sure. Like – like Isabelle.

GALLIMARD
(after a beat)

Oh, right.

MARC

What?

GALLIMARD

Nothing ...

MARC

What do you mean, 'Oh, right.'

GALLIMARD

Nothing. I hardly knew her.

(pause)

GALLIMARD

I still think Florette was a virgin.

MARC

I dunno. Maybe it's possible.

GALLIMARD
She wouldn't have lied to me.

MARC
I mean, it happened to Mary.

GALLIMARD
It was heavy petting.

MARC
Very heavy. Wait! Look at that letter again!

(Gallimard picks up one of the papers he's been stamping, and re-reads it.)

GALLIMARD (TO US:)
After six weeks, they began to arrive. The letters.

(Upstage special on Song, as Madame Butterfly.)

Sample 2

Act 3, Scene 2:
Scene synopsis:
In perhaps the most pivotal scene of the play, Gallimard finally confronts the true identity of Song, who strips off his Armani suit and reveals himself to his former lover.

Draft versions:
While the drafts below contain the core element of the scene (the stripping of Song),[5] Hwang is still experimenting with how Gallimard reacts to Song's[6] 20-year long deception and how Song handles Gallimard's rejection of him. In addition, Sample 2 also shows Hwang still experimenting with the play's narrative structure.

SOONG
You know something, Rene? Your mouth says 'no,' but your eyes say 'yes'. Turn them away. I dare you.

GALLIMARD

I don't have to! Every night I go through these events in my mind, and every night you stop! I beg you, and you stop!

SOONG

I guess that tonight is different.

GALLIMARD

Why? Why would that be?

SOONG

Maybe I've become frustrated. Maybe I'm saying, 'Look at me, you fool!' Or maybe I'm just feeling ... sexy.

(HE *is down to his briefs*)

GALLIMARD

Please. This is unnecessary. I know what you are.

SOONG

You do? What am I?

GALLIMARD

A – a man.

SOONG

You don't really believe that.

GALLIMARD

Yes, I do! I knew all the time somewhere that my happiness was temporary, my love a deception. But my mind kept the knowledge at bay. To make the wait bearable.

SOONG

M. Gallimard – the wait is over.

(HE *drops his briefs.* HE *is naked. Sound cue out.*)

Long silence. GALLIMARD *starts to laugh*)

SOONG (continued)
What are you doing?

GALLIMARD
You're a man – look at you! You're a man!

SOONG
Yes, I'm – I'm a man. Now, you believe me.

GALLIMARD
Of course I believe you. I can't very well – I mean, I'm not blind.

SOONG
Tell me – does it change your feelings for me one bit?

GALLIMARD
Now, that is a silly question.

SOONG
What are you saying?! You still love me, don't you?

GALLIMARD
How can I? You're a man.

SOONG
That shouldn't make any difference!

GALLIMARD
Don't be ridiculous. My Butterfly's a woman.

SOONG
Wait, wait. This skin. Touch it. It's the same skin you've worshipped for twenty years.

GALLIMARD
Yes, it does feel the same.

SOONG
Now, kiss me. These are the same lips that –

GALLIMARD
I'll take your word for it.

SOONG
Rene, ~~how can~~ you ... ~~resist~~ [*hand written* 'adore'] me?
(*Pause*)

[*Two lines of dialogue handwritten on the draft, but difficult to make out.*]⁷

GALLIMARD
It's very funny, isn't it? I suppose I ... see you for what you are. Like all the other men I pass in the halls. The ones I've gone camping with, traded dirty jokes with, complained with about women and their eccentricities. Like Marc. Or Toulon. Or Pinkerton. **Just a man.**

SOONG
You think so? Well, **what about this?**

(**HE starts to pick up BUTTERFLY's robes, dance around. No music**)

GALLIMARD
Yes, that's very nice. I have to admit.

SOONG
You see? I'm the same – '**How I wish there were even a** tiny café ...'

GALLIMARD
You do her well.

SOONG
'Do her well'? Rene! There's a reason for that!

GALLIMARD
Yes. Because ... you are an excellent actor.

SOONG

No! I *am* her!

GALLIMARD

Don't embarrass yourself. It won't do a bit of good. Looking at you now, I've learned – I've finally learned to tell fantasy from reality. And, knowing the difference, I choose fantasy.

SOONG

But *I'm* your fantasy.

GALLIMARD

You? You're as real as hamburger. Look at those. You dress like a pimp.

SOONG

These are Armani slacks and – oh, I'm not going to get caught up in this.

(He walks away from GALLIMARD, starts putting back on his clothes)

So, you never loved me ... not really me. Only when I was playing a part. Well, I should've realized – **Men**. You're like the rest of them. It's all in the way we dress, and make up our faces, and bat our eyelashes.

GALLIMARD

Didn't you know that?

SOONG

Of course I knew that. Don't tell *me* about! I know that a lot better than you.

GALLIMARD

So I would imagine.

SOONG

But **in the crush of your adoration** – the fact that I could hit you, mock you, knock you down and you'd coming bouncing back with an even greater love – **I thought you'd become ... something more. More like ... a woman.** Yes, I know all about men – about <u>us</u>. But I suppose, over time ... I forgot.

(HE *is dressed again in his suit*)

So – Rene, you're more pathetic than I ever imagined. I gave you too much credit. **You really have so little imagination!**

GALLIMARD

You, M. Soong? Accuse me of too little imagination? You, if anyone, should know – I am pure imagination. And in imagination, I will remain. Goodbye.

(*Pause*)

SOONG

I'm not impressed by your words – you'll be calling me back.

GALLIMARD

I think the judge is calling you back. To the stand. Where you're busy betraying me.

SOONG

I'm nailing your ass to the wall.

GALLIMARD

I expect nothing more from my fellow men. And, you might also like to know – I forgive you. Now, scoot!

(SOONG *turns Upstage, towards the stand*)

SOONG

Rene?

GALLIMARD

Will you get out of here? **I have a date with my Butterfly, and I don't want your body polluting the room!**

SOONG
Your Butterfly? I'll be waiting. For your pleas. Calling me back. To put on those robes again. Calling me back.

GALLIMARD
I suppose so. And, in waiting, will you complete your days.

(SOONG *takes his place back at the witness stand*)

SOONG
M. Gallimard would tell me where the Americans planned to bomb, and the Chinese government would pass this information on to the Viet Cong. So by the time the planes arrived …

(Lights fade out on SOONG)

Sample 3

Act 3, Scene 2
This draft version appeared later in the writing process and reflects Hwang's focus on Song's attempt to overcome Gallimard's rejection.

SONG
I want you to admit –

GALLIMARD
That you're a man?

SONG
– that, yes, I'm a man, but still –

GALLIMARD
Yes?

SONG
Still, **you … adore me.**

(*pause*)

GALLIMARD
That's a rather tall order. Particularly when you've just dropped your pants.

SONG
Rene, how can you resist me? **Touch it – this skin – it's the same skin you've worshipped for years.**

GALLIMARD
Yes, it does feel similar.

SONG
These lips. They're the same – Kiss them.

GALLIMARD
Get those old things away, will you? **Tonight, I've finally learned to tell fantasy from reality. And, knowing the difference, I choose fantasy.**

SONG
I'm your fantasy!

GALLIMARD
You? You're as real as hamburger. Now, get out of my life! I have a date with my Butterfly, and I don't want your body polluting the air.

SONG
You want me to put on the robes again, is that it?

GALLIMARD
No, I want you to put on your clothes! Or leave naked! Show the world you're a man! I don't care!

(He tosses Song's suit at him.)

GALLIMARD
Look at these – you dress like a pimp.

SONG

What do you mean? **These are Armani slacks and –!** Wait. I'm not going to get caught up in this ... tantrum of yours. **Let's just say I'm very ...** I'm disappointed. **Disappointed in you, Rene.**

(*He starts putting back on his clothes.*)

GALLIMARD

I don't care what you are so long as you're out of this room.

SONG

I should've known –. **Men. You're like the rest of them. It's all in the way we dress, and make up our faces, and bat our eyelashes.**

GALLIMARD

Don't you know that?

SONG

Of course I knew that. Don't tell me about –! I know that a lot better than you.

GALLIMARD

So I would imagine.

SONG

But **in the crush of your adoration** – the fact that I could hit you, mock you, knock you down and you'd come bouncing back with an even greater love – **I thought you'd become ... something more. More like ... a woman.** Yes, I know all about men – about us. But I suppose, over time ... I forgot.

(He is dressed again in his suit.)

Rene, I gave you too much credit. **You really have so little imagination!**

GALLIMARD

You, M. Song? Accuse me of too little imagination? You, if anyone, should know – I am pure imagination. And in imagination, I will remain. Now, get out! You've already stayed twenty years too long!

(Song starts to leave; then:)

SONG

You say you're meeting your Butterfly. Well, how? How, if not with me? And where? Where will you find her, if not by calling my name?

GALLIMARD

You think I'm going to tell you? Now, are you going to blabber all night or can we have some privacy?

(**Gallimard** starts to **bodily remove[s] Song from the stage.**)

SONG

What are you doing? **Rene! You'll be sorry! I'll never put on those robes again!**

GALLIMARD

You won't even touch the hem of her skirt! My Butterfly – I know where to find her! Tonight – she's returning to me – at last!

(Gallimard tosses Song offstage.)

Irene Fornes

The following three figures are some of many drafts from Fornes's The Danube *and* No Time *(later revised as* Conduct of Life*); they suggest that she was an obsessive editor who never saw her plays as truly finished.*

```
PAUL    Eve, there is no future for the children.
EVE     What do you mean?
PAUL    What they have today is what they will have tomorrow.
EVE     Let's hope they will have as much tomorrow.
PAUL    That's not enough. There's more to life.
EVE     What, Paul?
PAUL    A promise.
EVE     Is that how it should be?
PAUL    Yes.
                    (HE turns up his eyes. HE is trying to remember)
EVE     I never heard that, Paul.
PAUL    Well, I did.
EVE     I thought we lived because we wanted to.
PAUL    No. We live because of a promise.
EVE     I thought we did things because we wanted to.
PAUL    No, we do them because we hope for something.
```

Readers will note that these two conversations (in Figure 1 and Figure 2) between Eve and Paul are not included in the published PAJ version. Only their tone of frail intimacy can be seen in Scene 9, 'In the sanatorium', and through the devolution of their relationship.

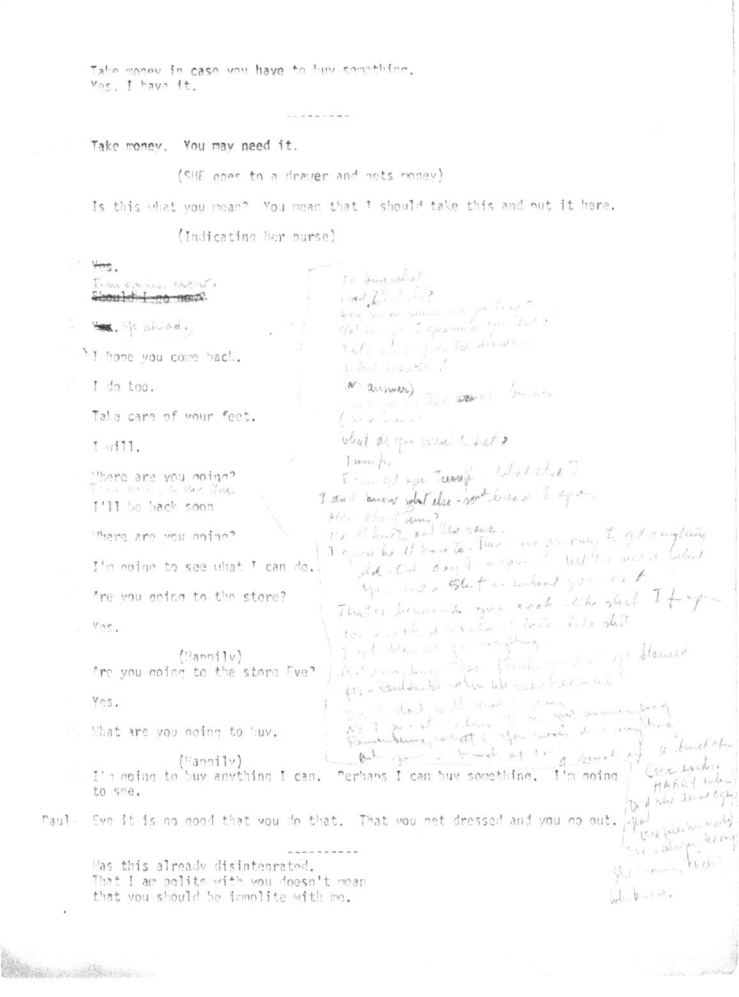

Figures 1 and 2 from the Maria Irene Fornés Papers, 'Script Fragments from The Danube', MSS 413, Box 3, Folder 4, the Fales Library & Special Collections, New York University; courtesy of David Lapinel and the Abrams Artists Agency.

```
ready to see her go. To let the whole thing go. To let it come
to an end. Even if it would be the end. How to hold it
any longer it was gainning momentum and it was pounding his skin.
His breast shut up fireworks. She moaned like a whale and he
screamed like one damned to hell. They orgasmed vibrantly and
collapsed pouring liquid from every way. Now she loved him because
it was the only time she had been loved. This was a boyfriend
she had when she had to move out and O. moved her out into a
room. He didn't know she had this man and this man was a revolut-
ionary and it was through him that she understood that she had
been mistreated before, but once she understood that she became
more political than him.
```

In this earlier draft of The Conduct of Life, *we see the relationship between characters who would morph into Orlando and Nena as one of consensual intimacy and sexual passion. Not only does this add a disturbing layer to the power dynamic in the published version of* Conduct, *it also indicates how characters and relationships would constantly evolve in Fornes's plays.*
Figure 3 from Maria Irene Fornes's personal papers, courtesy of the Fornes family.

August Wilson

From James Earl Jones and Mary Alice

Despite countless performances of August Wilson's Fences, *none surpasses that of acting duo James Earl Jones and Mary Alice, who etched the roles of Troy and Rose Maxson into the Broadway history books during the play's April 1985 performance at the Yale Repertory Theatre. In the following interview with Heather Henderson of* Theatre *magazine, 'Building Fences: An Interview with Mary Alice and James Earl Jones', published in autumn 1985, Jones and Alice speak candidly about the unique quality of August Wilson to capture the realities of this husband and wife of 1950s America.*

Henderson: What has it been like to work in an August Wilson play?

Jones: A dear friend of mine, a director, came backstage today and said that the play is unusual, and I agreed. You don't often find this kind of play. Steinbeck used to write about this stratum of life, but among American playwrights, it is rare. Few writers can capture dialect as dialogue in a manner as interesting and accurate as August's. My first experience with a play with the black sound was by a white writer, Howard Sacker – in the *Great White Hope*. That dialogue was not identifiable as Galveston, Texas; it was a poetic rendering of an *idea* of Southern dialect. August's dialogue is less 'invented'. Howard's dialogue was invented totally out of his imagination, which I admired. But August's language has a certain root – I've *heard* other people speak with the same kind of inarticulateness. You find it in other cultures – the uneducated Irish too sometimes speak with great floweriness, they use language very richly – and I think August is catching this sort of speech.

My dad, who was a Mississippian before I was, said don't ever lose touch with that sound; don't let your children lose touch with it. People do get educated out of it.

Alice: I have found this with other writers, too – Charles Gordone, who wrote *No Place to Be Somebody*, Lorraine Hansberry, Charles Fuller – the wonderful thing is that because they are writing about material they're very familiar with, they can create the proper language, which is very important. Also – and August has admitted this – they love actors. So they write interesting characters. No matter how small the roles are, the characters are always complete.[8]

'The Ground on Which I Stand'

In April 1996, August Wilson accepted an invitation to deliver the keynote address at the annual conference of the Theatre Communications Group held at Princeton University. Like Frederick Douglass, who famously 'went off script' during his speech titled 'What to the Slave Is the Fourth of July?', Wilson surprised the largely white, Ivy League academic audience with his unapologetic manifesto, 'The Ground on Which I Stand'. This document is decidedly the playwright's best articulation of what lies at the core of his aesthetic choices: an Afrocentric world-view. Following is an excerpt from his what has become his signature piece:

I am what is known, at least among the followers and supporters of the ideas of Marcus Garvey, as a race man. That is simply that I believe that race matters. That is the largest, most identifiable, and most important part of our personality. It is the largest category of identification because it is the one that most influences your perception of yourself, and it is the one to which others in the world of men most respond. Race is also an important part of the American landscape, as America is made up of an amalgamation of races from all parts of the globe. Race is also the product of a shared gene pool that allows for group identification, and it is an organizing principle around which cultures are formed. When I say culture, I am speaking about the behavior patterns, arts, beliefs, institutions, and all other products of human work and thought as expressed in a particular community of people.

There are some people who will say that black Americans do not have a culture. That cultures are reserved for other people, most notably Europeans of various ethnic groupings, and that black Americans make up a sub-group of American culture that is derived from the European origins of its majority population. But black Americans are Africans, and there are many histories and many cultures on the African continent.

Those who would deny black Americans their culture would also deny them their history and the inherent values that are a part of all human life.

Growing up in my mother's house at 1727 Bedford Avenue in Pittsburgh, Pennsylvania, I learned the language, the eating habits, the religious beliefs, the gestures, the notions of common sense, attitudes towards sex, concepts of beauty and justice, and the responses to pleasure and pain that my mother had learned from her mother and which you could trace back to the first African who set foot on the continent. It is this culture that stands solidly on these shores today as a testament to the resiliency of the African-American spirit.

The term black or African American not only denotes race; it denotes condition and carries with it the vestige of slavery and the social segregation and abuse of opportunity so vivid in our memory. That this abuse of opportunity and truncation of possibility is continuing and is so pervasive in our society in 1996 says much about who we are and much about the work that is necessary to alter our perceptions of each other and to effect meaningful prosperity for all. The problematic nature of the relationship between white and black for too long led us astray from the fulfillment of our possibilities as a society. We stare at each other across a divide of economics and privilege that has become an encumbrance on black Americans' ability to prosper and on the collective will and spirit of our national purpose.[9]

From Lloyd Richards

The following excerpt is from a published interview between Lloyd Richards and Wilson scholar Sandra Shannon that took place in June 1991 in Richards's office at the Yale School of Drama where he served as Dean at the time. At the time of this interview, Wilson and Richards had embarked upon an historic collaboration on a series of his early American Century Cycle plays, including Two Trains Running, which had been workshopped at the Yale Repertory Theater and had begun to make its way on to Seattle Rep and the Kennedy Center in Washington, DC.

Shannon: You and August Wilson seem to have such a pleasant working relationship. What is it about him and his work that makes this possible?

Richards: I guess we both listen to each other. I think there's a whole background that also makes it possible. We find that we are sensitive to the same things. We have many of the same values, value system, sense of fidelity, family, responsibility. I continually find that we're alike in many ways, though that is not always the insurance of good work. Sometimes to not be alike results in productive work.

Ours has worked because we've seen kind of eye to eye, which doesn't mean that we don't question one another.

Shannon: ... To what extent has being African-American helped your collaboration with him?

Richards: Oh, very much. Very much.

I think he has said that the first time that we went to the rehearsal and I talked to the cast about his play, he learned things and he learned that I understood his work and all of the ramifications of it and that it wasn't necessary for him to sit in the room and check me because we were both coming from the same place ...

Richards: The fact that a character has a weakness only means that he is human. I don't think that any of the characters that August writes are inhuman, which means that they have strengths and weaknesses, and that includes the women. I think they are wonderfully human given those weaknesses and strengths ...

Shannon: What effect do you think Wilson has had on American theatre?

Richards: Oh, I think he's had a wonderful effect upon the American theatre. I think that he has stimulated playwrights to write. He has stimulated black playwrights to write. Always when one looks at achievement, there is a stimulus in that. Someone will say 'Let me try that'. And that is very important. That is very, very important because it brought black people into the theatre in various areas of the country – all over the country. People want to go to the theatre and go places where they can see themselves reflected or their concerns reflected. And if they find that in the theatre, that's the place that they will go. And so people are coming into the theatre.

Shannon: ... One theatre critic wrote, 'Eugene O'Neill's bonafide successor in the American Theater may have emerged, and his name is August Wilson'. Do you think this is a fair comparison?

Richards: I think all comparisons are unfair. I don't think that August Wilson should be expected to live up to O'Neill or O'Neill to live up to August Wilson. I think they are both major playwrights that America should be proud of – all Americans.

Shannon: In general, how have white audiences responded to Wilson's work?

Richards: Very warmly. Very warmly. The major comments or the most universal comment that comes from a white audience is that 'It is not just a black play. It's also a play about me'. And they find their own identification within the work. Why? Because it's human. It's very, very human.[10]

From Suzan-Lori Parks

One of the many encomia about August Wilson in the 2015 documentary, August Wilson, The Ground on Which I Stand,[11] *is that of playwright Suzan-Lori Parks, who teared up at the sudden realization that the subject of her upcoming interview was facing imminent death. Hers was to be his final interview.*[12] *She had just learned in a phone call that the 60-year-old Wilson, whom she referred to as her 'literary hero', had been diagnosed with liver cancer and had only months to live. Following are excerpts from their last meeting strategically scheduled to complement the publication of* Radio Golf, *the last play in the American Century Cycle.*

Parks: There's that line in *Radio Golf*, 'You score too many points they'll change the rules'. Do you ever feel like there are the rules of the game of theatre, and then there are the rules of *writing* – that after you write two plays, three plays, four plays, winning your Pulitzers, your Tony, being the great writer that you are, did you feel like you were scoring too many points, that the muse would change the rules up on you?

Wilson: No, largely I was driven by things like this: I remember after I wrote *Piano Lesson*, I was doing an interview with a guy and he says, 'Well, Mr. Wilson, now that you've written these four plays and exhausted the black experience, what are you going to write about next?'

Parks: Oh, stop!

Wilson: I said, 'Wait a minute, the black experience is inexhaustible' ... I just told him I would continue to explore the black experience, whether he thought it was exhausted or not. And then my goal was to prove that it was inexhaustible, that there was no idea that couldn't be contained by black life. That's part of the thing that couldn't be contained by black life. That's part of the thing that drove me – I would go: Well, if that's all I have to do, then I'm confident I can do that. A lot of confidence was given to me by people negating the idea – what Albert Murray would call 'antagonistic cooperation'. They're cooperating with you in their antagonism. They are enabling you to do the work. I took that as fuel for confidence ...

Parks: What's great is you say there is no exhausting the African-American experience, and the architecture of your cycle of plays was never at odds with its subject. It's like Shakespeare's writing about kings in those great histories. You're writing about African-Americans, and you're putting us in this brilliant cycle, suddenly we can see ourselves in the constellations. It's such an empowering thing you've done for so many people.

Wilson: Well, thank you again. I'm glad it worked out that way; it didn't have to, but I was sure trying hard.[13]

From Denzel Washington and Viola Davis

Many argue that August Wilson's Fences *is his signature play as this instalment for the 1950s is perhaps most recognizable among the entire American Century Cycle. The excerpts from two interviews that follow represent an arc in performances of this Pulitzer Prize-winning play that span from 1987 to 2016 – with particular emphasis upon acting decisions made by James Earl Jones and Mary Alice, who portrayed Troy and Rose Maxson on Broadway, and by Denzel Washington and Viola Davis, who turned in more recent performances of the 1950s husband and wife in Paramount's much anticipated film release of the play.*

This interview between NBA legend and cultural commentator Kareem Abdul Jabbar, Viola Davis and Denzel Washington is one of several that were conducted in advance of the 2016 film release of Wilson's Fences. *Many will recall the historical implications of this moment as Wilson's much publicized demands for a black director in the early 1990s seem to have come full circle in 2016:* Fences, *the film, is directed by acclaimed actor and director Denzel Washington, who also plays the lead role of Troy Maxson. The following excerpts are taken from this session.*

Jabbar: August Wilson once said that his plays offer white Americans a different way to look at black Americans, and he hoped that they would change how they think and deal with black

Americans. What insights into black people and black life do you think white Americans will get from the film?

Washington: It could be that it's not that different. Circumstances, no matter what the colour is, could be similar. Troy's whole [resentment of his lack of success as a baseball player] ... was it his colour or was he just too old? I think he was just too old regardless of his colour. Or, as his friends said, 'He just come along too early'.

Davis: I think sometimes what people miss about black people is that we're complicated, that we are indeed messy, that we do our best with what we've been given. We come into the world exactly like you. It's just that there are circumstances in the culture that are dictated and put on our lives that we have to fight against.

Washington: And it's a curse and a blessing to have someone to blame. What about the guy in the mirror? ...

Jabbar: Wilson also said that all art is political. The play premiered in 1985. Why do you think the story still is relevant after thirty years, especially after the recent presidential election that we've been through?

Washington: The circumstances, again, are universal. It could happen to anyone. I don't know if it's more political now given the election or whatever, but it's a long way from Troy to now because now we're post-Obama even.

Davis: I don't know why I don't see the play as political. I don't see it as representing something any bigger than a family and a man being born into a set of circumstances and maybe not taking ownership of how he's poisoning his family, which most of us don't. Some of us go to our grave never taking ownership. We just cause destruction around us. Arthur Miller said it, and August Wilson said it: When you notice all of the sins of your father, hopefully you can approach it with forgiveness and illumination. That's just life ...

Jabbar: I read that Hollywood wanted to film *Fences* years ago with a white director, but Wilson refused. He thought that the director needed to have lived the culture of black Americans. Do you think he was right?

Washington: Scorsese probably could have directed *Schindler's List* and Spielberg probably could have directed *Goodfellas*. But it's as much to do with the difference in culture as it is with race. We know what hair smells like when a hot comb hits it. That's a cultural thing. We know what that smells like on Sunday mornings, usually church-related or something. In my house, it was getting ready for church and your sister was getting her hair fried ...

Jabbar: Troy talks a lot about what it means to be a man, particularly a black man, but his ideas often are delusional. What do you think the film says about being a black man?

Washington: Well, I love the things he says to his son about responsibility and taking care of his family. 'Mr. Rand don't give me my money because he like me. He give it to me because he owe me'. In my own life, I had a male teacher who was trying to teach me things that I didn't believe – how you should treat women and things like that – but I knew better. But Cory doesn't know better.

Davis: They're all trying to find this reason to matter, a place in the world. When I look at *Fences*, with Cory needing a connection with his father, Troy, his disconnect from his father to me is even more relevant in his life than not making it to the football league. That is a theme in all of Wilson's plays, the need to matter ...[14]

NOTES

1 Introduction to the 1980s

1. U.S. Soviet Relations, 1981–91, 'Milestones: 1981–1988', https://history.state.gov/milestones/1981-1988/u.s.-soviet-relations (accessed 17 March 2017).
2. Robert Parry, 'Ronald Reagan: Worst President Ever?', Consortiumnews.com: Independent Investigative Journalism Since 1995, 6 February 2014, https://consortiumnews.com/2014/02/06/ronald-reagan-worst-president-ever-2/ (accessed 17 March 2017).
3. U.S. History: Pre-Columbian to the New Millennium, 'The New Right', http://www.ushistory.org/us/58e.asp (accessed 5 September 2016).
4. Ibid.
5. Parry, 'Ronald Reagan'.
6. The U.S. Economy: A Brief History, Ch. 3, http://usa.usembassy.de/etexts/oecon/chap3.htm (accessed 16 November 2016).
7. American History from the Revolution to the Reconstruction and Beyond, 'The Economy in the 1980s and 1990s', http://www.let.rug.nl/usa/outlines/economy-1991/a-historical-perspective-on-the-american-economy/the-economy-in-the-1980s-and-1990s.php (accessed 19 October 2016).
8. Ibid.
9. Tru Love Stories, 'The Woman of the 1980s', http://trulovestories.com/love-stories/the-woman-of-the-1980s/ (accessed 21 October 2016).
10. Katelyn Scammell, *Family Life: 1980s*, 3 December 2013, https://prezi.com/xqubflaygmqw/family-life-1980s/ (accessed 17 March 2017).
11. Ibid.
12. Ibid.

13. Graham Thompson, *American Culture in the 1980s* (Edinburgh: Edinburgh University Press, 2007), 108.
14. The Reagan Era, 'Race in the Reagan Era', http://www.shmoop.com/reagan-era/race.html (accessed 2 November 2016).
15. Josh Levin. 'The Welfare Queen', *Slate*, 19 December 2013, http://www.slate.com/articles/news_and_politics/history/2013/12/linda_taylor_welfare_queen_ronald_reagan_made_her_a_notorious_american_villain.html (accessed 17 March 2017).
16. Nadya Agrawal, 'Latino Voices: Six Decades of Mexican and Mexican-American Style Evolution', *Huffington Post*, 10 October 2016, http://www.huffingtonpost.com/entry/6-decades-of-mexican-and-mexican-american-style-evolution_us_56211041e4b069b4e1fbc1e6 (accessed 23 January 2017).
17. Mary Institute and St. Louis Country Day School, 'American Race and Racism 1970 to Present', https://sites.google.com/a/micds.org/american-race-and-racism-1970-to-present/home/19 (accessed 2 November 2016).
18. Elin Woodger and David F. Burg, *Eyewitness History: The 1980s* (New York: Facts on File, 2006).
19. Gay in the 1980s: From Fighting for Our Rights to Fighting for Our Lives, 'A Pivotal Era in LGBT History', http://www.gayinthe80s.com/ (accessed 4 November 2016).
20. Ronald Roach, 'Concerns about Use of Standardized Tests a Constant over the Years', 20 March 2014, http://diverseeducation.com/article/61309/ (accessed 17 March 2017).
21. Diane Ravitch, 'Education in the 1980's: A Concern for "Quality"', *Education Week*, http://www.edweek.org/ew/articles/1990/01/10/09200009.h09.html (accessed 4 November 2016).
22. 'The Way It Was: Mass Media Landscape, 1983', http://harwoodp.people.cofc.edu/MMMTheWayitWasIntroduction.pdf (accessed 4 November 2016).
23. History, 'The 80s', http://www.history.com/topics/1980s (accessed 4 November 2016).
24. 'Fox Broadcasting Company', https://en.wikipedia.org/wiki/Fox_Broadcasting_Company (accessed 4 November 2016).
25. 'Archive of American Television', http://www.emmytvlegends.org/resources/tv-history (accessed 24 January 2017).
26. Tru Love Stories, 'The Woman of the 1980s', http://trulovestories.

com/love-stories/the-woman-of-the-1980s (accessed 21 October 2016).

27 Bob Batchelor (ed.), *American Pop Culture Decade by Decade*, 4 vols (Westport, CT: Greenwood, 2008).

28 Ibid., Vol. 3: 1960–89, '1980s as Travel Decade', 321, 325.

29 The Eighties Club: Politics and Popular Culture in the 1980s, 'The American Scene', http://eightiesclub.tripod.com/id44.htm (accessed 12 November 2016.).

30 Jian Deleon, 'The 80 Greatest '80s Fashion Trends', Complex, http://www.complex.com/style/the-80-greatest-80s-fashion-trends/ (accessed 17 March 2017).

2 American Theatre in the 1980s

1 Bradford Martin, *The Other Eighties: A Secret History of America in the Age of Reagan* (New York: Hill and Wang, 2011), ix.

2 Helen Chinoy and Linda Jenkins, *Women in American Theatre*, rev. and expand. 3rd edn (New York: Theatre Communications Group, 2006), xviii.

3 Martin Banham. *The Cambridge Guide to Theater* (Cambridge: Cambridge University Press, 1995), 365.

4 Ibid., xviii.

5 Jane T. Peterson and Suzanne Bennett (eds), *Women Playwrights of Diversity: A Bio-bibliographical Sourcebook* (Westport, CT: Greenwood Press, 1997), 11.

6 Carlos Cortés (ed.), *Multicultural America: A Multimedia Encyclopedia* (Thousand Oaks, CA: Sage, 2013), 1523.

7 Sydne Mahone (ed.), *Moonmarked and Touched by the Sun* (New York: Theatre Communications Group, 1994), 283.

8 Jeffrey Huntsman, 'Introduction', in *New Native American Drama: Three Plays by Hanay Geiogamah* (Norman: Oklahoma Univeristy Press, 1980), ix.

9 Banham, *The Cambridge Guide to Theatre*, 351.

10 Scott Miller, *Strike up the Band: A New History of Musical Theatre* (Portsmouth, NH: Heinemann, 2006), 156.

11 Miranda Lundskaer-Nielsen, *Directors and the New Musical Drama: British and American Theatre in the 1980s and 90s* (New York: Springer, 2008), 2.

12 Miller, *Strike up the Band*, 156.
13 Ibid.

3 David Mamet

1 Frank Rich, 'Theater: Al Pacino in "American Buffalo"', *New York Times*, 5 June 1981.
2 Christopher Bigsby, *David Mamet* (London and New York: Methuen, 1985), 12.
3 David Mamet, *The Cabin, Reminiscence and Diversions* (New York: Turtle Bay Books, 1992), 3–12.
4 Bruce Weber, 'At 50, a Mellower David Mamet May Be Ready to Tell His Story', *New York Times*, 16 November 1997.
5 Samuel G. Freedman, 'The Gritty Eloquence of David Mamet', *New York Times*, 21 April 1985.
6 John Lahr, 'Fortress Mamet', *The New Yorker*, 17 November 1997.
7 David Mamet, *American Buffalo* (New York: Grove Press, Inc., 1975), 10.
8 Lahr, 'Fortress Mamet'.
9 Don Shewey, 'David Mamet Puts a Dark Urban Drama on Stage', *New York Times*, 24 October 1982.
10 David Mamet, *Make-Believe Town: Essays and Remembrances* (Boston and New York: Little, Brown and Company, 1996), 4–5.
11 David Mamet, *True and False: Heresy and Common Sense for the Actor* (New York: Pantheon Books, 1997), 9–10.
12 Ibid., 12.
13 Ibid., 62.
14 Shewey, 'David Mamet Puts a Dark Urban Drama on Stage'.
15 Ibid.
16 Mimi Leahey, 'The American Dream Gone Bad', *Other Stages*, 4 November 1982, 3.
17 Brenda Murphy, *Understanding David Mamet* (Columbia: University of South Carolina Press, 2011), 107
18 Ibid., 72.
19 Arthur Miller, *Timebends: A Life* (New York: Harper and Row, 1987), 184

20 David Worster, 'How to Do Things with Salesmen: David Mamet's Speech-Act Play', in Leslie Kane (ed.), *David Mamet's Glengarry Glen Ross: Text and Performance* (New York and London: Garland Publishing, Inc., 1996), 63–80.
21 Leslie Kane, 'A Conversation with Sam Mendes', in Leslie Kane (ed.), *David Mamet's Glengarry Glen Ross: Text and Performance* (New York and London: Garland Publishing, Inc., 1996), 245–62, 256
22 Leslie Kane, *Weasels and Wisemen: Ethics and Ethnicity in the Work of David Mamet* (New York: St. Martin's Press, 1999), 59.
23 David Mamet, 'The Human Stain', *Guardian*, 6 May 2005.
24 Bigsby, *David Mamet*, 113.
25 Ibid., 121.
26 Geoffrey Norman and John Rezek, 'Working the Con', in Leslie Kane (ed.), *David Mamet in Conversation* (Ann Arbor: University of Michigan Press, 2001), 123–42, 134–5.
27 Kane, 'A Conversation with Sam Mendes', 258.
28 Steven Price, 'Disguise in Love: Gender and Desire in *House of Games* and *Speed-the-Plow*', in Christopher C. Hudgins and Leslie Kane (eds), *Gender & Genre: Essays on David Mamet* (New York: Palgrave, 2001), 41–59, 55.
29 Murphy, *Understanding David Mamet*, 93.
30 Richard Stayton, 'Enter Scowling', *Los Angeles Times Magazine*, 23 August 1992.
31 Megan Rosenfeld, 'Exit the Audience, Arguing', *Washington Post*, 30 April 1993.
32 Stayton, 'Enter Scowling'.
33 Deborah Tannen, 'He Said … She Said … Who Did What?', *New York Times*, 15 November 1992.
34 Bruce Weber, 'On Stage, and Off', *New York Times*, 30 October 1992.
35 Charlie Rose, 'On Theater, Politics, and Tragedy', in Leslie Kane (ed.), *David Mamet in Conversation* (Ann Arbor: University of Michigan Press, 2001), 163–81.
36 Bruce Weber, 'At Home with: David Mamet', *New York Times*, 17 November 1994.
37 Frank Rich, '"Oleanna"; Mamet's New Play Detonates the Fury of Sexual Harassment', *New York Times*, 26 October 1992.
38 Arthur Holmberg, *David Mamet and American Macho* (Cambridge: Cambridge University Press, 2012), 210.

39 Dorothy H. Jacobs, 'Levene's Daughter: Positioning the Female in *Glengarry Glen Ross*', in Leslie Kane (ed.), *David Mamet's Glengarry Glen Ross: Text and Performance* (New York and London: Garland Publishing, Inc., 1996), 107–22, 120.
40 David Mamet, *Writing in Restaurants* (New York: Penguin Books, 1986), 44.
41 Stayton, 'Enter Scowling'.
42 Norman and Rezek, 'Working the Con', 132.
43 Price, 'Disguise in Love', 158.
44 David K. Sauer, *David Mamet's Oleanna* (London: Continuum, 2008), 3–4.
45 Weber, 'At Home with: David Mamet'.
46 Tannen, 'He Said … She Said'.

4 David Henry Hwang

1 Jeremy Gerard, 'David Hwang: Riding on the Hyphen', *New York Times Magazine*, 13 March 1988, http://www.lexisnexis.com (accessed 10 June 2011).
2 Bruce Weber, 'A Family's Tales of China as a Path to Theatre Fame', *New York Times*, 30 March 1998, http://www.proquest.com (accessed 6 June 2011).
3 David Henry Hwang, 'Worlds Apart', *American Theatre* (January 2000): 56.
4 Ibid.
5 Weber, 'A Family's Tales of China'.
6 Gerard, 'David Hwang'.
7 In 2007, Rich would write an effusive foreword to the published version of Hwang's *Yellow Face*.
8 Hwang, 'Worlds Apart', 51.
9 See Esther Kim Lee, *The History of Asian American Theatre* (Cambridge: Cambridge University Press, 2011), 129–37; this section contains a detailed discussion of the history behind Hwang's theatrical breakthrough.
10 Eric Pace, 'I write plays to claim a place for Asian-Americans', *New York Times*, 12 July 1981, 2:4.
11 Hwang, Kotanda and Houston comprised a second wave of

Asian-American writers and performers who began to make a significant impact for Asian-Americans in the theatre in the 1980s. For a more detailed discussion of this wave of writers/performers, see Lee's *A History of Asian American Theatre*, 124–54.

12 Dinitia Smith, 'Face Values: The Sexual and Racial Obsessions of David Henry Hwang', *New York* 26, no. 2 (11 January 1993): 44.

13 Ibid., 42.

14 For a larger discussion of the direction of Asian-American literature during this era, see Stephen H. Sumida, 'The More Things Change: Paradigm Shifts in Asian American Studies', *American Studies International* 38, no. 2 (June 2000): 97–114.

15 Eve Oishi argues that the struggle in the play between the three characters is a metaphor for Hwang's own struggle to reconcile his views and developing writing style with that of Chin and Kingston. She notes that 'Hwang casts the literary battle as a love triangle between himself, Kingston, and Chin by restaging the battle between the two writers as a fight between two Chinese mythological figures.' Eve Oishi, 'The Asian American Fakeness Canon, 1972–2002', *Aztlán: A Journal of Chicano Studies* 32, no. 1 (Spring 2007): 200.

16 David Savran, 'David Hwang', in *In Their Own Words: Contemporary American Playwrights* (New York: Theatre Communication Group, 1988), 123.

17 Joe Brown, 'On Wings of a "Butterfly": Playwright David Henry Hwang, Broadway Bound', *Washington Post*, 10 February 1988, B1, http://www.lexisnexis.com (accessed 10 June 2011).

18 Bonnie Lyons, '"Making His Muscles Work for Himself": An Interview with David Henry Hwang', *Literary Review* 33 (1990): 240.

19 Lee, *The History of Asian American Theatre*, 133.

20 David Henry Hwang, *FOB*, *Trying to Find Chinatown: The Selected Plays* (New York: Theatre Communication Group, 2000), 7.

21 James S. Moy, *Marginal Sights: Staging the Chinese in America* (Iowa City: University of Iowa Press, 1993), 126.

22 Ban Wang, 'Reimagining Political Community: Diaspora, Nation-State, and the Struggle for Recognition', *Modern Drama* 48, no. 2 (2005): 264.

23 Smith, 'Face Values', 43.

24 Pace, 'I write plays', 2:4.

25 Ibid.
26 Smith, 'Face Values', 44.
27 Hsiu-Chen Lin, 'Staging Orientalia: Dangerous "Authenticity" in David Henry Hwang's M. Butterfly', *Journal of American Drama and Theatre* 9, no. 1 (1997): 27.
28 Hwang, *The Dance and the Railroad*, Trying to Find Chinatown, 67.
29 Lyons, 'Making His Muscles Work for Himself', 236.
30 Hwang, 'Worlds Apart', 50.
31 Savran, 'David Hwang', 125–6.
32 Hwang, *Family Devotions*, Trying to Find Chinatown, 97.
33 Pace, 'I write plays', 2:4.
34 Smith, 'Face Values', 43.
35 John Louis DiGaetani, 'M. Butterfly: An Interview with David Henry Hwang', *Drama Review* 33 (Fall 1989): 143.
36 David Henry Hwang, 'Afterword', *M. Butterfly* (New York: Plume, 1989), 95.
37 Gerard, 'David Hwang'.
38 Hwang, *M. Butterfly*, 83, 82.
39 Rocio G. Davis, '"Just a Man": Subverting Stereotypes in David Henry Hwang's M. Butterfly', *Hitting Critical Mass* 6, no. 2 (2000): 68.
40 DiGaetani, 'M. Butterfly', 146.
41 Ruth Leon, 'One fine play we will see', *The Times*, 17 March 1989, http://www.lexisnexis.com (accessed 9 June 2011).
42 Gerard, 'David Hwang'.
43 Douglas Kerr, 'David Henry Hwang and the Revenge of Madame Butterfly', *Asian Voices in English* (1991): 125.
44 Ibid., 128.
45 Moy, *Marginal Sights*, 124.
46 Josephine Lee. *Performing Asian America: Race and Ethnicity on the Contemporary Stage* (Philadelphia: Temple University Press, 1997), 114.
47 Angela Pao, 'M. Butterfly by David Henry Hwang', in Sau-Ling Cynthia Wong and Stephen H. Sumida (eds), *A Resource Guide to Asian American Literature* (New York: Modern Language Association, 2001), 201.

48 Ibid.
49 James S. Moy, 'David Henry Hwang's *M. Butterfly* and Philip Kan Gotanda's *Yankee Dawg You Die*: Repositioning Chinese American Marginality on the American Stage', *Theatre Journal* 42, no. 1 (March 1990): 54.
50 Lin, 'Staging Orientalia', 31.
51 Pao, '*M. Butterfly*', 201.
52 Williamson B. C. Chang, '*M. Butterfly*: Passivity, Deviousness, and the Invisibility of the Asian-American Male', in Linda A. Revilla, Shirley Hune and Gail M. Nomura (eds), *Bearing Dreams, Shaping Visions: Asian Pacific American Perspectives* (Pullman: Washington State University Press, 1993), 182.
53 Ibid., 183.
54 David Henry Hwang, 'Evolving a Multicultural Tradition', *MELUS* 16, no. 3 (Fall 1989–90): 17.
55 Lin, 'Staging Orientalia', 29.
56 Jon Rossini, 'From *M. Butterfly* to *Bondage*: David Henry Hwang's Fantasies of Sexuality, Ethnicity, and Gender', *Journal of American Drama and Theatre* 18, no. 3 (2006): 56.
57 Ryan McKittrick, 'Words from a Zen Garden', *ARTicles*, 1 June 2003, http://www.americanrepertorytheater.org (accessed 12 December 2011).
58 Robert Cooperman, 'New Theatrical Statements: Asian–Western Mergers in the Early Plays of David Henry Hwang', in Marc Maufort (ed.), *Staging Difference: Cultural Pluralism in American Theatre and Drama* (New York: Peter Lang, 1995), 208.
59 Hwang, 'David Henry Hwang', 93.
60 McKittrick, 'Words from a Zen Garden'.
61 Kerr, 'David Henry Hwang', 93.
62 Gerard, 'David Hwang'.
63 Hwang, 'Evolving a Multicultural Tradition', 17.
64 Gerard, 'David Hwang'.
65 Hwang, 'Evolving a Multicultural Tradition', 17.
66 Gerard, 'David Hwang'.
67 Frank Rich, '*Rich Relations*, From David Hwang', *New York Times*, 22 April 1986, C15, http://www.proquest.com (accessed 7 June 2012).
68 Smith, 'Face Values', 44.

69 For a detailed discussion of the *Miss Saigon* protest, see Lee's *A History of Asian American Theatre*, 177–99.

5 Maria Irene Fornes

1 While more recent scholarship on Fornes includes diacriticals, Fornes did not. Therefore, this chapter will print her name without accent marks, while noting that this is a strong example of Fornes's complicated relationship with her Latina identity.
2 Thanks to my students in the 'Major Playwrights: Fornes' seminar held at New York University during the autumn of 2014, especially Hanna Novak, Megan Emilio and Zoe Curzi, for helping me develop many of the ideas in this chapter. Thanks also to Scott T. Cummings for graciously reading earlier drafts of this chapter, and Nishad More for assistance with editing.
3 For a book-length study of Fornes's influence on a younger generation of Latina playwrights, see Anne García-Romero's *The Fornes Frame: Contemporary Latina Playwrights and the Legacy of Maria Irene Fornes* (Tucson: University of Arizona Press, 2016).
4 For a sampling of feminist scholarship on Fornes's work, see Helen Keyssar (ed.), *Feminist Theatre and Theory* (New York: St Martin Press, 1996); Diane L. Moroff, *Fornes: Theater in the Present Tense* (Ann Arbor: University of Michigan Press, 1996); Gayle Austin, 'The Madwoman in the Spotlight: Plays of Maria Irene Fornes,' in Linda Hart (ed.), *Making a Spectacle: Feminist Essays on Contemporary Women's Theatre* (Ann Arbor: University of Michigan Press, 1989); Assunta Kent, *Maria Fornes and Her Critics* (Westport, CT: Greenwood Press, 1996); and Beverly B. Pevitts, 'Review of *Fefu and Her Friends*,' in Helen K. Chinoy and Linda W. Jenkins (eds), *Women in American Theatre* (New York: Theatre Communications Group, 1987).
5 Maria Irene Fornes, 'Creative Danger', in Marc Robinson (ed.), *The Theater of Maria Irene Fornes* (Baltimore, MD: Johns Hopkins University Press, 1999), 230–3.
6 Rachel Wetzsteon, 'Irene Fornes: The Elements of Style,' *The Village Voice*, 29 April 1986.
7 Maria Irene Fornes, '"Seeing with Clarity: The Visions of Maria Irene Fornes" An Interview by Scott Cummings', *Theater* 17, no. 1 (1985): 52.

8   Scott T. Cummings, *Maria Irene Fornes* (London and New York: Routledge, 2013), 64–84.
9   For further discussion of Fornes's role as a director, see Susan Letzler Cole, '"To be quiet on stage": Fornes as Director', in Marc Robinson (ed.), *The Theater of Maria Irene Fornes* (Baltimore, MD: Johns Hopkins University Press, 1999), 140–55.
10 Fornes, 'Seeing with Clarity', 9.
11 Steven Drukman, 'Notes on Fornes (with apologies to Susan Sontag)', *American Theatre* 17, no. 7 (2000): 36–9, 85.
12 Maria Irene Fornes, *Letters from Cuba and Other Plays* (New York: PAJ Publications, 2007), 9.
13 Throughout this chapter, I use the idea of 'environment' both to refer to Fornes's integration of locations when staging a piece, her attention to landscape and ecology (in *The Danube* in particular), and the larger genre of environmental theatre as genre, founded by Richard Schechner and others in New York City in the late 1960s and 1970s.
14 Maria Irene Fornes, 'From an Interview with Allen Frame', in Marc Robinson (ed.), *The Theater of Maria Irene Fornes* (Baltimore, MD: Johns Hopkins University Press, 1999), 224–9.
15 Maria Irene Fornes interview with Rod Wooden from Maria M. Delgado and Paul Heritage (eds), *In Contact with the Gods?: Directors Talk Theatre* (Manchester and New York: Manchester University Press, 1996), 102.
16 Fornes, 'From an Interview with Allen Frame', 228.
17 Sally Porterfield, 'Black Cats and Green Trees: The Art of Maria Irene Fornes', *Modern Drama* 43, no. 2 (2000): 204–17, 215.
18 Caridad Svich and Maria Delgado (eds), *Conducting a Life: Reflections on the Theater of Maria Irene Fornes* (New York: Smith and Krauss, 1999). Indeed Fornes was working on a book titled *Anatomy of Inspiration* that would have set down her teaching exercises in print. Sadly, this book was never completed. A brief compendium of her exercise was gathered by Svich and published in *PAJ* 31, no. 3 (2009).
19 Even as I write this chapter, I am inundated by the legacy of Fornes as dozens of posts are forwarded to my inbox from the Latina/o Theatre Commons, an advocacy group fostering the work of Latina/o playwrights in the United States today.
20 Richard Schechner, *Between Theatre and Anthropology* (Philadelphia: University of Pennsylvania Press, 1985).

21 Maria Irene Fornes, *Plays* (New York: PAJ Publications, 1986), 42–3.
22 Cummings, *Maria Irene Fornes*, 84
23 Frank Rich, 'The Danube at the American Place,' *New York Times*, 13 March 1984, Theater section.
24 Bill Worthen, 'Still Playing Games: Ideology and Performance in the Theater of Maria Irene Fornes', in Marc Robinson (ed.), *The Theater of Maria Irene Fornes* (Baltimore, MD: Johns Hopkins University Press, 1999), 61–75.
25 Una Chaudhuri. *Staging Place: The Geography of Modern Drama* (Ann Arbor: University of Michigan Press, 1997), 166–7.
26 See Cummings, *Maria Irene Fornes*, 83.
27 Fornes, 'Creative Danger', 231–2.
28 Fornes, 'From an Interview with Allen Frame', 227.
29 Fornes, *Plays*, 19.
30 Cummings, *Maria Irene Fornes*, 104–5.
31 Fornes, *Plays*, 27.
32 Maria Irene Fornes, 'Introduction to *Conducting a Life*', in M. Elizabeth Osborn (ed.), *On New Ground: Contemporary Hispanic American Plays* (New York: Theatre Communications Group, 1987), 46–9. See the earlier draft of *No Time* included in the Documents section for an interaction between this, very different, pairing of Nena and Orlando.
33 Fornes, *Plays*, 66.
34 Ironically, according to Michelle Memran, this 'pause', and the consequent dramatic shift in this scene, came from the actress who was playing Nena turning the pages of the script incorrectly. Fornes, with her prescient ability to recognize strong segues, turned this chance event into the finalized version of the monologue.
35 Worthen, 'Still Playing Games', 68.
36 Deborah R. Geis, 'Wordscapes of the Body: Performative Language as "Gestus" in Maria Irene Fornes's Plays', *Theatre Journal* 42, no. 3 (1990): 291–307.
37 Fornes quoted in David Savran (ed.), *In their Own Words: Contemporary American Playwrights* (NewYork: Theatre Communications Group, 1988), 68.
38 Worthen, 'Still Playing Games', 72.

39 Fornes, *Plays*, 71.
40 For views on this ending, see Austin, 'The Madwoman in the Spotlight', 76–85.
41 Maria Irene Fornes, *The Conduct of Life*, in M. Elizabeth Osborn (ed.), *On New Ground: Contemporary Hispanic American Plays* (New York: Theatre Communications Group, 1987), 72.
42 Linda Kintz, 'Permeable Boundaries, Femininity, Fascism, and Violence: Fornes's *The Conduct of Life*', *Gestos* 6, no. 11 (1991): 79–89.
43 Cummings, *Maria Irene Fornes*, 79.
44 Stephen J. Bottoms, 'Sympathy for the Devil?: Maria Irene Fornes and *The Conduct of Life*', *Journal of American Drama and Theatre* 16, no. 3 (2004): 19–38, 21.
45 On this point, see Stacy Wolf, 'Re/Presenting Gender, Re/Presenting Violence: Feminism, Form and the Plays of Maria Irene Fornes', *Theatre Studies* 37 (1992): 17–31.
46 Fornes, interview with Rod Wooden, 105.
47 Drukman, 'Notes on Fornes', 13.

6 August Wilson

1 'Preface', *King Hedley II* (New York: Theatre Communications Group, 2005), viii–ix.
2 'The Play', *Joe Turner's Come and Gone* (New York: New American Library, 1988).
3 Harry Elam, *The Past as Present in the Drama of August Wilson* (Ann Arbor: University of Michigan Press, 2005), xi.
4 John Lahr, 'Been here and Gone', in *The Cambridge Companion to August Wilson* (New York: Cambridge University Press, 2007), 35.
5 Ibid., 36.
6 Laurence Glasco and Christopher Rawson, *August Wilson: Pittsburgh Places in His Life and Plays*, 2nd edn (Pittsburgh: Pittsburgh History & Landmarks Foundation, 2015), 23, 14.
7 Ibid., 14.
8 August Wilson, *Joe Turner's Come and Gone* (New York: Plume, 1988).
9 Ibid.

10 David Savran, 'August Wilson', in David Savran (ed.), *In Their Own Words: Contemporary American Playwrights* (New York: Theater Communication Group, 1988), in Jackson R. Bryer and Mary C. Hartig (eds), *Conversations with August Wilson* (Jackson: University of Mississippi Press, 2006), 26.

11 August Wilson, 'Foreword', in Myron Schwartzman, *Romare Bearden: His Life and Art* (New York: Abrams, 1990), 8.

12 Ibid., 8.

13 Bill Moyers, 'August Wilson: Playwright', in Bill Moyers, *Bill Moyers: A World of Ideas – Conversations with Thoughtful Men and Women About American Life Today and the Ideas Shaping Our Future* (New York: Doubleday, 1989), 77.

14 Samuel Friedman, 'A Playwright Talks about the Blues', *New York Times*, 13 April 1984, C3.

15 Richard Christiansen, 'New Playwright Ignites with *"Ma Rainey's Black Bottom"*', *Chicago Tribune*, 15 October 1984, 1–2.

16 Stanley Kauffmann, 'Bottoms Up', *Saturday Review* 11 (January/February 1985): 83, 90.

17 Robert Isaacs, 'You Don't Get "Ma Rainey", but Play Has Good Moments', *Waterbury Republican*, 13 April 1984.

18 John Fisher, 'Ma Rainey's Statement Needs Some Refinement', *Buck County Courier Times*, 26 September 1984.

19 August Wilson's *King Hedley, II*, set in Pittsburgh's Hill District during the mid-1980s, arguably demonstrates an even greater degree of destitute conditions that blacks faced in blighted, drug infested, crime-ridden urban areas in America.

20 *The Homecoming*, Wilson's as-yet unpublished one-act play written in 1976, was first produced by Kuntu Theatre, a local amateur group in Pittsburgh. Wilson dedicates the seventeen-page script 'to the memory of Blind Lemon Jefferson and to the countless "unknown" blues singers, whose story remains largely untold'.

21 'Blind' Lemon Jefferson (1893–1929) was an American blues and gospel singer, guitarist and songwriter from Texas. He was one of the most popular blues singers of the 1920s, and has been called 'Father of the Texas Blues'.

22 Dennis Watlington, 'Hurdling Fences', *Vanity Fair*, April 1989, 110.

23 Ibid., 106.

24 David Savran, 'August Wilson', in David Savran (ed.), *In Their*

Own Words: Contemporary American Playwrights (New York: Theatre Communications Group, 1988), 302.

25 Also known as the Cult of Domesticity, the Cult of True Womanhood is a term identifying a nineteenth-century ideology that women's nature suited them especially for tasks associated with the home. The ideology held that the role of the 'true woman' was to perform the domestic chores of the household or oversee their performance by others (usually women) hired for that purpose. She prepared nutritious meals, nurtured her children both physically and spiritually, comforted her husband and soothed away the wounds of his encounters with the outside world, and stood as an invincible sentinel at the portals of the home to keep worldly pollution from entering and despoiling the family.

26 Clive Barnes, 'Fiery Fences', *New York Post*, 27 March 1987, 23.

27 *Fences* is a 2016 American drama film directed by Denzel Washington and written by August Wilson, based on his Pulitzer Prize-winning play of the same name. The film stars Washington, Viola Davis, Stephen Henderson, Jovan Adepo, Russell Hornsby, Mykelti Williamson and Saniyya Sidney.

28 Ulysses, the hero of Homer's Greek epic poem *The Odyssey*, spends ten years trying to get back home to Ithaca after the Greeks win the Trojan War.

29 Ishmael Reed, 'In Search of August Wilson', *Connoisseur* 217 (March 1987): 95.

30 Ibid.

31 Bill Moyers, *Bill Moyers: A World of Ideas – Conversations with Thoughtful Men and Women about American Life Today and the Ideas Shaping Our Future* (New York: Doubleday, 1989), 178.

32 Savran, 'August Wilson', 34.

33 Kim Powers, 'An Interview with August Wilson', in Bill Moyers, *Bill Moyers: A World of Ideas – Conversations with Thoughtful Men and Women about American Life Today and the Ideas Shaping Our Future* (New York: Doubleday, 1989), 9.

34 The term Post-Blackness was coined by Thelma Golden and Glenn Ligon to describe 'the liberating value in tossing off the immense burden of race-wide representation, the idea that everything they do must speak to or for or about the entire race'.' Darryl Pinkney, 'Big Changes for Black America?', *New York Review of Books*, 24 May 2012, http://www.nybooks.com/

articles/2012/05/24/big-changes-black-america/?pagination=false (accessed 17 March 2017).

35 Michele Norris, Interview, 'Toure Discusses What It Means to be Post-Black', *All Things Considered*, NPR, 27 September 2011, http://www.npr.org/2011/09/27/140854965/toure-discusses-what-it-means-to-be-post-black (accessed 17 March 2017).

36 August Wilson, *The Ground on Which I Stand* (New York: Theatre Communications Group, 1996), 12.

37 Sandra G. Shannon. *The Dramatic Vision of August Wilson* (Washington, DC: Howard University Press, 1995), 216.

38 Sandra G. Shannon and Dana A. Williams (eds), *August Wilson and Black Aesthetics* (New York: Palgrave-McMillan, 2004), 3–4.

39 Sandra G. Shannon, 'The Role of Memory in August Wilson's Four-Hundred-Year Autobiography', in Amritjit Singh et al. (eds), *Memory & Cultural Politic: New Approaches to American Ethnic Literatures* (Boston: Northeastern University Press, 1996), 180.

40 Mervyn Rothstein, 'Round Five for the Theatrical Heavyweight', *New York Times*, 15 April 1990, sec. 2, 8.

41 Paul Carter Harrison (ed.), *August Wilson: Three Plays* (Pittsburgh: Pittsburgh University Press, 1984), xii.

42 Savran, 'August Wilson', 34.

Afterword

1 Richard Zoglin, 'The Downward Spiral of David Mamet', *Time*, 11 January 2010, http://content.time.com/time/magazine/article/0,9171,1950955,00.html (accessed 17 March 2017).

2 Hilton Als, 'Exit the Dragon: Asian-American Artists Defy Stereotype through the Decades', *New Yorker*, 10 February 2014, http://www.newyorker.com/magazine/2014/02/10/exit-the-dragon (accessed 28 January 2017).

3 Her later work has been written about less, but is the focus of Scott Cummings's recent monograph, *Maria Irene Fornes*, which many find to be a good resource guide. It not only analyses all of the later plays in detail, but also has a useful appendix with the dates and locations of all of Fornes's productions.

Documents

1. President Ronald Reagan, 12 June 1987, 'Tear Down This Wall', The History Place: Great Speeches Collection, http://www.historyplace.com/speeches/reagan-tear-down.htm (accessed 30 December 2016).
2. 'Pneumocystis Pneumonia – Los An*geles*', *CDC*, Epidemiologic Notes and Reports, MMWR 30, no. 21 (5 June 1981): 1–3, https://www.cdc.gov/mmwr/preview/mmwrhtml/june_5.htm (accessed 17 March 2017)
3. Matthew Roudane, 'An Interview with David Mamet', December 1984, http://www.upstartfilmcollective.com/portfolios/jcharnick/mamet-museum/old-interview.html (accessed 17 March 2017).
4. Seth Abramovitch, 'David Mamet's Master Class Memo to the Writers of *The Unit*', Movie Line, 23 March 2010, http://movieline.com/2010/03/23/david-mamets-memo-to-the-writers-of-the-unit/ (accessed 17 March 2017).
5. In an email (10 February 2016) to William C. Boles, Hwang revealed that when he first began writing the play, he did not originally have Song stripping before Gallimard.
6. In earlier versions of the draft Song is spelled 'Soong'. As the play drew closer to its premiere in Washington, DC, Soong was changed to Song.
7. The handwriting that can be made out says, 'That's a rather tall [illegible]. Particularly when you're just [illegible] you [illegible].' The dialogue appears to be attributed to Gallimard.
8. Heather Henderson, 'Building Fences: An Interview with Mary Alice and James Earl Jones', *Theatre* 16, no. 3 (Summer/Fall 1985).
9. August Wilson, *The Ground on Which I Stand* (New York: Theatre Communications Group, 2001), 13–17.
10. Sandra Shannon, 'From Lorraine Hansberry to August Wilson: An Interview with Lloyd Richards', *Callaloo* 14, no. 1 (1991): 126, 130–1.
11. *August Wilson: The Ground on Which I Stand*, dir. Sam Pollard (American Masters, 2015).
12. During the summer of 2015, publishers of *American Theatre* recruited Suzan-Lori Parks to interview August Wilson for a special edition they were preparing that includes the complete script for *Radio Golf*.

13 Suzan-Lori Parks, 'The Light in August: An African Spiritual Strength Born of Adversity Undergirds August Wilson's 10-play Cycle', *American Theatre* (November 2005): 25, 74.

14 Kareem Abdul Jabbar, 'Race, Family, and Fences in the Trump Era: An Interview with Denzel Washington and Viola Davis', *Hollywood Reporter*, 30 November 2016, http://www.hollywoodreporter.com/features/denzel-washington-viola-davis-interviewed-by-kareem-abdul-jabbar-race-family-fences-trump-e (accessed 17 March 2017).

BIBLIOGRAPHY

'The 80s'. *History*. Available online: http://www.history.com/topics/1980s (accessed 4 November 2016).

Als, Hilton. 'Exit the Dragon: Asian-American Artists Defy Stereotype through the Decades'. *New Yorker*, 10 February 2014. Available online: http://www.newyorker.com/magazine/2014/02/10/exit-the-dragon (accessed 28 January 2017).

'Archive of American Television'. Available online: http://www.emmytvlegends.org/resources/tv-history (accessed 24 January 2017).

The August Wilson Century Cycle. New York: Theatre Communications Group, 2007.

Austin, Gayle. 'The Madwoman in the Spotlight: Plays of Maria Irene Fornes', in Linda Hart (ed.), *Making a Spectacle: Feminist Essays on Contemporary Women's Theatre*. Ann Arbor: University of Michigan Press, 1989.

Banham, Martin. *The Cambridge Guide to Theatre*. Cambridge: Cambridge University Press, 1995.

Barnes, Clive. 'Fiery Fences'. *New York Post*, 27 March 1987, 23.

Batchelor, Bob, ed. *American Pop Culture Decade by Decade*. Westport, CT: Greenwood, 2008.

Bean, Kellie. 'A Few Good Men: Collusion and Violence in *Oleanna*', in Christopher C. Hudgins and Leslie Kane (eds), *Gender and Genre: Essays on David Mamet*, 109–23. New York: Palgrave, 2001.

Bigsby, Christopher. *David Mamet*. London and New York: Methuen, 1985, 12.

Bigsby, Christopher, ed. *The Cambridge Companion to David Mamet*. Cambridge and New York: Cambridge University Press, 2004/2007.

Blansfield, Karen C. 'Women on the Verge, Unite!', in Christopher C. Hudgins and Leslie Kane (eds), *Gender and Genre: Essays on David Mamet*, 125–42. New York: Palgrave, 2001.

Bloom, Harold, ed. *August Wilson*. Bloom's Modern Critical Views Series. New York: Chelsea House, 2001.

Bogumil, Mary L. *Understanding August Wilson*. Columbia: University of South Carolina Press, 2011.

Boles, William C. *Understanding David Henry Hwang*. Columbia: University of South Carolina Press, 2013.

Bottoms, Stephen J. 'Sympathy for the Devil?: Maria Irene Fornes and *The Conduct of Life*'. *Journal of American Drama and Theatre* 16, no. 3 (2004): 19–38, 21.

Bragg, Melvyn. 'The South Bank Show', in Leslie Kane (ed.), *David Mamet in Conversation*, 143–56. Ann Arbor: University of Michigan Press, 2001.

Brown, Joe. 'On Wings of a "Butterfly": Playwright David Henry Hwang, Broadway Bound'. *Washington Post*, 10 February 1988, B1. Available online: http://www.lexisnexis.com (accessed 10 June 2011).

Brucher, Richard. 'Prophecy and Parody in *Edmond*', in Christopher C. Hudgins and Leslie Kane (eds), *Gender and Genre: Essays on David Mamet*, 61–76. New York: Palgrave, 2001.

Bryer, Jackson R. and Mary C. Hartig, eds. *Conversations with August Wilson*. Jackson: University of Mississippi Press, 2006.

Chang, Williamson B. C. 'M. *Butterfly*: Passivity, Deviousness, and the Invisibility of the Asian-American Male', in Linda A. Revilla, Shirley Hune and Gail M. Nomura (eds), *Bearing Dreams, Shaping Visions: Asian Pacific American Perspectives*. Pullman: Washington State Press, 1993.

Chaudhuri, Una. *Staging Place: The Geography of Modern Drama*. Ann Arbor: University of Michigan Press, 1997.

Chinoy, Helen and Linda Jenkins. *Women in American Theatre*, rev. and exp. 3rd edn. New York: Theatre Communications Group, 2006.

Christiansen, Richard. 'New Playwright Ignites with "*Ma Rainey's Black Bottom*"'. *Chicago Tribune*, 15 October 1984, 1–2.

Cody, Gabrielle. 'David Hwang's *M. Butterfly*: Perpetuating the Misogynist Myth'. *Theater* 20, no. 2 (1989): 24–7.

Cole, Susan Letzler. '"To be quiet on stage": Fornes as Director', in Marc Robinson (ed.), *The Theater of Maria Irene Fornes*, 140–55. Baltimore, MD: Johns Hopkins University Press, 1999.

Cooperman, Robert. 'New Theatrical Statements: Asian–Western Mergers in the Early Plays of David Henry Hwang', in Marc Maufort (ed.), *Staging Difference: Cultural Pluralism in American Theatre and Drama*. New York: Peter Lang, 1995.

Cortés, Carlos, ed. *Multicultural America: A Multimedia Encyclopedia*. Thousand Oaks, CA: Sage, 2013.

Cummings, Scott T. *Maria Irene Fornes*. London and New York: Routledge, 2013.

Davis, Rocio G. '"Just a Man": Subverting Stereotypes in David Henry Hwang's *M. Butterfly*'. *Hitting Critical Mass* 6 (2) (2000): 68.

Dean, Ann. *David Mamet: Language as Dramatic Action*. Madison, NJ: Fairleigh Dickinson University Press, 1990.
Deleon, Jill. 'The 80 Greatest '80s Fashion Trends'. *Complex*. Available online: http://www.complex.com/style/the-80-greatest-80s-fashion-trends/ (accessed 17 March 2017).
DiGaetani, John Louis. '*M. Butterfly*: An Interview with David Henry Hwang'. *Drama Review* 33 (Fall 1989): 143.
Drukman, Steven. 'Notes on Fornes (with apologies to Susan Sontag)'. *American Theatre* 17, no. 7 (2000): 36–9, 85.
'The Economy in the 1980s and 1990s'. *American History from the Revolution to the Reconstruction and Beyond*. Available online: http://www.let.rug.nl/usa/outlines/economy-1991/a-historical-perspective-on-the-american-economy/the-economy-in-the-1980s-and-1990s.php (accessed 19 October 2016).
'The Eighties Club: Politics and Popular Culture in the 1980s, *The American Scene*'. Available online: http://eightiesclub.tripod.com/id44.htm (accessed 12 November 2016).
Elam, Harry J. Jr. *The Past as Present in the Drama of August Wilson*. Ann Arbor: University of Michigan Press, 2006.
Elkins, Marilyn, ed. *August Wilson: A Casebook*. New York: Garland, 1994.
Fisher, John. 'Ma Rainey's Statement Needs Some Refinement'. *Buck County Courier Times*, 26 September 1984.
Fornes, Maria I. '"Seeing with Clarity: The Visions of Maria Irene Fornes, An Interview by Scott Cummings'. *Theater* 17, no. 1 (1985): 52.
Fornes, Maria I. *Plays*. New York: PAJ Publications, 1986.
Fornes, Maria I. *The Conduct of Life*, in M. Elizabeth Osborn (ed.), *On New Ground: Contemporary Hispanic American Plays*. New York: Theatre Communications Group, 1987.
Fornes, Maria I. 'Introduction to *Conducting a Life*', in M. Elizabeth Osborn (ed.), *On New Ground: Contemporary Hispanic American Plays*, 4–9. New York: Theatre Communications Group, 1987.
Fornes, Maria I. *Promenade and Other Plays*. New York: PAJ Publications, 1987.
Fornes, Maria I. *Fefu and Her Friends*. New York: PAJ Publications, 1990.
Fornes, Marie I. Interview with Rod Wooden, in Maria M. Delgado and Paul Heritage (eds), *In Contact with the Gods?: Directors Talk Theatre*. Manchester and New York: Manchester University Press, 1996.
Fornes, Maria Irene. 'Creative Danger', in Marc Robinson (ed.), *The Theater of Maria Irene Fornes*, 230–3. Baltimore, MD: Johns Hopkins University Press, 1999.
Fornes, Marie Irene. 'Interview with Allen Frame', in Marc Robinson

(ed.), *The Theater of Maria Irene Fornes*, 224–9. Baltimore, MD: Johns Hopkins University Press, 1999.

Fornes, Maria I. *Letters from Cuba and Other Plays*. New York: PAJ Publications, 2007.

Fornes, Maria I. *What of the Night?: Selected Plays*. New York: PAJ Publications, 2008.

Friedman, Samuel G. 'A Playwright Talks about the Blues'. *New York Times*, 13 April 1984, C3.

Freedman, Samuel G. 'The Gritty Eloquence of David Mamet'. *New York Times*, 21 April 1985.

Garber, Marjorie. *Vested Interests: Cross-Dressing and Cultural Anxiety*. New York: Routledge, 1992.

García-Romero, Anne. *The Fornes Frame: Contemporary Latina Playwrights and the Legacy of Maria Irene Fornes*. Tucson: University of Arizona Press, 2016.

Geis, Deborah R. 'Wordscapes of the Body: Performative Language as "Gestus" in Maria Irene Fornes's Plays'. *Theatre Journal* 42, no. 3 (1990): 291–307.

Gerard, Jeremy. 'David Hwang: Riding on the Hyphen'. *New York Times Magazine*, 13 March 1988. Available online: http://www.lexisnexis.com (accessed 10 June 2011).

Glasco, Laurence A. and Christopher Rawson, eds. *August Wilson: Pittsburgh Places in His Life and Plays*, 2nd edn. Pittsburgh: Pittsburgh History and Landmarks Foundation, 2015.

Goldman, Andrew. 'Always Be Changing'. *New York Times Magazine*, 29 May 2011.

Habib, Imtiaz. 'Demotic Male Desire and Female Subjectivity in David Mamet: The Split Space of the Women of *Edmond*', in Christopher C. Hudgins and Leslie Kane (eds), *Gender and Genre: Essays on David Mamet*, 77–94. New York: Palgrave, 2001.

Haedicke, Janet V. 'Plowing the Buffalo, Fucking the Fruits: (M)others in *The American Buffalo* and *Speed-the-Plow*', in Christopher C. Hudgins and Leslie Kane (eds), *Gender and Genre: Essays on David Mamet*, 27–40. New York: Palgrave, 2001.

Harrison, Paul Carter, ed. *August Wilson: Three Plays*. Pittsburgh: Pittsburgh University Press, 1984.

Harrison, Paul Carter. 'August Wilson's Blues Poetics', in *Three Plays by August Wilson*, 291–317. Pittsburgh: University of Pittsburgh Press, 1991.

Herrington, Joan. *I Ain't Sorry for Nothin' I Done: August Wilson's Process of Playwriting*. New York: Limelight, 1998.

Hitchens, Christopher. 'The Antagonist'. *New York Times Book Review*, 19 June 2011.

Holmberg, Arthur. *David Mamet and American Macho*. Cambridge: Cambridge University Press, 2012.
Hudgins, Christopher C. and Leslie Kane (eds). *Gender and Genre: Essays on David Mamet*. New York: Palgrave, 2001.
Huntsman, Jeffrey. *New Native American Drama: Three Plays by Hanay Geiogamah*. Norman: University of Oklahoma Press, 1980.
Hwang, David Henry. *M. Butterfly*. New York: Plume, 1989.
Hwang, David Henry. 'Evolving a Multicultural Tradition'. *MELUS* 16, no. 3 (Fall 1989–90): 17.
Hwang, David Henry. *FOB and Other Plays*. New York: Plume, 1990.
Hwang, David Henry. *Trying to Find Chinatown: The Selected Plays*. New York: Theatre Communication Group, 2000.
Hwang, David Henry. 'Worlds Apart'. *American Theatre* (January 2000): 56.
Isaacs, Robert. 'You Don't Get "Ma Rainey", but Play Has Good Moments'. *Waterbury Republican*, 13 April 1984.
Jacobs, Dorothy H. 'Levene's Daughter: Positioning the Female in *Glengarry Glen Ross*', in Leslie Kane (ed.), *David Mamet's Glengarry Glen Ross: Text and Performance*, 107–22. New York and London: Garland Publishing, Inc., 1996.
Kane, Leslie. *David Mamet: A Casebook*. New York and London: Garland Publishing, Inc., 1992.
Kane, Leslie. 'Stirring Controversy at the MLA', 1992. David Mamet Society website. Available online: http://mamet.eserver.org/review/1992-94/meetings.html (accessed 17 March 2017).
Kane, Leslie. 'A Conversation with Sam Mendes', in Leslie Kane (ed.), *David Mamet's Glengarry Glen Ross: Text and Performance*, 245–62. New York and London: Garland Publishing, Inc., 1996.
Kane, Leslie. *Weasels and Wisemen: Ethics and Ethnicity in the Work of David Mamet*. New York: St. Martin's Press, 1999.
Kane, Leslie, ed. *David Mamet's Glengarry Glen Ross: Text and Performance*. New York and London: Garland Publishing, Inc., 1996.
Kane, Leslie, ed. *David Mamet in Conversation*. Ann Arbor: University of Michigan Press, 2001.
Kauffmann, Stanley. 'Bottoms Up'. *Saturday Review* 11 (January/February 1985): 83, 90.
Kent, Assunta. *Maria Fornes and Her Critics*. Westport, CT: Greenwood Press, 1996.
Kerr, Douglas. 'David Henry Hwang and the Revenge of Madame Butterfly'. *Asian Voices in English* (1991): 125.
Keyssar, Helen, ed. *Feminist Theatre and Theory*. New York: St Martin Press, 1996.

Kintz, Linda. 'Permeable Boundaries, Femininity, Fascism, and Violence: Fornes's *The Conduct of Life*'. *Gestos* 6, no. 11 (1991): 79–89.
Lahr, John. 'Fortress Mamet'. *New Yorker*, 17 November 1997.
Lahr, John. 'Been here and Gone', in *The Cambridge Companion to August Wilson*. New York: Cambridge University Press, 2007.
Leahey, Mimi. 'The American Dream Gone Bad'. *Other Stages*, 4 November 1982, 3.
Lee, Esther Kim. *The History of Asian American Theatre*. Cambridge: Cambridge University Press, 2011.
Lee, Esther Kim. *The Theatre of David Henry Hwang*. New York: Bloomsbury Methuen Drama, 2015.
Lee, Josephine. *Performing Asian America: Race and Ethnicity on the Contemporary Stage*. Philadelphia: Temple University Press, 1997.
Leogrande, Ernest. 'A Man of Few Words Moves on to Sentences', in Leslie Kane (ed.), *David Mamet in Conversation*, 27–30. Ann Arbor: University of Michigan Press, 2001.
Leon, Ruth. 'One fine play we will see'. *The Times*, 17 March 1989. Available online: http://www.lexisnexis.com (accessed 9 June 2011).
Levin, Josh. 'The Welfare Queen'. *Slate*, 19 December 2013. Available online: http://www.slate.com/articles/news_and_politics/history/2013/12/linda_taylor_welfare_queen_ronald_reagan_made_her_a_notorious_american_villain.html (accessed 17 March 2017).
Lin, Hsiu-Chen. 'Staging Orientalia: Dangerous "Authenticity" in David Henry Hwang's *M. Butterfly*'. *Journal of American Drama and Theatre* 9, no. 1 (1997): 26–35.
Lundskaer-Nielsen, Miranda. *Directors and the New Musical Drama: British and American Theatre in the 1980s and 90s*. New York: Springer, 2008.
Lyons, Bonnie. '"Making His Muscles Work for Himself": An Interview with David Henry Hwang'. *Literary Review* 33 (1990): 240.
Mamet, David. *American Buffalo*. New York: Grove Press, Inc., 1975.
Mamet, David. *The Water Engine and Mr. Happiness*. New York: Grove Press, 1978.
Mamet, David. *Glengarry Glen Ross*. New York: Grove Press, Inc., 1983.
Mamet, David. *The Shawl and Prairie du Chien*. New York: Grove Press, 1985.
Mamet, David. *Writing in Restaurants*. New York: Penguin Books, 1986.
Mamet, David. *Speed-the-Plow*. New York: Grove Press, 1988.
Mamet, David. *The Cabin: Reminiscence and Diversions*. New York: Turtle Bay Books, 1992.
Mamet, David. *Oleanna*. New York: Pantheon Books, 1992.
Mamet, David. *The Woods, Lakeboat, Edmond*. New York: Grove Press, 1994.

Mamet, David. *Make-Believe Town: Essays and Remembrances*. Boston and New York: Little, Brown and Company, 1996.
Mamet, David. *True and False: Heresy and Common Sense for the Actor*. New York: Pantheon Books, 1997.
Mamet, David. *The Old Neighborhood*. New York: Vintage Books, 1998.
Mamet, David. *3 Uses of the Knife: On the Nature and Purpose of Drama*. New York: Columbia University Press, 1998.
Mamet, David. 'The Human Stain'. *Guardian*, 6 May 2005.
Mamet, David. 'Why I Am No Longer a "Brain-Dead Liberal": An Election-Season Essay'. *Village Voice* 11 (March 2008).
Mamet, David. 'We Can't Stop Talking About Race in America'. *New York Times*, 13 September 2009.
Mamet, David. *The Secret Knowledge: On the Dismantling on American Culture*. New York: Sentinel, 2011.
Martin, Bradford. *The Other Eighties: A Secret History of America in the Age of Reagan*. New York: Hill and Wang, 2011.
McKittrick, Ryan. 'Words from a Zen Garden'. *ARTicles*, 1 June 2003. Available online: http://www.americanrepertorytheater.org (accessed 12 December 2011).
Middeke, Martin, Peter Paul Schnierer, Christopher Innes and Matthew C. Roudane (eds). *The Methuen Guide to Contemporary Playwrights*. London: Bloomsbury Methuen Drama, 2014.
'Milestones: 1981–1988'. *U.S. Soviet Relations, 1981–1991*. Available online: https://history.state.gov/milestones/1981-1988/u.s.-soviet-relations (accessed 17 March 2017).
Miller, Arthur. *Timebends: A Life*. New York: Harper and Row, 1987.
Miller, Scott. *Strike up the Band: A New History of Musical Theatre*. Portsmouth, NH: Heinemann, 2006.
Moroff, Diane L. *Fornes: Theater in the Present Tense*. Ann Arbor: University of Michigan Press, 1996.
Moy, James S. 'David Henry Hwang's *M. Butterfly* and Philip Kan Gotanda's *Yankee Dawg You Die*: Repositioning Chinese American Marginality on the American Stage'. *Theatre Journal* 42, no. 1 (March 1990): 48–56
Moy, James S. *Marginal Sights: Staging the Chinese in America*. Iowa City: University of Iowa Press, 1993.
Moyers, Bill. 'August Wilson: Playwright', in Bill Moyers, *Bill Moyers: A World of Ideas – Conversations with Thoughtful Men and Women about American Life Today and the Ideas Shaping Our Future*, 77. New York: Doubleday, 1989.
Moyers, Bill. *Bill Moyers: A World of Ideas – Conversations with Thoughtful Men and Women about American Life Today and the Ideas Shaping Our Future*. New York: Doubleday, 1989.

Murphy, Brenda. *Understanding David Mamet*. Columbia: University of South Carolina Press, 2011.
Nadel, Alan, ed. *May All Your Fences Have Gates: Essays on the Drama of August Wilson*. Iowa City: University Iowa Press, 1994.
Nadel, Alan, ed. *August Wilson: Completing the Twentieth-Century Cycle*. Iowa City: Iowa University Press, 2010.
Nadel, Ira. *David Mamet: A Life in the Theatre*. New York: Palgrave Macmillan, 2008.
'The New Right'. *U.S. History: Pre-Columbian to the New Millennium*, 5 September 2016. Available online: http://www.ushistory.org/us/58e.asp (accessed 17 March 2017).
Norman, Geoffrey and John Rezek. 'Working the Con', in Leslie Kane (ed.), *David Mamet in Conversation*, 123–42. Ann Arbor: University of Michigan Press, 2001.
Norris, Michele. Interview, 'Toure Discusses What It Means to be Post-Black'. *All Things Considered*, NPR, 27 September 2011. Available online: http://www.npr.org/2011/09/27/140854965/toure-discusses-what-it-means-to-be-post-black (accessed 17 March 2017).
Oishi, Eve. 'The Asian American Fakeness Canon, 1972–2002'. *Aztlán: A Journal of Chicano Studies* 32, no. 1 (Spring 2007): 200.
'Ole Bull's Colony Historical Marker'. ExplorePAhistory.com. Available online: http://explorepahistory.com/hmarker.php?markerId=1-A-3D5 (accessed 17 March 2017).
Pace, Eric. 'I write plays to claim a place for Asian-Americans'. *New York Times*, 12 July 1981, 2:4.
Pao, Angela. '*M. Butterfly* by David Henry Hwang', in Sau-Ling Cynthia Wong and Stephen H. Sumida (eds), *A Resource Guide to Asian American Literature*, 201. New York: Modern Language Association, 2001.
Parry, Robert. 'Ronald Reagan: Worst President Ever?'. Consortiumnews.com: Independent Investigative Journalism Since 1995, 6 February 2014. Available online: https://consortiumnews.com/2014/02/06/ronald-reagan-worst-president-ever-2/ (accessed 17 March 2017).
Peterson, Jane and Suzanne Bennett, eds. *Women Playwrights of Diversity: A Bio-bibliographical Sourcebook*. Westport, CT: Greenwood, 1997.
Pevitts, Beverly B. 'Review of *Fefu and Her Friends*', in Helen K. Chinoy and Linda W. Jenkins (eds), *Women in American Theatre*. New York: Theatre Communications Group, 1987.
Piette, Alain. 'The 1980s', in Christopher Bigsby (ed.), *The Cambridge Companion to David Mamet*, 74–88. Cambridge: Cambridge University Press, 2004.
Pinkney, Darryl. 'Big Changes for Black America?' *New York Review*

of Books, 24 May 2012. Available online: http://www.nybooks.com/ articles/2012/05/24/big-changes-black-america/?pagination=false (accessed 17 March 2017).

'A Pivotal Era in LGBT History'. *Gay in the 1980s: From Fighting for Our Rights to Fighting for Our Lives*, 4 November 2016. Available online: http://www.gayinthe80s.com/ (accessed 17 March 2017).

Porterfield, Sally. 'Black Cats and Green Trees: The Art of Maria Irene Fornes'. *Modern Drama* 43, no. 2 (2000): 204–17.

Powers, Kim. 'An Interview with August Wilson', in Jackson R. Bryer and Mary C. Hartig (eds), *Conversations with August Wilson*, 9. Jackson: University Press of Mississippi, 2006.

Price, Steven. 'Disguise in Love: Gender and Desire in *House of Games* and *Speed-the-Plow*', in Christopher C. Hudgins and Leslie Kane (eds), *Gender and Genre: Essays on David Mamet*, 41–59. New York: Palgrave, 2001.

'Race in the Reagan Era'. *The Reagan Era*, 2 November 2016. Available online: http://www.shmoop.com/reagan-era/race.html (accessed 17 March 2017).

Ravitch, Diane. 'Education in the 1980's: A Concern for "Quality"'. *Education Week*, 4 November 2016. Available online: http://www.edweek.org/ew/articles/1990/01/10/09200009.h09.html (accessed 17 March 2017).

Reed, Ishmael. 'In Search of August Wilson'. *Connoisseur* 217 (March 1987): 95.

Rich, Frank. 'Theater: Al Pacino in "American Buffalo"'. *New York Times*, 5 June 1981.

Rich, Frank. '*The Danube* at the American Place'. *New York Times*, 13 March 1984, Theater section.

Rich, Frank. '*Rich Relations*, From David Hwang'. *New York Times*, 22 April 1986, C15. Available online: http://www.proquest.com (accessed 7 June 2012).

Rich, Frank. '"Oleanna"; Mamet's New Play Detonates the Fury of Sexual Harassment'. *New York Times*, 26 October 1992.

Richards, Sandra L. 'Yoruba Gods on the American Stage: August Wilson's "Joe Turner's Come and Gone"'. *Research in African Literature* 30, no. 4 (Winter 1999): 92–105.

Robinson, Marc, ed. *The Theater of Maria Irene Fornes*. Baltimore, MD: Johns Hopkins University Press, 1999.

Rose, Charlie. 'On Theater, Politics, and Tragedy', in Leslie Kane (ed.), *David Mamet in Conversation*, 163–81. Ann Arbor: University of Michigan Press, 2001.

Rosenfeld, Megan. 'Exit the Audience, Arguing'. *Washington Post*, 30 April 1993.

Rossini, Jon. 'From *M. Butterfly* to *Bondage*: David Henry Hwang's Fantasies of Sexuality, Ethnicity, and Gender'. *Journal of American Drama and Theatre* 18, no. 3 (2006): 54–76.

Rothstein, Mervyn. 'Round Five for the Theatrical Heavyweight'. *New York Times*, 15 April 1990, sec. 2, 8.

Roudane, Matthew C. 'Something out of Nothing', in Leslie Kane (ed.), *David Mamet in Conversation*, 46–53. Ann Arbor: University of Michigan Press, 2001.

Sauer, David K. *David Mamet's Oleanna*. London: Continuum International Publishing Group, 2008.

Savran, David. 'August Wilson', in David Savran (ed.), *In Their Own Words: Contemporary American Playwrights*, New York: Theatre Communications Group, 1988. From Jackson R. Bryer and Mary C. Hartig (eds), *Conversations with August Wilson*, 26, 34. Jackson: University of Mississippi Press, 2006.

Savran, David. 'August Wilson: An Interview', in David Savran (ed.), *In Their Own Words: Contemporary American Playwrights*, 302. New York: Theatre Communications Group, 1988.

Savran, David. 'David Hwang', in David Savran (ed.), *In Their Own Words: Contemporary American Playwrights*, 123. New York: Theater Communication Group, 1988.

Savran, David. 'Maria Irene Fornes: An Interview', in David Savran (ed.), *In their Own Words: Contemporary American Playwrights*, 68. New York: Theatre Communications Group, 1988.

Scammell, Katelyn. *Family Life: 1980s*. 3 December 2013. Available online: https://prezi.com/xqubflaygmqw/family-life-1980s/ (accessed 17 March 2017).

Schechner, Richard. *Between Theatre and Anthropology*. Philadelphia: University of Pennsylvania Press, 1985.

Schvey, Henry I. 'Celebrating the Capacity for Self-Knowledge', in Leslie Kane (ed.), *David Mamet in Conversation*, 60–71. Ann Arbor: University of Michigan Press, 2001.

Shannon, Sandra G. *The Dramatic Vision of August Wilson*. Washington, DC: Howard University Press, 1995.

Shannon, Sandra G. 'The Role of Memory in August Wilson's Four-Hundred-Year Autobiography', in Amritjit Singh, Joseph T. Skerrett Jr and Robert E. Hogan (eds), *Memory and Cultural Politic: New Approaches to American Ethnic Literatures*, 180. Boston: Northeastern University Press, 1996.

Shannon, Sandra G. *August Wilson's Fences: A Reference Guide*. Westport, CT: Greenwood, 2003.

Shannon, Sandra G., ed. *August Wilson's Pittsburgh Cycle: Critical Perspectives on the Plays*. Jefferson, NC: McFarland, 2016.

Shannon, Sandra G. and Sandra L. Richards, eds. *Approaches to*

Teaching the Plays of August Wilson. New York: Modern Language Association, 2016.
Shannon, Sandra G. and Dana A. Williams, eds. *August Wilson and Black Aesthetics*, 3–4. New York: Palgrave McMillan, 2004.
Shewey, Don. 'David Mamet Puts a Dark Urban Drama on Stage'. *New York Times*, 24 October 1982.
Skloot, Robert. '*Oleanna*, or, The Play of Pedagogy', in Christopher C. Hudgins and Leslie Kane (eds), *Gender and Genre: Essays on David Mamet*, 95–108. New York: Palgrave, 2001.
Smith, Dinitia. 'Face Values: The Sexual and Racial Obsessions of David Henry Hwang'. *New York* 26, no. 2 (11 January 1993): 44.
Stayton, Richard. 'Enter Scowling'. *Los Angeles Times Magazine*, 23 August 1992.
Sumida, Stephen H. 'The More Things Change: Paradigm Shifts in Asian American Studies'. *American Studies International* 38, no. 2 (June 2000): 97–114.
Svich, Caridad. 'The Legacy of Maria Irene Fornes: A Collection of Impressions and Exercises'. *PAJ: The Journal of Performance and Art* 31, no. 3 (September 2009): 1–32.
Svich, Caridad and Maria Delgado, eds. *Conducting a Life: Reflections on the Theater of Maria Irene Fornes*. New York: Smith and Krauss, 1999.
Tannen, Deborah. 'He Said … She Said … Who Did What?'. *New York Times*, 15 November 1992.
Templeton, David. 'Oleanna: The Ole Bull Colony'. *Strings*, November / December 2002. Available online: http://www.allthingsstrings.com/Reviews/Editions/Oleana-The-Ole-Bull-Colony (accessed 17 March 2017).
Thompson, Graham. *American Culture in the 1980s*. Edinburgh: Edinburgh University Press, 2007.
The U.S. Economy: A Brief History, Ch. 3. Available online: http://usa.usembassy.de/etexts/oecon/chap3.htm (accessed 16 November 2016).
U.S. History: Pre-Columbian to the New Millennium. Available online: http://www.ushistory.org/us/58e.asp (accessed 5 September 2016).
Wang, Ba. 'Reimagining Political Community: Diaspora, Nation-State, and the Struggle for Recognition'. *Modern Drama* 48, no. 2 (2005): 264.
Watlington, Dennis. 'Hurdling Fences'. *Vanity Fair*, April 1989, 110.
'The Way It Was: Mass Media Landscape, 1983'. Available online: http://harwoodp.people.cofc.edu/MMMTheWayitWasIntroduction.pdf (accessed 4 November 2016).
Weber, Bruce. 'On Stage, and Off'. *New York Times*, 30 October 1992.
Weber, Bruce. 'At Home with: David Mamet'. *New York Times*, 17 November 1994.

Weber, Bruce. 'At 50, a Mellower David Mamet May Be Ready to Tell His Story'. *New York Times*, 16 November 1997.
Weber, Bruce. 'A Family's Tales of China as a Path to Theatre Fame'. *New York Times*, 30 March 1998. Available online: http://www.proquest.com (accessed 6 June 2011).
Wetzsteon, Rachel. 'Irene Fornes: The Elements of Style'. *Village Voice*, 29 April 1986.
Wikipedia. 'Fox Broadcasting Company'. Available online: https://en.wikipedia.org/wiki/Fox_Broadcasting_Company (accessed 4 November 2016).
Wilson, August. *Ma Rainey's Black Bottom*. New York: New American Library, 1985.
Wilson, August. *Fences*. New York: New American Library, 1986.
Wilson, August. *Joe Turner's Come and Gone*. The Play. New York: Plume, 1988.
Wilson, August. *The Piano Lesson*. New York: Plume, 1990.
Wilson, August. *Two Trains Running*. New York: Plume, 1993.
Wilson, August. *The Ground on Which I Stand*. New York: Theater Communications Group, 1996.
Wilson, August. *Seven Guitars*. New York: Dutton, 1996.
Wilson, August. 'Foreword', in Myron Schwartzman, *Romare Bearden: His Life and Art*, 8. New York: Abrams, 1998.
Wilson, August. Preface, *King Hedley II*, viii–ix. New York: Theatre Communications Group, 2005.
Wilson, August. *Gem of the Ocean*. New York: Theatre Communications Group, 2007.
Wilson, August. *Jitney*. New York: Overlook, 2001; Theatre Communications Group. 2007.
Wilson, August. *Radio Golf*. New York: Theatre Communications Group, 2007.
Wolf, Stacy. 'Re/Presenting Gender, Re/Presenting Violence: Feminism, Form and the Plays of Maria Irene Fornes'. *Theatre Studies* 37 (1992): 17–31.
'The Woman of the 1980s'. *Tru Love Stories*. Available online: http://trulovestories.com/love-stories/the-woman-of-the-1980s/ (accessed 21 October 2016).
Woodger, Elin and David F. Burg. *Eyewitness History: The 1980s*. New York: Facts on File, 2006.
Worthen, Bill. 'Still Playing Games: Ideology and Performance in the Theater of Maria Irene Fornes', in Marc Robinson (ed.), *The Theater of Maria Irene Fornes*, 61–5. Baltimore, MD: Johns Hopkins University Press, 1999.
Worster, David. 'How to Do Things with Salesmen: David Mamet's

Speech-Act Play', in Leslie Kane (ed.), *David Mamet's Glengarry Glen Ross: Text and Performance*, 63–80. New York and London: Garland Publishing, Inc., 1996.

Zoglin, Richard. 'The Downward Spiral of David Mamet'. *Time*, 11 January 2010. Available online: http://content.time.com/time/magazine/article/0,9171,1950955,00.html (accessed 17 March 2017).

INDEX

9 Plays by Black Women 34
42nd Street 38
'42nd Street' 38
46th Street Theatre (New York City) 137
49 (Geiogamah) 36

ABC (American Broadcasting Network) 17, 20
Abingdon Square (Fornes) 103, 105, 121, 157, 158
Abstinence (L. Wilson) 42
Abu Ghraib 121
Actor's Nightmare, The (Durang) 41
Actors Studio (New York) 101, 102
Actors Theatre of Louisville 154
Africa 2
    African belief systems 132
African-Americans 11, 40
Africans in America 125
Afrocentrists 149
Agrawal, Nadya 13
Aida (Verdi) 97, 155
AIDS
    AIDS epidemic 29, 90
    AIDS-related illness 11, 27, 35, 157
Ain't Supposed to Die a Natural Death (Van Peebles) 34
Airplane! 24
album-oriented rock (AOR) 18
Alice, Mary 142

Alice in Wonderland (Carroll) 155
Allegheny Repertory Theatre (Pittsburgh) 128
Als, Hilton 156
AM radio 18
Amadeus (Shaffers) 88
America's Got Talent 21
American Century Cycle 41, 129, 132, 150, 152, 158, 159, 161 *see also* Pittsburgh Cycle
American Historical Society 161
American Idol 7
American Indians 13, 14
American Masters 160
American Place Theatre (New York City) 32
American Playhouse 154
American Repertory Theatre (Cambridge) 63
Angels Fall (L. Wilson) 42
Angels in America (Kushner) 69, 121, 157
antifeminist 3
Archives in American Television 20
Area Playwrights Workshop 84
Arena Stage (Washington, DC) 155
Aristotelean convention 144
Armstrong, Louis 133
'the art of the deal' 154
Arthur, Beatrice 21
Asante, Molefi 149

Ashley, Robert 157
Asian-Americans 40, 76, 77, 82, 86, 89, 91, 92, 95, 97
　Asian-American actors 75
　Asian-American play 35, 71, 75, 76, 95
　Asian-American Theatre Company 75
　Asian male stereotype 91
　Asian theatre 35
　Northwest Asian American Theatre (Seattle) 75
　Pan Asian Repertory Theatre (New York City) 75
Aspects of Love (Webber) 39
At the Foot of the Mountain Theatre (Minneapolis) 33
Audition, The (Fornes) 158
August Wilson and Black Aesthetics 150
August Wilson Center (Pittsburgh) 160
August Wilson Estate 161
August Wilson Theatre 160 *see also* Virginia Theatre
Avocado Kid, The (Gotanda) 75

baby boomer 9, 17
Baby with the Bathwater 41
Baldwin, James 132, 133
BAM Harvey Theatre 34
Banham, Martin 31
Baraka, Amiri 130, 132, 133, 149
Barvarian State Opera 155
Bay Area Playwrights Festival 156
BBC 68
Beals, Jennifer 26
Bearden, Romare 130–2, 144
Beckett, Samuel 54, 60
Bedford Avenue (Pittsburgh) 127
Bee Gees 79
Before It Hits Home (West) 34

Beijing 20
Bell, James 'Cool Papa' 127
Bell, Terrel 15
Bennett, Suzanne 34
Berlin Wall 20
Bettelheim, Bruno 46
Beyond Therapy (Durang) 41
Big Chill, The 10
Big Deal, The 39
Bigsby, Christopher 45, 57
black aesthetic 150
Black Power movement 149, 150
Blakey, Art 127
Blessing, Lee 42
blues 130
Blues for Mr. Charlie (Baldwin) 133
Body Indian (Geiogamah) 36
Borges, Jorge Louis 130, 132
Bosley, Tom 21
Bossum Buddies 21
Bottoms, Stephen 121
Branagh, Kenneth 52
Breakfast Club, The 19
Bridge, The: or Radiation and the Half-Life of Society. A Study of Decay 58, 64
Bright Lights, Big City 10
Bring Back Birdie 39
Brinkley, David 20
British Invasion 36
British and American Musical Theatre in the 1980s (Lundskaer-Nielsen) 37
Broadway 32, 34, 36, 37, 38, 39, 43, 44, 58, 72, 76, 96, 98, 128, 133, 143, 150, 151, 152, 153, 154, 160, 161
Broderick, Matthew 22
Brokaw, Tom 20
Brown, Doug 58–61
Brown v. Board of Education 138

Brustein, Robert 160
Bryant, Paul 155
Buchner, George 47
Buck County Courier Times 134
Bureau of Indian Affairs 14
Burke, Edmond 47
Burn This (L. Wilson) 42
Burton, Brenda 150
Bush, George H. W. 12, 15
Butler, Samuel 63

Cabin, The (Mamet) 45
California Institute of the Arts 116
Cambridge Guide to Theatre (Banham) 36
Caouette, Jonathan 155
Carroll, Lewis 155
Carsey-Warner Productions 21
Carter, Jimmy 12
Cats 37
Catholic Church 15
Catholic organizations 15
CBS 17, 20, 154
Century Plays 137 *see also* American Century Cycle; Pittsburgh Cycle
Challenger space shuttle 20
Chang, Williamson 91
Charisse, Cyd 37
Chess (Rice) 39
Chicago Tribune 133
Chicago Tribune Literary Prize for Lifetime Achievement 160
Chicken Coup Chinaman (Chin) 75
Chin, Frank 75–7
Chin, Unsuk 155
China 85
Chinatown 155
Chinese Americans 40, 74, 76, 82, 84–7
Chinese 'dragon lady' 91

Chinoy, Helen 30, 33
Chisholm, Anthony 161
Christian belief systems 132
Christian Broadcast Network 4
Christiansen, Richard 133
Chrysler 23
Chung, Connie 17
City of Angels 37
Civil War 145
colour blind casting 149
Comedy Arts Festival (Aspen, CO) 160
Congress 6
Conn, Billy 159
Chinglish 97
Civil Liberties Act 14
Clinton, Bill 15, 129, 160
CNN 17, 19, 20, 22, 27
Cold War 2, 3, 27
Conduct of Life, The: Reflections on the Theater of Maria Irene Fornes 106
conspicuous consumption 9
Cooperman, Robert 93
Cort Theatre (New York) 161
Cortes, Carlos 33
Cosby, Bill 21
Cosby Show, The 19, 21, 22
Costner, Kevin 58
Cotton Club 39
Crimes of the Heart (Henley) 30–2, 100
Cronkite, Walter 20
Crouse, Lindsay 45, 68
Cruise, Tom 26
Cruz, Migdalia 106, 158
Cruz, Nilo 35, 106, 158
Cryptogram, The (Mamet) 47
Cult of Domesticity 142
Culture Club 19
Cummings, Scott 103, 114, 121
Cutler (*Ma Rainey's Black Bottom*) 136

Dabney, Sheila 106
Dachau 63
Dallas 10, 21, 23
'Dames' 38
Dancing with the Stars 21
Darwinian jungle 154
David Letterman Show, The 21
Davis, Rocio 89
Davis, Viola 142, 152, 161
Deena (*Dreamgirls*) 38
Deleon, Jan 24
Democratic Party 4
DeNiro, Robert 58
DePalma, Brian 58
Diary of Anne Frank, The 63
'Disguise in Love' (Price) 68
Distinguished Artist Award 157
Divine, Loretta 34
Donmar Warehouse (London) 57
Don't Play Us Cheap (Van Peebles) 34
Doonesbury 39
Douglass, Michael 136
Drama Desk Award 42
Dream Girls 34, 38
Dream of the Red Chamber (Hwang and Sheng) 155
'Dreams, The' 38
Dreamettes 38
DreamWorks Animation 155
Drukman, Steven 104, 123
Duran Duran 19
Durang, Christopher 41
Dutchman (Baraka) 133
Dutton, Charles 150
Dutton publishers 162
Duval, Robert 43
Dynasty 10, 21, 23

Early, James 'Thunder' 38
East-West Players (Los Angeles) 75, 76
Eastern aesthetics 93–4

Ebb, Fred 39
effeminization 91 *see also* Asian male stereotype
Effie (*Dreamgirls*) 38
Eisenstadt, Debra 68
Elam, Harry 126, 137
Ellington, Duke 39
Ellison, Ralph 133
Elton John and Tim Rice's Aide (Mamet and Falls) 155
Emancipation Proclamation 148
Ensemble Theatre 34, 41
environmentalism 104
Equal Rights Amendment 3, 32
Equus (Shaffers) 88
Esbjornson, David 111
ESPN 17, 22
E.T.: The Extra-Terrestrial 19
Ethel Barrymore Theatre (New York) 151
Ethnic Theatre 36
Etwaroo, Indira 161
Eugene O'Neill Festival 74, 75
Eugene O'Neill Theatre Center 128, 133, 144
Euro-American stereotypes 34
Evangelical Christians 3
Evita 37
Executive Order 9066 14

Fairness Doctrine 18
Fall Guy, The 21
Family Ties 19, 21, 22
Falls, Robert 155
Fatal Attraction 90
Father Dowling Mysteries 21
Federal Communications Commission 18
federal deficit 6, 7
Federal Reserve 6
feminine or feminist aesthetic 33
feminist politics 113
'feminine sensitivity' 7

feminist theatre 100
feminist theory 113
pro-feminist 7
Second Wave Feminism 31
US feminism 33, 100, 101
Ferra, Max 106
Ferris Beuller's Day Off 10, 22
Fields, Joseph 155
First (Siegel), The 34
Fisher, John 134
Flash Dance 26
Flower Drum Song (Rodgers and Hammerstein) 97, 155
FM radio 18
Foghorn (Geiogamah) 36
Fonda, Jane 26
Forgotten Arm, The (Mann) 155
Fornes Frame, The (Romero) 158
Fornes, Maria Irene 35, 40, 73, 99–123
   Abingdon Square 103, 105, 121, 157, 158
      Marion 177
   Conduct of Life, The 40, 99, 101, 103, 106, 111, 112, 115–20, 122
      Leticia 114, 116, 118, 119, 120, 122
      Nena 106, 115–20, 122
      Olimpia 116–19, 122
      Orlando 116–19
   Danube, The 40, 99, 103 107–11, 114
   Dr. Kheal 120
   Drowning 103
   Enter the Night 158
   Evelyn Brown 103, 118
   Fefu and Her Friends 101–5, 112, 118, 120, 121
      Julia 117
   Hunger 158
   Ibsen and the Actress 158

Letters from Cuba 104, 105, 157, 158
   Joseph 104
Lust 158
Manual for a Desperate Crossing/Balseros 157, 158
Mud 35, 40, 99, 103, 105, 111–15, 122
   Henry 113
   Lloyd 113, 114
Nadine 158
Promenade 102
Springtime 158
Tango Palace 114, 120
Terre Incognito 158
Vietnamese Wedding 102
'Fortress Mamet' (Lahr) 45
'found objects' 105
Fox cable network 20
Fox, Michael J. 21
Freedman, Samuel, G. 160
Freedom of Speech Award 160
Friedman, Samuel 133
Frye, Cameron 22
Fuller, Charles 133

'gang comedy' 57
Gee, Pop! (Chin) 77
Geiogamah, Hanay 36
Gekko, Gordon 10, 22, 136
'Gems from the Gambler's Bookshelf' (Mamet) 47
Gender & Genre Essays on David Mamet (Kane) 67, 68
gender neutral language 8
General Hospital 21
Geneva nuclear arms talks 42
Getting Out (Norman) 31
Gibson, Josh 127
'Girls Just Want to Have Fun' 18
Glass, Philip 94, 97, 154
Golden Girls, The 22

Goodman Theatre 56
Gorbachev, Mikhail 2–3
Gotanda, Philip Kan 36, 75
Grand Hotel 37
Graves, Peter 24
Great Depression 41
Great Migration 41, 131, 145, 148
Great White Way 135
Greenspan, Alan 6
Grier, David Alan 34
Grey, Jennifer 22
Grind 39
Guggenhein Foundation 157
Guns n' Roses 19
Gwan Gung 77, 78, 81–4

Hamlet 144
Hammerstein, Oscar 155
Haney, Eric L. 154
Hanks, Tom 21
Hansberry, Lorraine 128, 133, 144
Harlem Renaissance 127, 136
Harper Collins 17
Harrigan 'n Hart 39
Hasa Houston, Velina 36, 75
HBO (Home Box Office) 152
hedonism 9
Heidi Chronicles, The (Wasserstein) 30, 31, 32, 42, 100
Heinz Award in the Arts and Humanities 160
Henderson, Stephen McKinley 161
Henley, Beth 30, 31, 100
Hill, Anita 63
Hill District 41, 126, 129, 160, 161 *see also* Hill, the
Hill, the 127, 128 *see also* Hill District
Hill–Thomas hearings 63
Hispanic/Latino theatre 35

Hitchcock, Alfred 49
HIV *see* AIDS
Hoffa 45
Hofman, Hans 101
Holliday, Jennifer 34
Hollywood 46, 58, 69
Homecoming, The (Wilson) 136–7
How to Do Things with Salesmen: David Mamet's Speech-Act Play (Worster) 52
House of Ramon Iglesia (Rivera) 35
Hubert-Whitten, Janet 34
Hudson, Rock 11
Hughes, John 21, 79
Hughes, Langston 133
Humana Festival 154
Huntsman, Jeffrey 36
Hwang, David Henry 35, 40, 41, 71–98, 100
  1000 Airplanes on the Roof 97
  Cain and Abel 155
  The Dance and the Railroad 71, 81–4, 85, 87, 93
  Face Value 96
  Family Devotions 41, 71, 84–7, 93, 95, 96
    Ama 84, 85, 86
    Chester 84–7, 96
    Christianity in, Di-gou 85–7
    Hannah 84, 85
    Jeanne 84, 85
    Jenny 84–6
    Popo 84, 86
    Robert 84, 85
    Wilbur 84, 85
  FOB 71, 73–81, 82, 84, 86, 87, 93, 95
    Dale 77–80, 82, 85, 86
    Grace 77–80
    Steve 77, 78, 80

Golden Child 97, 154
Golden Gate 154
House of Sleeping Beauties, The 93
M. Butterfly 35, 40, 71, 72, 76, 87–92, 96, 97, 154
   Boursicot, Bernard 88
   Comrade Chin 88
   Dragon Lady 91
   Gallimard 88–92
   Helga 90
   Pinkerton 88, 90, 92
   Liling, Song 88, 90, 91, 92, 97
   Rich Relations 74, 95–6
   Hinson 96
   Keith 96
Hwang, Dorothy 72

'I Only Have Eyes for You' 38
Ibsen, Henrik 157
Imperceptible Mutabilities of the Third Kingdom (Parks) 34
'In a Sentimental Mood' 39
Inside Delta Force (Haney) 154
INTAR Hispanic Playhouse Lab 106, 115, 156
Isaacs, Robert 133
Isn't It Romantic? (Wasserstein) 41
'It Don't Mean a Thing If It Aint Got that Swing' 39
It Takes a Nation of Millions to Hold Us Back (Public Enemy) 19
It's Alright to be a Woman Theatre (New York) 32
It's Showtime at the Apollo 21

Jackson, Michael 17, 19
Jacobs, Dorothy H. 67
Japanese culture 93
   Japanese-Americans 13, 14, 75
Jay, Ricky 46
Jazz Age 136
Jeannie (*Ferris Beuller's Day Off*) 22
Jefferson, Blind Lemon 137
Jenkins, Linda 30
John Gossner Outer Critics Circle Award 137
Jones, James Earl 143
Jones, Jeffrey 22
Joseph and the Amazing Technicolor Dreamcoat 39
Judson Poets 102
Julia Miles Women's Project 32
'Just say no!' 11

Kander, John 39
Kane, Leslie 52, 56, 67
Kaufman, Stanley 133
Kawabata, Yasunari 94
Kerr, Douglass 90
Khomeini, Ayatolla Ruhollah 1
King, Martin Luther, Jr. 12, 127
Kingston, Maxine Hong 77
Kintz, Linda 120
Kittel, Frederick A. (Fritz) 126
Kittel, Frederick 'Freddy' August *see* Wilson, August
Kowalski, Stanley 133
Kung Fu 92, 97, 155
Kushner, Tony 44, 67, 69, 121, 157

La Cage Aux Folles 37
LA Law 149
Lady Day at Emerson's Bar and Grill 39
Lahr, John 45, 126
Lakeboat 48, 51, 59, 68
'land of the Gold Mountain' 77
Landskaer-Nielsen, Miranda 37
The Lark (New York) 97, 156

INDEX

Latin-American 35
   Latin-American plays 121, 156, 157
   Latin-American Writers Workshop 156
   Latina/o playwrights 99, 100, 106, 158
Laughing Wild (Durang) 41
Lauper, Cindy 18
Laurel and Hardy 60
Leader of the Pack 39
Lee, Bruce 92, 155
Lee, Esther Kim 78
Lee, Josephine 91
Legs Diamond 39
Leon, Kenny 150, 161
Leopold (*Tango Palace*) 114
Les Miserables 37, 38
Letters from Cuba and Other Plays 157
Lewis, Bobby 102
LGBT community 11, 14, 15
Lifestyles of the Rich and Famous 21
Lin, Hsui-Chen 82, 91, 92
Lin, Justin 155
The Living Theatre 32
Loman, Linda (*Death of a Salesman*) 57
Loman, Willie (*Death of a Salesman*) 56, 138, 144
Lone, John 78, 81–4, 87
Long Duck Dong 79
Lorrell 38
Louis, Joe 159
'Lullaby of Broadway' 38
Lunt-Fontanne Theatre 39
Lupone, Patti 153

Ma, Tzi 81–3, 85
Machado, Eduardo 106, 158
Mackintosh, Cameron 97
Macy, William H. 52, 58, 63, 67

Madonna 10, 17, 18
Mae (*Mud*) 105, 111, 112, 113, 114, 119, 122
Magnum P.I. 21
Majestic Theatre 38
Major League baseball 138
Mahone, Sydne 34
Majors, Lee 21
Mako 78
Mamet, David 40, 43–69, 153–4
   American Buffalo 43, 44, 46, 52, 61, 66, 67, 153
   Anarchist, The 46, 153
   Boston Marriage 153
   China Doll 46, 153
   Disappearance of the Jews, The 56
   Edmond 47–52, 57, 66, 69
   Glengarry Glen Ross 40, 44–6, 48, 52–7, 58, 61, 62, 67, 153, 154
      Aaranow 54, 55, 57, 65
      Graff, Jerry 54, 68
      Levene, Shelley 53, 54, 56, 57, 59, 65, 67
      Levites 56
      Lingk, James 55, 56
      Lingk, Jenny 68
      Murray 54
      Moss 54, 55, 65
      Nyborg, Harriet 68
      Williamson, John 53, 55–7
   Heist 46
   House of Games 45
   'Human Stain, The' 56
   Life in the Theatre, A 48
   Make Believe Town 47
   'Mametspeak' 40, 44, 154
   Oleanna 40, 44, 51, 56, 59, 60, 62–8
      Carol 45, 62, 64–6, 68
      John 63, 64, 65, 66
      Pidgeon 63

Perversity 51
Postman Always Rings Twice, The 45
Race 46, 67
'Rake, The' 45
Romance 67
Sexual Perversity in Chicago 48, 68
Shawl, The 46
Speed-the-Plow 40, 44, 56, 58–62, 63, 67, 154
   Bob 61
   Dubrow, Donny 62
   Fox, Charlie 59–62
   Gould 58–62
   Karen 58, 60-2
The Spanish Prisoner 46
True and False: Heresy and Common Sense for the Actor 48
'True Stories of Bitches' 68
Verdict, The 45, 68
'Why I am No Longer a Brain-Dead Liberal' 44
Mamet, Bernie 45
Mamet, Lynn 45
Mann, Aimee 155
Mann, Emily 31
Mantegna, Joe 44
Marie Irene Fornes (Cummings) 103
Mark Taper Forum (Los Angeles) 161
Martin, Bradford 29, 30
Marriage of Bette and Boo, The (Durang) 41
Married with Children 19, 22
M-A-S-H 20
'Material Girl' 10
materialism 9
McClinton, Marion 150
'Me Decade' 40
Me and My Girl 37

Memran, Michelle 158
Mendes, Sam 53, 57
Merlin 39
Metallica 19
Mexican-Americans 40
MGM 37
Miami Vice 26
Middle Passage 146, 151
Mill Hand's Lunch Bucket (Wilson) 131, 144
Miller, Arthur 44, 52, 53, 67, 143
Miller, Scott 36, 39
Miss Firecracker Contest, The (Henley) 31
Miss Saigon (Mackintosh) 37, 97, 98
Mitch (*Glengarry Glen Ross*) 54
MLA Special Session on Mamet and Pinter 67
The Mojo and the Sayso (Rahman) 34
Molly's Dream 102, 104
Moon Marked and Touched by the Sun (Mahone) 34
Moonlighting 21
Moraga, Cheri 106, 158
Morrison, Toni 160
Moses (*Glengarry Glen Ross*) 56
'Mountain of Gold' (*FOB*) 80
Moy, James 79, 90, 91
Moyers, Bill 132, 147
Multicultural America: A Multimedia Encyclopedia (Cortes) 34
multicultural theatre 35–6
Murder She Wrote 21
Murdoch, Rupert 17
Murphy, Brenda 51, 52
Music Lessons (Yamauchi) 75
Music Television (MTV) 17–19, 22
musical theatre 36–9
   British Invasion 36–7

mega-musicals 36
Mysteries, The 155

NASA 20
Nation at Risk, A: The Imperative for Educational Reform 15
National Commission on Excellence in Education 15
National Endowment for the Arts (NEA) 157
National Humanities Medal 129, 160
National Museum of African American History and Culture 160
National Playwright's Conference (Connecticut) 128, 134
National Register of Historic Places 161
National Theatre (London) 52
Native Americans 14, 43
  Native American theatre 35, 36
  Native American women 33
Native Son (Wright) 47, 136
NBC 17, 20, 21
Neblett, Toure 149
Negro National League baseball 11, 127, 138, 139
New American Library 162
New City Theatre (Seattle) 111
New Dramatists (New York City) 102
New Man 7
New Right 3, 4
New York Drama Critics' Circle Award 31, 42, 137, 159, 160
New York Public Theatre 71, 72, 74, 75
New York Theatre Strategy 102

Relativity Media Lab 104
Newhart, Bob 21
News Corporation 17
Nickelodeon 17, 22
Nicklaus, Jack 26
Night Mother (Norman) 30–2
No Child Left Behind 15
Nobel Prize 159
'Nobody Can Bake a Sweet Jelly Roll Like Mine' (Smith) 130
Norman, Marsha 30, 31
November (Mamet) 46, 67, 153
nuclear family 9

Obie Award 41, 78, 98, 102, 103, 111, 116, 123, 154, 157
Off Broadway 31, 43, 74, 154, 155, 158
Off-Off Broadway 31, 99
Oleanna (Mamet) 40, 44, 51, 56, 59, 60, 62–8
Omaha Magic Theatre 111
Open Theatre, The (New York) 32, 102
Oprah Winfrey Show, The 21
Orient 89
  Orientalia 92, 95
  Orientalism 72, 91
Oregon Shakespeare Festival 155
Oscar and Bertha (Fornes) 158
Other Eighties, The: A Secret History in the Age of Reagan (Martin) 27
Overlook Press 162
Oyamo, David 74, 75

Pacino, Al 43, 153
Padua Hills Playwrights Festival 106 111, 112, 116, 156
Paige, Satchel 127
'PAJ plays' 103, 104, 157

PAJ press 103
Pao, Angela 91
'Papa Don't Preach' 18
Papp, Joseph 71, 74, 78
Paramount Pictures 22
Parks, Suzan-Lori 34
Past as Present in the Drama of August Wilson, The (Elam) 137
PBS (Public Broadcast System) 160
Pendennis (Thackeray) 59
Penny, Rob Lee 128
Performance Group, The 32
People Finder, The (*Joe Turner's Come and Gone*) 145, 146, 148
Peterson, Janet T. 33
Peterson, Sloan 22
Phantom of the Opera 37, 38
Pidgeon, Rebecca 45
Pinter, Harold 52, 54, 60, 73, 78
Pinteresque 68
Pittsburgh Cycle 129 *see also* American Century Cycle
Pittsburgh, PA 41, 126, 127, 128, 144, 161
  Pittsburgh's Hill District 160 *see also* the Hill; Hill District
Plays by African Americans 34
Playboy 68
Playwright's Horizon (New York) 41, 42
Plume 162
Plymouth Theatre (New York) 42
Pollard, Sam 160
Pope John Paul II 15, 18
Porterfield, Sally 106
post-black 149
postmodern 67
pre-Civil Rights era 41
pre-Obama era 41

Pressley, Priscilla 24
Pretty in Pink 19
Price, Steven 58, 68
Prince 26
Promise, The (Rivera) 35
Pryce, Jonathan 97
Pu, Shi Pei 88
Public Enemy 19
Public Theatre 34, 74, 92
Puccini, Giacomo 88
Pulitzer Prize 30, 32, 35, 40, 41, 42, 45, 87, 103, 129, 137, 144, 154, 157, 159
Purdy, Claude 127, 128

Qui magazine 45

Raggedy Ann 39
Rahman, Aisha 34
Rainey, Gertrude Pridgett 'Ma' 133, 134
Raisin in the Sun (Hansberry) 128, 133, 134, 144, 151
Raiders of the Lost Ark 19
Ralph, Sheryl Lee 34
Rashad, Phylicia 34, 160, 161
Rather, Dan 20
Reagan, Nancy 11
Reagan, Ronald 1–6, 9, 11–15, 17, 19, 20, 25, 29, 44, 125
  Reagan Democrats 5
  Reagan era 27, 136
  Reagan-inspired tax cuts 6
  Reagan right 29
  Reaganomics 9
Reconstruction 41, 144
Republican Party 1, 5, 12
  politics 125
Rest I Make Up, The (Memran) 158
Resurrection Blues (Miller) 53

resurrection motif 96
Return of the Jedi 19
Rice, Tim 39
Rich, Frank 44, 65, 74, 160
Richards, Lloyd 128, 133, 134, 144, 151
Rink, The (Kander and Ebb) 39
Rivera, Jose 35
Robertson, Pat 4
Robinson, Jackie 34, 138
Rockefeller Foundation 157
Rodgers and Hammerstein 97
Rodgers, Richard 155
Roe vs. Wade 3
Roma, Rich 55, 56, 57, 61
Romero, Anne Garcia 158
Romero, Constanza 159, 161
Rooney, Edward 22
Rose, Charlie 63
Roseanne 21
Rosencrantz and Guildenstern Are Dead (Stoppard) 77
Ross, Diana 34
Ross (*Speed-the-Plow*) 61
Rossini, Jon 92
Roth, Richard 20
Ruck, Alan 22
Rust Belt 4

Samuel Friedman Theatre (New York) 161
San, Cio-Cio 88–90, 92
San Francisco Opera 155
Santiago-Hudson, Ruben 161
Sara, Mia 22
Sarafina 39
Sarita (Fornes) 101, 103
'Satin Doll' 39
Saturday Review, The 133, 136
Sauer, David K. 67
Savran, David 130, 141, 147, 151
Sawyer, Peggy 38

School of Arts at Columbia University 97, 156
Science Museum of Minnesota 128
Search for Signs of Intelligent Life in the University (Tomlin and Wagner) 32
Seattle Repertory Theatre 42
Second World War 6, 14, 41
Secret Knowledge, The (Mamet) 44, 57
See-go-poh (*Family Devotions*) 85, 86
Selleck, Tom 21
Shaffer, Peter 88
Shakespeare, William 144
Sheng, Bright 156
Shepard, Sam 73, 78, 84, 93, 122
Sher, Bartlett 149–50
shopaholic 9
'Shuffle Off to Buffalo' 38
Signature Theatre (New York) 99, 111, 155, 157
Silver, Ron 45
Silverman, Shell 45
Simon and Simon 21
Simpson, O. J. 24
Singing in the Rain 39
Sister Mary Ignatius Explains It All for You (Durang) 41
Sixteen Candles (Hughes) 79
Slow Drag (*Ma Rainey's Black Bottom*) 135
Smile 39
Smith, Bessie 130
Soap 20
Soldier's Play, A (Fuller) 133
Solid Gold 21
Some Kind of Wonderful 19
Son, Diana 98
Sontag, Susan 101, 103, 104
Sophisticated Ladies 38, 39

Soul Train Music Awards 21
Sound and Beauty (Hwang) 74
  89, 93, 94
Sound of a Voice, The (Hwang)
  40, 93
South Coast Repertory 154
Soviet Union 1–3
Speak Easy era 39
Spiderwoman Theatre (New
  York) 33
'Stairway to Heaven' 18
St. James Theatre 38
St. Paul, Minnesota 128
Star Search 21
Star Wars *see* Strategic Defense
  Initiative
Starlight Express 37, 39
Still Life (Mann) 31
Stone, Oliver 44, 136
Stop Kiss (Son) 98
Stoppard, Tom 73, 78, 93
Strasberg, Lee 101
Strategic Defense Initiative (SDI)
  2
Sturdyvant (*Ma Rainey's Black
  Bottom*) 135, 136
Substance abuse 9
Sumida, Stephen H. 76
Summer in Gossensass, The
  (Fornes) 157, 158
Supremes, The 34, 38
Susan Smith Blackburn Prize 30,
  42
Svich, Caridad 158
Sweeney Todd 39

'Take the A-Train' 39
Tale Told, A (L. Wilson) 42
Tanglewood 102
Tannen, Deborah 63, 68
Tap Dance Kid, The 39
Tarzan 97
Taxi 20

Taylor, Curtis 38
Teddy and Alice 39
Tender Offer (Wasserstein) 41
Thackeray, William 59
Theatre Communications Group
  (TCG) 141
Theatre for a New City (TNC)
  103, 111
Third World 3
Things Change (Mamet and
  Silverman) 45
thirtysomething 10, 21
This Week with David Brinkley
  20
Thomas, Clarence 63
Thriller 17, 19
Timebends (Miller) 52
TNZ 116
Tomlin, Lily 32
Tony Award for Best Musical
  37–8
Tony Award for Best Play 35, 42,
  87, 129, 137, 154, 159,
  161
Travolta, John 79
Trump, Donald 11, 27
Turner, Joe 145, 147, 148, 151
Turner, Pete 147
Turner, Ted 18, 20
Turrentine, Stanley 127
Twentieth Century Fox 17

Uncommon Women and Others
  (Wasserstein) 31
Unit, The 154
United States Supreme Court 8
Untouchables, The (DePalma), 58
Urban American capitalism 44
US Court of Appeals 15
US State Department Office 1
USA Today 19
The Uses of Enchantment
  (Betelheim) 46

Van Peebles, Melvin 34
Vatican 18
Verdi, Giuseppe 155
Vietnam War 6, 21
Village Voice 44
Virginia Theatre (New York) 160
    see also August Wilson
    Theatre
Volcker, Paul 6

Wagner, Jane 32
Walk in the Woods, A (Blessing)
    42
Wall Street 5, 27
Wall Street (Stone) 10, 22, 44, 136
'walking blues' 141
Walters, Barbara 17
Wan, Ban 79
Water Engine, The (Mamet) 51
Washington, Denzel 12, 161, 162
Wasserstein, Wendy 30, 31, 41,
    100
Waterbury Republican 134
Way of All Flesh, The (Butler) 63
Weasels and Wisemen (Kane) 52,
    56
Weber, Bruce 63
'We're in the Money' 38
West, Cheryl 34
West Coast Playwrights 156
West, Cornell 40, 149
West End (London) 39
What of the Night (Fornes)
    103–21, 157, 158
White House 17, 20, 25
'Who's That Girl' world tour 18
William Inge Theatre Festival
    (Independence, KS) 159
William Inge Award 159
Williams, Billy Dee 142
Wilson, August 33, 40, 41, 69,
    71, 72, 100, 125–52,
    158–62

1727 Bedford Avenue
    (Pittsburgh) 161
Fences 125, 126, 129, 130,
    134, 137–44, 152, 159,
    161, 162
    Alberta 139, 140, 143
    Bono, Jim 138
    Death 140 *see also* Grim
        Reaper
    Gabriel 141
    generational plays 140–1
    Grim Reaper 140
    Maxson, Cory 138–42
    Maxson, Rose 139, 141–3,
        161
    Maxson, Troy 138–44, 161
    Mr. Lubin 141
    Raynelle 139
Freddie 127
Fullerton Street 159
Gem of the Ocean 41, 125,
    129, 159, 161
*The Ground on Which I
    Stand* (2015 Wilson
    documentary) 152, 160
'The Ground on Which
    I Stand' (Wilson's
    1996 keynote at TCG
    conference) 159
*How I Learned What I
    Learned* (Wilson) 160
Jitney 71, 128, 129, 138, 143,
    152, 159, 160, 161
Joe Turner's Come and Gone
    125, 126, 129, 131, 132,
    138, 144–52, 159, 161,
    162
    African spirituality 146
    'blood memory' 151
    Christianity 146
    Holly boarding house 146
    Loomis, Herald 145–8, 150
    Loomis, Martha 145, 146,

150 (a.k.a Martha
      Pentecost)
   Selig, Rutherford 145
   Walker, Bynum 146, 148
   King Hedley, II 129, 159
   Ma Rainey's Black Bottom
      125, 126, 128–31
      Irvin 135, 136
      Levee 131, 134–6
   The Piano Lesson 129, 131,
      132, 138, 144, 159, 160,
      162
   Radio Golf 41, 125, 129, 138,
      152, 159
   Seven Guitars 129, 130, 159
   Two Trains Running 129, 144,
      159
   Toledo 134, 135, 136
Wilson, Daisy 126, 127
Wilson, Lanford 42
Winfrey, Oprah 17
Winger, Debra 153
Winter Garden Theatre 38
Wise Gu 21
Wiz, The 39

Wolfe, George C. 33
Wolverton, Linda 155
Woman Warrior, The (Kingston)
   77
Women in American Theatre
   (Chinoy and Jenkins) 30
Women's Project (New York) 157
women's theatre 30–4
The Wonder Years 22
Wong, B. D. 97
Woods, The (Mamet) 51, 68
Worster, David 52
Worthen, W. B. 117
Woyzeck (Buchner) 47
Wright, Richard 47, 133

Yale Repertory Theatre 128, 133,
   134, 144, 151
Yale School of Drama 128, 134
Yamauchi, Wakako 75
'yellow-face casting' 74
Yellow Face (Hwang) 97, 98
YouTube 155
Younger, Walter Lee 144
yuppies 10

www.ingramcontent.com/pod-product-compliance
Lightning Source LLC
Chambersburg PA
CBHW070030010526
44117CB00011B/1774